SUPERNATURAL LOVE

Releasing the Compassion of Jesus Through the Gifts of the Spirit

IHERINGIUS

ISBN 978-0-9575354-6-6

A CIP catalogue record for this book is available from the British Library.

Iheringius
An imprint of
Joensuu Media Ltd
20-22 Wenlock Road
London
N1 7GU
England

www.iheringius.com

SUPERNATURAL LOVE

Releasing the Compassion of Jesus Through the Gifts of the Spirit

MARKO JOENSUU

Now when He was asked by the Pharisees when the kingdom of God would come, He answered them and said, "The kingdom of God does not come with observation; nor will they say, 'See here!' or 'See there!' For indeed, the kingdom of God is within you." (Luke 17:20-21)

CONTENTS

ACKNOWLEDGEMENTS

My greatest gratitude is to the Holy Spirit who gave me the idea for this book nearly twenty-five years ago. Without You, I wouldn't have had the courage to write and publish this book.

Thank you Ikwu Amiaka for your prophetic words that confirmed to me at the right time that this is a direction I should take.

Thank you my friends Esteban Gecchelin, Markku Koivisto, Peter Gayer and Yoshua Zimmerman with whom I have had countless of conversations about the spiritual gifts and the difficulties linked to them. These conversations have shaped the content of this book profoundly, although all mistakes are mine.

Thank you Mum and Dad; without you, I wouldn't be on this planet, and neither would I have ever been able to make this spiritual journey without the model of uncompromising, hospitable, honest and forgiving discipleship that you have given to me.

Thank you my son Joshua and wife Daniella for sharing this long journey with me, and for loving me unconditionally.

Marko Joensuu
London, August 2016

INTRODUCTION

The Azusa Street Revival that began in Los Angeles in 1906 was instrumental in bringing an awareness about the nine gifts of the Spirit in 1 Corinthians 12:7-11 back to the Church.

There had been many revival movements emphasising the gifts of healings in the 19th century, and in other revivals some of the other gifts had erupted spontaneously. But it was the Pentecostal revival of Azusa Street that began to bring knowledge about the nine spiritual gifts—the word of wisdom, the word of knowledge, faith, gifts of healings, working of miracles, prophecy, discerning of spirits, different kinds of tongues and interpretation of tongues—back to the Church.

The revival in Los Angeles was by no means the only revival at the time, but perhaps the most significant one, as it would influence the global Church with the theology and phenomena of the Pentecost, eventually birthing the Charismatic movement in the 1960s.

There were many revivals around the globe at the time. For example, the Welsh Revival started in 1904, the Korean Revival in 1903; there was a revival in India in 1905, and in Chile in 1908-1909.[1]

The Welsh Revival preceded the Azusa Street Revival, and stories about it inspired the Azusa Street Revival, but its nature was remarkably different, as it focused mainly on conversions. So, none of the other revivals of the time were particularly focused on spiritual gifts.

The Azusa Street Revival began in a city that would soon become the entertainment capital of the world. Looking back, it is easy to see how this birthing place has profoundly shaped and affected the Pentecostal and Charismatic movements—even when they have often protested loudly against the 'corrupting' influence of Hollywood.

Yet, today we don't seem to know any more about the spiritual gifts than the Pentecostal pioneers did. It appears to me that over hundred years of studying the charismata—the gifts of the Spirit—have made us none the wiser.

What the over hundred-year history of Pentecostalism and fifty years of the Charismatic movement have taught us is that focus on spiritual gifts doesn't often produce holiness or love. Also, rarely have we seen an individual that has been able to hold onto the gifts at high level over a lifetime.

We have seen that the use of the gifts ebbs and flows much like our revivals. We have seen the Charismatic church in a never-ending and ever-failing search of the supernatural, in the rhythm of the comings and goings of revivals.

Many Christians begin to operate in the gifts at some stage of their lives, often as a result of receiving them during some revival. But only a few years later they will usually have lost them. For example, a minister, who prophesied to me during an offshoot of the Toronto Blessing in 1995 at Kensington Temple in Notting Hill Gate, London, has not only lost his prophetic gift, but, today, he is an atheist.

Nevertheless, many remember the days when they were able to minister with the spiritual gifts fondly, and they either long for another revival to rekindle them, or chase revivals around the world, creating the phenomenon of 'revival tourism'.

It might not be your impression that spiritual gifts are dead, as there is a lot of noise about them. But if you look closer, you soon realise that much of that noise is merely there to conceal the lack of substance and genuine understanding about them.

But spiritual gifts have never needed a revival to function properly. In fact, it is the other way around! It is the spiritual gifts that trigger revivals and renewal of the Church, when they are functioning in a mature way. Neither do the spiritual gifts need a particularly charismatic atmosphere, or even a faith-filled church. If you look at the early church, you see that it was the use of the gifts that helped to grow the Church. Yes, there was an initial outpouring of the Spirit, but the apostle Paul didn't ever need a revival before he could begin to make an impact on a city. Instead, he went into a city and ministered through the gifts. And people came to Christ and were equipped to serve Him as the end result.

There are *three* major reasons why we have not learned that much about the gifts in the last hundred years.

First, we have failed to make *love* the glue and the unifying factor, when it comes to understanding the dynamics of the gifts.

Paul says in 1 Corinthians 14:1,

> Pursue love, and desire spiritual gifts, but especially that you may prophesy.

It is not a coincidence that love and spiritual gifts are brought together in this verse, or that 1 Corinthians 13, perhaps the most profound passage ever written about love, is sandwiched between instructions on the use of spiritual gifts. It is astonishing to me that 1 Corinthians 13 might not have even been written, had Paul not needed to teach the Corinthians how to use the gifts.

1 John 4:8 says,

> He who does not love does not know God, for God is love.

Your gifts won't ever reach maturity, unless you learn to live in love. Love is the essence of the spiritual gifts.

Second, our teaching about the gifts was created largely as a counterargument against cessationists, who claim that the gifts ceased to function soon after the New Testament was completed.

In our eagerness to defend the gifts, we have often defended supernatural phenomena whose origins have been spurious and ministers whose theology borders on heresy. In our eagerness to take a stand for the gifts, we have often glossed over issues that demand critical reflection before they can become genuine learning experiences. We have been eager to use the gift of discerning spirits in the world, but avoided it in the Church, and this has led us to lose it altogether.

But any encouragement in the use of spiritual gifts must be accompanied with a functioning gift of discerning spirits in the Church, as otherwise, the Church will accept all supernatural phenomena and open the door to demonic forces and deception.

Third, our understanding about the gifts has been largely experiential, rather than theological, or when it has been theological, it has mostly been abstractly so, without any practical application.

This has led us to accepting phenomena, experiences and ministries solely based on their perceived impact, without assessing their spiritual roots.

Because of our eagerness to defend the supernatural, we have looked for phenomena that appear to demonstrate the power of God—often around well-known Charismatic ministers—considering theological issues related to the gifts to be of secondary importance.

We haven't inspected the work and theology of the previous generations critically, but rather we have used their work as evidence for the supernatural, without questioning it at all. As a result, the streams of revival that might have once run with pure water have become polluted, and we have come to accept clearly unbiblical doctrines. Because of that, the Charismatic movement has been drinking from polluted fountains for a long time.

For example, many know Smith Wigglesworth as an "apostle of faith and healing", and they often refer to any healing stories linked to him uncritically, believing that it all happened.

But in Smith Wigglesworth's understanding, over 90% of healings were the result of casting out demons from people he prayed for[2]—and these people were mostly Christians. His rather unbiblical belief that Christians can be possessed by demons could certainly have led to the high number of 'declared' healings in his ministry.

The explanation is quite simple. According to his doctrine, if a demon had been cast out, he could declare healing. This didn't demand any medical evidence, only theological belief about God being more powerful than the demons.

If an illness had been caused by a demon, and God is more powerful than demons, then casting out a demon in Jesus' name would automatically bring healing—and there was no medical evidence or verification needed.

All that was needed for the audience to accept that was the belief that God is more powerful than the demons. And because most people in the audience were Christians, they would have naturally accepted that premise.

Wigglesworth's theology and demonology had a deep impact on his methodology. He used to punch a sick person, as in his mind he was punching a demon rather than sickness. And many defend Wigglesworth's punching of the people today, because they believe that he had a great healing ministry.

But if you believe, like most people do, that sicknesses are genuine physical conditions, rather than caused by demonisation or demon-possession, you will end up questioning the declared healings rather than defending the methodology of 'knocking out' demons.

Often, we accept the healing stories of past revivalists, such as Wigglesworth, uncritically—a bit like the medieval Christians would have accepted the miracle stories about medieval saints uncritically until the Reformation, when the reformers began to openly question those stories.

But before we base our methodology on the ministry of some healer, have we first verified that healings actually took place?

Many Christians are frightened of testing anyone's work, as they are terrified of the potential consequences of touching the 'Lord's anointed'. But the Bible is not asking us to remain quiet if we see something we suspect to be false.

The apostle John writes:

> Beloved, do not believe every spirit, but test the spirits, whether they are of God; because many false prophets have gone out into the world. (1 John 4:1)

Also, Paul writes,

> Let two or three prophets speak, and let the others judge.
> (1 Corinthians 14:29)

I was raised within the Pentecostal movement, and for most of my working life, I have served within the more Charismatic end of it. And I have come to understand that much of what we 'know' about the gifts is fraudulent and untruthful, although often unintentionally so, as we pass on the teachings of the past generations without actually paying much attention to them.

Much of our understanding about the spiritual gifts is based on a false model of ministry that has been shaped of the legends of the Healing Revival and accepted by us without any inspection, mainly as so many preachers in the Charismatic movement promote the Healing Revival as one of the greatest eras in church history.

The Healing Revival is a term used by many American Charismatics in reference to a revival movement in the late 1940s and 1950s. Oral Roberts was perhaps the leading figure of the movement, but William Branham is widely regarded as the initiator of the revival.

So, before we move on to inspect how the genuine gifts of the Spirit function, we must first break out of the false ministry model that dominates our understanding. And as we inspect the gifts individually, we will soon find out that the false ministry model keeps on haunting us.

The seeds of this book were sown through a simple vision in the early 1990s, but it has taken nearly twenty-five years for my understanding of these issues mature enough for me to be able to share it.

One day, as I was praying, I saw a vision. It was a single image of a tractor ploughing the field. On its own, this image had little meaning, and I could have missed it easily. But I sensed that it was a vision from the Lord, although I was puzzled by it. Then I switched on the TV and caught a programme about a tractor drag race with super-powerful racing tractors competing against by pulling heavy loads. The difference between the lonesome tractor ploughing the field and the racing tractors celebrated by the cheering audience was striking. Then I switched on to another channel and saw a Charismatic well-known pastor 'demonstrating' the power of God on a large stage.

"This is all just fireworks," I heard the Holy Spirit say, interrupting my flow of thoughts. "All this energy is just wasted." I reflected on what I had seen and heard, and saw that there is a ministry that makes a lot of noise and achieves very little, and there is a ministry that often seems invisible, but achieves a lot. It all depends on where all the power and energy is spent on—a stage performance or real work.

It is when I was praying regarding writing this book and questioning the reason for writing it that the Holy Spirit gave me the words "a false model" that reminded me of this vision, and made me look at the roots of the prevalent ministry model in detail.

This book has been written for every 'doubting Thomas' out there, wanting to experience more of God, but also desperate to be certain that those experiences are real.

After the resurrection of Jesus, He appeared to His disciples, but for some reason Thomas missed the meeting.

> Now Thomas, called the Twin, one of the twelve, was not with them when Jesus came. The other disciples therefore said to him, "We have seen the Lord." So he said to them, "Unless I see in His hands the print of the nails, and put my finger into the print of the nails, and put my hand into His side, I will not believe."
>
> And after eight days His disciples were again inside, and Thomas with them. Jesus came, the doors being shut, and stood in the midst, and said, "Peace to you!" Then He said to Thomas, "Reach your finger here, and look at My hands; and reach your hand here, and put it into My side. Do not be unbelieving, but believing."
>
> And Thomas answered and said to Him, "My Lord and my God!" Jesus said to him, "Thomas, because you have seen Me, you have believed. Blessed are those who have not seen and yet have believed." (John 20:24-29)

Thomas' bad reputation as a doubter seems at least partially unwarranted, as he wanted to believe, but he also wanted to be certain that the other disciples had truly seen the resurrected Jesus, and not some angel or a ghost.

It is remarkable that Thomas was looking for the *marks of the cross* as evidence for the resurrected Jesus. Likewise, we also must be looking for the marks of the cross in every supernatural story before accepting them as a demonstration of God's power.

Thomas wasn't satisfied with a second hand experience, but desired to see Jesus with his own eyes. And because of that experience, it is Thomas who first exclaims, "My Lord and my God".

Thomas didn't want to be deceived by a *ghost story*. Only the resurrected Lord with the marks of the cross was enough for him.

In many ways, this book is continuation of my earlier book *Five Movements: Winning the Battle for Your Prophetic Gift*, which looks at the five spiritual movements in the Lord's Prayer. They are movements into God's presence, perspective, provision, nature and freedom. But whereas the previous book was focused on the journey, this one is focused on the endpoint.

The nine spiritual gifts can only operate fully and healthily when they flow from a lifestyle saturated in the presence of God, focused on learning and doing His will. It is a lifestyle that rejects greed, is full of forgiveness and able to discern and resist the devil's wile schemes.

Spiritual gifts are all about the second spiritual movement in the Lord's Prayer: *Your Kingdom come, Your will be done*. But I will also touch on the fifth spiritual movement: *Do not lead us into temptation, but deliver us from evil*, as that is the sphere for the gift of discerning spirits.

1

FROM COMMUNITY TO STAGE PERFORMANCE

Before we move into the general dynamics of the gifts and how the individual gifts operate, we need to uproot a misguided model that dominates our understanding about the gifts.

The false ministry model that I will outline is what I call the *stage performance model* that is primarily designed to deliver a great show. In essence, most churches today have been built around a stage performance experience, rather than to be expressions of a genuine Christian community. But gifts of the Spirit fit rather unwell into this stage performance environment.

The first phase in the development of the false ministry model began quite soon after the birth of the Pentecostal movement at 312 Azusa Street, Los Angeles, in 1906.

The rapid expansion of the Pentecostal movement into the world was made possible by two new technologies—steam ships and telegraph. The Azusa Street Revival was the first revival where ships and telegrams played a major role; the Welsh Revival that started two years earlier was the first revival spread by newspapers.

New developments in communication technology and media have always played a major part in spreading revivals and religious movements. Even the Protestant Reformation was made possible by the invention of mass printing. And it was the vast network of Roman roads that helped to spread the Good News into the Roman Empire.

But communication technologies have always also profoundly shaped all religious movements.

The building where the first Pentecostal revival started, 312 Azusa Street, was the humblest of buildings, located in an industrial area of Los Angeles. It had once been a Methodist church. The bottom floor had been converted into a horse stable. The floor was covered with sawdust, and planks were nailed to wooden barrels for use as pews. There was no platform, and William Seymour, the African-American minister who served as a catalyst for the revival, sat on the same level as the congregation.

The benches were arranged in such a way that the congregation faced each other, to symbolise the *equality* and *brotherhood* of all believers. And from that small space and insignificant-looking pulpit, the ideas and understanding of Pentecostalism spread rapidly into the world, making the resulting Pentecostal-Charismatic movement one of the largest Christian movements on earth today.

But just because the Pentecostal-Charismatic movement has spread rapidly, it doesn't mean that everything is or has always been well within it. For example, even a casual look at the current prophetic movement in the Charismatic church reveals that it has suffered a spiritual bankruptcy. What many perceive as prophecy today is in fact nothing more than a product of a *profetainment* industry— entertainment geared at producing emotions of fear or hope in Christians who consume events, prophecies and conferences. Much like any good entertainment, prophecies stir our emotions—but then a new prophecy is released! There is hardly any accountability, as even well-known prophetic figures seems to get away with false prophecies, and the prophecies that you can't prove to be false are infallible only because they are as vague as horoscopes.

The same low standards apply to our claims for healings. I, and many of you, have been to many healing meetings where healing has been proclaimed with congregation members standing on stage declared healed, but only a few days later it seems clear that hardly anyone was ever healed.

The issues linked to claims related to healing aren't any fringe issues, as the *Pew Forum on Religion and Public Life's Spirit and Power: A 10-Country Survey of Pentecostals* singles out "divine healing" more than any other factor, including speaking in tongues and financial prosperity, as distinguishing Pentecostals and Charismatics from other Christians.

In every country surveyed, large majorities (more than 70% in 8 of 10 countries) of Pentecostals reported having personally experienced or witnessed the "divine healing" of an illness or an injury. In the Latin American, Asian, and African countries, where Pentecostal growth is occurring most rapidly, as many as 80-90% of first-generation Christians attribute their conversions primarily to having received divine healing for themselves or a family member.[1]

So, faith in healing seems to unite most Charismatics and Pentecostals, regardless of their views on other matters. But although we believe in healing, it doesn't necessarily mean that we experience it as much as we think we do. The sad truth is that the Pentecostal and Charismatic world is full of healing claims—but most of them have never been verified.

A campaign run by a church I know illustrates this adequately. Some years ago, the church conducted a series of healing services. They lasted for some time and there were regular healing meetings at the church. The idea for the campaign came when a healing evangelist came to minister for one weekend.

During the service, a congregation member was healed of partial deafness. This sparked a lengthy campaign, and during the campaign many people went on stage and confessed their healing. But in real terms, not all of them were healed. Most of these healing stories were quite minor, with the initial healing from partial deafness remaining the most outstanding healing. Retrospectively, it seems clear to me that a lot more people were healed in small groups, regular church services and evangelistic outreaches of that church than during those services dedicated to healing.

You might think that this was some low-performing campaign, as this wasn't some famous church, but, in fact, it would have been pretty standard. Many similar campaigns, such as the Lakeland Revival in 2008, resort to increasing their healing numbers by doing very little verification and by attributing any healings in their vicinity to their own campaign. For example, the Lakeland Revival boasted of about thirty resurrections from dead, but according to *Christianity*

Today of 12th August, 2008, no one actually had actually met any of these resurrected people in person—all these claims had been based on unverified phone calls, texts or emails.[2] Retrospectively, all of the resurrections turned out to be urban myths, although there was one case of someone having been resuscitated after his heart had already stopped. But that 'resurrection' had nothing to do with the Lakeland Revival. But it happened in a hospital in Florida, which was enough for the revival to 'claim' it.

If the apostle John wrote his letters today, he might write, "My children, do not believe every email, Facebook post or revival report."

The stage performance model is based on inviting people to be prayed for on stage or front, and declaring healing or a working of a gift on the spot—without proper verification before or after. Often getting the "right answers" on stage can take some level of coaxing.

Anyone in the audience, or watching the events on TV, has very little or no background information about the real medical condition of the people on stage, such as the seriousness of their illness, so it is practically impossible to assess whether a healing or word of knowledge is genuine.

Unfortunately, this prevalent model of healing ministry in Charismatic churches worldwide has more to do with show business than real ministry.

Of course, this doesn't mean that healings can't take place in a public space, or even on stage. It is God who heals, and if He decides to perform a miracle, it is up to Him to choose the time and place. But much of the time, stage performance preachers aren't even interested in discovering whether a real healing has taken place or not—they are only concerned of how it all looks, as how it looks affects the bottom line through discouraging or encouraging donations and offerings.

The development of this stage performance model reached its culmination point during the era of the American healing evangelists in the late 1940s.

One of the central arguments of this book is that when God gave us the gifts of the Spirit, they were given to a community to be tools of *love*, but we have made them into stage performance. And that has twisted our understanding and obstructed us in reaching full maturity in using them.

It is interesting to read how William Seymour organised the meeting room of Azusa Street. Clearly he had an understanding about how the architecture of a meeting place affects our worship.

> Seymour designed an unusual seating arrangement. He placed the pulpit in the center of the room with the altar in front of it, serving as a bench for persons to use following the invitation. The pews formed a circle surrounding the pulpit and altar—all on one level. This plan reflected the oneness in equality Seymour envisioned. Worshippers gathered in a new way completely equal in the house of God, the body of Christ not a collection of individuals looking over the back of many heads simply to the clergy or choir but an intimate whole serving one another.[3]

The humble church building on Azusa Street was built to be a community where no man would be raised above another, and where focus would be on Jesus. But in today's stage performance setting the minister becomes a star and everything is focused on him or her.

The Azusa Street Revival, which was a spontaneous work of God, gave us a taste of revivals, and soon we sought for methods to reproduce that revival experience with the help of rapidly improving communication technologies of microphones and loudspeakers, which made regular large gatherings possible.

If you compare the church buildings built until the late 19th century with contemporary church buildings, you can see a remarkable difference. In the old churches, the pulpit was elevated high above the pews for largely acoustic purposes. The downside of the old-fashioned pulpit was that it restricted movement. Today's pulpits are mostly on theatrical stages positioned a lot lower than the old pulpits, and often in large auditoriums with effective sound systems. Our open stages can give an appearance of informality and intimacy, but their intimacy is often illusory and carefully managed—a bit like chat shows on TV.

Media theorists talk about "mediated intimacy", which is essentially "non-reciprocal intimacy at a distance".[4] Our media and entertainment industries have been built on that, and our churches have been built on that. But it is not real intimacy.

From the early 20th century onwards, the successful ministers have been the ones who have been able to harness, first the microphone, then radio and TV into their use, and are comfortable in this theatrical stage environment.

This development reflects a general shift in society. The Oscar and Bafta-winning film *The King's Speech* illustrates the early stages of this development. *The King's Speech* is a 2010 British historical drama directed by Tom Hooper and written by David Seidler. In the film, Colin Firth plays King George VI, who, to cope with a stammer, sees Lionel Logue, an Australian speech and language therapist, played by Geoffrey Rush. The men become friends as they work together, and after his brother abdicates the throne, the new king relies on Logue to help him make his first wartime radio broadcast on Britain's declaration of war on Germany in 1939.

By 1939, radio had changed the expectations when it came to the king. During World War 1, the king wasn't expected to make speeches that would reach the whole nation, and little bit of stammering wouldn't have mattered much. Now the whole nation was expecting to hear the king's speech on radio, and that speech had a huge significance, as it would communicate Britain's resolve to fight the Nazis.

Suddenly, it was all about the king's voice.

It has been said that Winston Churchill—the great Prime Minister of Britain, whose determination was vital when it came to winning World War 2—would have been unelectable in the era of TV, as he wasn't physically as attractive as most contemporary party leaders. But if you hear his radio speeches, you will soon realise how well he mastered radio.

Today, the people who get to lead our political system have to look good or at least sound good hence big part of politics is to project an impression of being a strong and charismatic leader. Politics is now personified in the party leader, and what matters is his or her *perceived* character, not who they really are. In many ways, politics is now *show business*.

We can see a parallel development in the Charismatic and Pentecostal movements that got their models for supernatural ministry largely from the 1946-1957 Healing Revival in America. During that time, there were around seventy full-time healing evangelists travelling with their tents across America and overseas. As part of the revival, many of these healing evangelists emphasised the baptism and the gifts of the Holy Spirit, divine healing, and the power of prayer and fasting. Some proclaimed the restoration of the fivefold ministry—the ministry of apostles, prophets, evangelists, pastors and teachers, according to Ephesians 4, and all of them subscribed to the ability to impart supernatural power through the laying on of hands.

Most of these healing evangelists have all passed away, but what they left behind is their ministry model, which has survived the Charismatic Renewal with only minor alterations.

And that ministry model is fundamentally broken.

There were two preachers that influenced the development of this ministry model more profoundly than most.

GIFTS AS THEATRE

Aimee Semple McPherson had a huge impact on how we understand public ministry today. In 1919, Aimee took the Pentecostal church on stage of the theatre.[5] Prior to her conversion experience, it had been her greatest ambition to become an actress. Now the Pentecostal movement moved from tents to auditoriums. Later on, she would build the large Angelus Temple in Los Angeles—the birthing place of both the Pentecostal movement and Hollywood.

Des Moines-Register Tribune of 13th July 1920 wrote about Aimee:

> To begin with, Aimee is beautiful, and she is artistic. The very tips of her fingers are eloquent with artistry . . . Winning, pleading, triumphant, running the entire gamut of emotion in an instant from ecstasy to woe . . . All the subtle artistry of the finished actress belongs to Aimee.[6]

Aimee founded a large denomination with millions of members today, her example liberated countless of women to minister, and we should be partially thankful to her for five-day working week, so in many ways, her legacy is a positive one.

It is a little-known fact that Gray Rochester, the owner of Rochester Can Company, introduced the shorter five-day working week most people in the developed countries enjoy today, because his heart had been touched and warmed by Aimee's ministry.[7] Soon, Ford came to study his factory, as it was more productive than any other factory in America, adopted the shorter working week, and five-day working week began to spread globally.

But Aimee also brought healing services on stage. In Aimee's divine healing service seven chairs were placed on the platform. In front of the chairs, there was a small table upon which rested a silver urn of anointing oil. The order of prayers followed the numbers given on printed cards.

The cards had been distributed days ago.

They had been numbered in order that they were handed out.

They asked for sufferer's name, church or faith, and nature of disease.[8]

Reporter Don Ryan wrote in Los Angeles Record of 2nd January 1923 about the opening of Angelus Temple,

> If Aimee Semple McPherson had not chosen to be a revivalist, she would have been a queen of musical comedy. She has a magnetism such as few women since Cleopatra have possessed . . . Standing beneath the dome the revivalist explained her inspiration for the temple. "I wanted it like God's own outdoors," she said. "So the gypsies and people of that sort would feel more at home. The churches seem to have lost the intimacy we get in theatres. I tried to get that intimacy here . . . The cheerful intimacy of the theater had been achieved. The building is much like a theater. It has numerous foyers. The seats are opera chairs. The only churchly touch is in the windows."[9]

In an interview in 1978, Aimee's daughter Roberta said,

> All she had was drama lessons in High School. So she read the Bible as an actress. She put back the drama that was already there.[10]

Aimee was very aware of entertainment as her main competition, and she taught young preachers,

> Remember you have competition. There are the movies and the boxing-galleries and the bowling allies. Students, beat the old devil at his game and come prayed through, with the power of God upon you and every means you can at your disposal to get the message over.[11]

In many ways, Aimee's life resembled that of the Hollywood movie stars. She divorced twice, once before she became famous and once during her career as the senior minister of Angelus Temple. She died of an overdose of sleeping pills. She lived the showbiz life and died the showbiz death.

Angelus Temple was the first *megachurch*, and thousands of megachurches have since followed her architecture. She built a theatre, so now we have thousands of churches built like theatres.

And in a *theatre* all that matters is maintaining the illusion.

Uri Geller, an Israeli illusionist, says,

> In entertainment, there is a kind of acceptability to deceive. It is like there are two Picasso paintings on the wall. One of them is real. One of them is fake. But it doesn't really matter. There is no harm in that.[12]

Media researcher Simone Natale argues that the rise of the spiritualist movement in the Victorian era was closely connected to the evolution of the media entertainment industry. Spiritualist mediums and leaders employed some of the same advertising strategies, performance practices and spectacular techniques that were being developed within the field of spectacular entertainments.

The performances of spiritualist mediums often had theatrical character. Seances were held in theatres and public halls, establishing a situation where the medium played the role of the performer, and the sitters the role of spectators.[13]

Showmen such as P.T. Barnum understood that doubts about the authenticity of their spectacular feats only added to their appeal, and they would thus openly stimulate public controversies as an advertising scheme. Moreover, spiritualism benefited from the powerful publicising mechanism connected to celebrity culture. Frequently, it was the appeal of the famous mediums featured in the popular press that attracted the attention of the public.[14]

Spiritualism and magic brought illusion to the centre of the entertainment business, where it has remained ever since. This is not meant to demonise entertainment, but as Uri Geller says, entertainment industries have been built on an illusion.

One of the fads of the spiritualist movement was "spirit photography"—taking pictures of different environments where the "spirits" appeared in the pictures. It remained influential in the spiritualist field for decades, starting to decline in popularity only in the middle decades of the twentieth century.[15] This was the precursor of cinematic tricks and special effects, and it might be one of the reasons why film and literature are still full of ghosts and supernatural fantasy.

William Branham, whose ministry will be discussed in the next chapter, was famous for a mysterious pillar of fire that once appeared above his head on a photograph. Many have taken it as a sign from God, but these kinds of photographs were always part of the spiritualists' playbook.

The entertainment model has worked its way through our society so pervasively that it has twisted our understanding of Christianity, to the point that we need reformation as badly as the Church in the Middle Ages. Whereas the medieval Church sold salvation to people frightened of hell, we are selling emotional experiences to a generation that has been so shaped by entertainment that they can't discern a difference between true and fake, simply, as on stage, the difference between them doesn't really matter.

2

THE FALSE MINISTRY MODEL

Aimee only began the developing of the stage performance model, and it would take the Healing Revival to perfect it. A broad consensus of church historians, Charismatic writers and ministers perceives William Branham as the man who started the revival.

Paul Keith Davis, writing in March 2009 on 'The Elijah List', a leading prophetic website, says about Branham:

> I believe he was a token or prototype of an entire body of people who will emerge as Jesus' bridal company. By his own acknowledgment, Branham was a harbinger of something new and fresh the Lord planned for the last days. This supernatural dimension will be commonplace in end-time life and ministry . . . A platform had been established for heavenly truth, and we must comprehend the significance of this type of ministry for our generation. These events were much more than revival; they were the beginning of end-time ministry; they pointed to a generation of destiny prophesied in Scripture.[1]

Paul Cain, another leading figure in the American prophetic movement, called Branham "the greatest prophet that ever lived."

So, who was this remarkable man so many seem to respect?

Branham was indeed the first revivalist in the Healing Revival. He was known for healing and for allegedly accurate words of knowledge.

Kris Valloton, a prophetic leader at Bethel Church, Redding, tells in one video available on YouTube that he once asked God, "Would you give me the mantle of William Branham?" He says that God's answer was that Branham's mantle would destroy him, and that it would be too heavy to be carried by one man.[2]

And surely Branham's mantle would destroy anybody.

According to Branham himself, over 15,000 people were healed through his prayers in 1946 alone, the year when the Healing Revival started.

C. Douglas Weaver, Professor of Religion and Director of Undergraduate Studies in the Department of Religion in Baylor University writes,

> The influence of William Branham did not end with his death. His ministry has made a significant impact upon the broader Pentecostal movement of this day. As the pacesetter for revival, Branham was a primary source of inspiration in the development of other deliverance ministries.[3]

According to Weaver, "Branham's ministry must also be considered, at least in part, as a precursor of the Faith/Confession movement..."[4]

So, according to many, William Branham is the prototype of the end-time ministry, and we should all follow his lead. Bill Johnson, Senior Minister of Bethel Church, Redding, writes about Branham,

> It is very possible that no one since Jesus Himself carried this particular measure of anointing. But he was not without faults. The strangeness of his doctrine later in life has caused many to once again "throw out the baby with the bath-water." It seems easier to reject a person for error than it is to learn to eat the meat and throw out the bones. One response only needs an opinion; the other requires maturity.[5]

Bill Johnson refers to Branham's "faults", but he doesn't seem to perceive them as significant. According to this view, Branham's doctrine "later in life" is the problem, but his ministry model still remains the gold standard in the Charismatic ministry.

Derek Prince looked at Branham's ministry more critically after sharing a platform with him on few occasions.

> Unfortunately, after exercising his gift two or three times, he just collapsed and his men came and gathered him up and carried him away. He explained that by the statement of Jesus, "The power has gone out of me." But Jesus did not collapse. I do not believe that was the Holy Spirit. I believe it was demonic.[6]

In Derek Prince's view, Branham operated under the influence of a demonic spirit at least part of the time. And yet many expect us to accept Branham's ministry uncritically.

Branham's teachings and life history indicate that, contrary to what he insisted, he might not have been called into ministry by God at all.

Branham had many doctrines that were clearly wrong. For instance, he affirmed the Old Testament law that man had the right to divorce his wife, if she cut her hair short.[7]

But Braham's most infamous teaching was the doctrine of the serpent's seed. According to Branham, Eve gave birth to Cain through sexual intercourse with the snake; consequently every woman potentially carried the literal seed of the devil.[8] He also taught that denominations were the mark of the beast.

Most alarmingly, Branham said, "Trinitarianism is of the Devil. I say 'Thus saith the Lord.'"[9]

So, here we have a religious leader, venerated by many, who denies one of the fundamental Christian doctrines about the nature of God.

Based on Branham's teachings, his ministry must be rejected on theological grounds. Had he really known God, he could not have made these kinds of statements.

I don't have the space to write about Branham's many false prophecies, but even a cursory glance at them, all available online, soon reveals that rather than being an accurate prophet, most of his prophecies were clearly off the mark.

But what all these Charismatic leaders are referring to are Branham's seemingly accurate words of knowledge, and they are willing to ignore any error because of them. That is why we need to look at them in more detail.

THE METHODOLOGY OF A FAKE HEALER-SEER

If you look at any videos of Branham's stage ministry, you can easily come to the conclusion that Branham had a powerful gift of the word of knowledge. But it is possible that Branham was one of the best illusionists the church has ever seen, or as Derek Prince said, Branham might have been channelling a demonic spirit.

But whatever conclusion you make, if you look at Branham's methodology, you encounter such a high level of manipulation that his ministry needs to be rejected on *ethical* grounds.

If you watch any Branham's videos, many of them available online, what seems to happen is that he invites people randomly on stage, tells intimate details of their life, and then heals them.

And like any illusion artist worthy of their profession, Branham went to the grave without revealing the exact way he performed his illusion act. But it was preceded by an extreme level of manipulation and preparation that caused the crowd to see what Branham wanted them to see.

First, Branham insured himself against anyone not getting healed by claiming that any failure was never his fault. According to F.F. Bosworth, a healing evangelist that assisted Branham,

> If a sick person did not receive healing, the problem was either some unconfessed sin or the presence of a demon.[10]

Branham used fear and intimidation to manipulate his audiences. He said that the exorcised demons looked for new inhabitants and warned that the demons would enter the sceptics, asking them to leave before the healing stage of the service. He was convinced that it was lack of faith that obstructed people from getting healed. He admonished audiences to persevere in their faith, and said that some healings were gradual. Branham's response to temporary healing was that healing could be lost. Healing lasted only as long as unwavering faith lasted.[11]

You wouldn't want to become demon-possessed simply by disbelieving that a miracle had taken place, would you?

Other ministers often led the morning services. The purpose of these meetings was to increase the 'level of faith' for the evening services.

The use of the prayer line was Branham's primary method of ministering to the sick. After 1949, when Branham added the gift of "discernment" to his methodology, the fast lane was disbanded. Slow lane had people in wheelchairs, but now there was only one queue. People were instructed to line up on his right side, since that was the side where "the angel" stood, as Branham needed the presence of an "angel" for healings.

Branham insisted that healing demonstrations indicated God's presence at the meeting. When those seated in the audience witnessed a healing on stage, additional healings could occur as the 'level of faith' was raised. This justified praying for a limited number of persons each night. When Branham started his ministry, all people were allowed in the line. But soon, Branham was exhausted. After that, one hundred cards were given out for each service. I don't know exactly when Branham introduced the prayer cards, but I would conjecture that the timing was somewhat linked to the introduction of his new gift of "discernment"—the word of knowledge.

Each person was instructed to write the nature of their illness and other personal details on the card. As he passed through the prayer line, a Branham team member collected the card.[12]

Bosworth said,

> Branham does not begin to pray for the healing of the afflicted in body in the healing line each night, until God anoints him for the operation of the gift, and until he is conscious of the presence of the Angel with him on the platform. Without this consciousness, he seems to be perfectly helpless . . . When he is conscious of the angel's presence, he seems to break through the veil of the flesh into the world of the spirit, to be struck through and through with a sense of the unseen.[13]

Initially, Branham asserted that it was 'the angel' that performed the healing. But later on, Branham rarely spoke about 'the angel'. The presence of 'the angel' enabled Branham to perform his role in the healing process.

It is mostly because of Branham that many healing evangelists have developed 'healing' ministries that apparently rely on angels.

Branham alleged that he utilised two signs—the detection of disease by a vibration of the left hand, and the discernment of the secrets of a person's heart. The operation of the gift occurred after the angel 'anointed' Branham.

What is noteworthy is that it wasn't the Holy Spirit but 'the angel' that performed the healing. But this is a radical departure from the biblical understanding of God as the Healer. Also, the person being prayed for had to believe in *Branham* as the prophet and healer for healing to take place.

For the person to be healed, he or she had to affirm that God had given Branham a special gift of healing.

Branham asked the people in the prayer line:

> Sir, do you believe me? Do you accept me as God's servant? Do you believe that I am his prophet that was sent here for your purpose that you might be healed, and will you obey what I tell you to do? . . . You have arthritis . . . Jump up like this on the platform like this. You're healed my brother.[14]

There are so many layers of manipulation in Branham's methodology that it seems difficult to believe that he was allowed to operate as a healing evangelist.

Often, Branham 'healed' people of sicknesses they didn't even know they had. But because of high level of manipulation and subtle intimidation, not many people would have protested, with most believing afterwards that they had in fact had the sickness.

Like with today's healing evangelists, many criticised Branham because his healings didn't last. But in the Bible no one ever lost their healing.

But how did Branham acquire his seemingly accurate words of knowledge?

They would have been easily taken from the prayer cards, as most of his words of knowledge referred to people's sicknesses and their home addresses.

What Branham needed for his word of knowledge to operate was a good memory. He either read and prayed for the cards before the service, or he was in regular contact with his assistants that collected the cards during the service. Then Branham asked the people to get on stage based on the number in the cards.

You must ask the question—if both the 'words of knowledge' and the prayer cards contained the same information, what is the most likely source for the 'words of knowledge'?

Or to put it another way: why would God give Branham a word of knowledge about an illness if he already had the information on the card?

And Branham always insisted that the sick would be ordered to be in line according to the number in the card. If they were in the wrong order, or if anyone with the card hadn't actually turned up, the gift often stopped working—until the line was reordered according to Branham's requirements.

So, here we can see the model for healing meetings, but as most healing revivalists don't know about Branham's methodology, they often attempt to create the same effect without realising that all along, it is probable that Branham's act was an illusion.

Also, a serious question must be asked about Branham's source of information and calling.

According to Branham's own story, as a still unbelieving teenager, he went to a carnival.

One of the fortune-tellers approached him and said,

> Say, do you know that you were born under a sign, and there is a star following you? You were born with a gift.[15]

So, according to William Branham himself, he received his calling from a fortune-teller. And Branham seemed fairly comfortable with the occult even in the early days of his ministry. In 1933, when he received the prophecy of the seven major events that were to come to pass before the return of Jesus—which has been proven to be a false prophecy many decades ago—he was conducting services in the old Masonic Hall on Meggs Avenue in Jeffersonville.[16]

So, it is clear that even in the early stages of his ministry Branham was giving out false prophecies, which debunks the theory that he started well but finished badly. He both started and finished badly.

As a prophetic minister, I find it troubling that Branham was happy to minister prophetically in a masonic temple. Around one in ten Americans were freemasons at the time, and the temples were useful if you wanted to bring together a crowd from all denominations, which explains it, but it doesn't seem that he took any precautions when ministering in such a spiritually hostile environment.

In fact, Branham never condemned freemasonry, and even his gravestone is a pyramid, a masonic symbol.

It seems that Branham gave clear clues about the source of his power at every opportunity, but for some reason, many Charismatic ministers seem to disregard them.

What launched Branham's healing ministry was an appearance of an angel in 1946. According to Branham, the angel told him,

> Fear not. I am sent from the presence of Almighty God to tell you that your peculiar life and your misunderstood ways have been to indicate that God has sent you to take a gift of divine healing to the people of the world. If you will be sincere, and can get the people to believe you, nothing shall stand before your prayer, not even cancer.[17]

This 'angel' encouraged Branham to get people believe in him—not in God.

The apostle Paul writes in Galatians 1:8,

> But even if we or an angel from heaven should preach a gospel other than the one we preached to you, let them be under God's curse!

Any revelation that contradicts the Bible should be rejected outright. I am not sure if an angel ever appeared to Branham, or if he made up the story, but if it truly was an angel, it couldn't have been an angel of the Lord.

This acceptance of any supernatural phenomena by many Charismatics can only be understood in the historical context of defending the supernatural gifts against the doctrine of cessationism. But when our theology is formed through an argument with other Christians, it will automatically lead to imbalance. Put simply, we stop looking for the truth, as our only concern is to win the argument.

> Jesus answered and said to them, "You are mistaken, not knowing the Scriptures nor the power of God." (Matthew 22:29)

Some of the Reformers generated partially erroneous theology, as they denied the power of God with the doctrine of cessationism. Their goal was not to deny the power of God, but rather to defend the Word. Equally, the goal of many Charismatics isn't to deny the Bible, but to defend the supernatural. Unfortunately, the way we go about it is based on ignoring large parts of the Scripture, including the demand for discernment.

We must know the Scriptures, but also the power of God. But we must also know the Scriptures and not just the power of God.

But because of our disregard for truth, it is no wonder that the genuine gift of discerning Spirits is nearly non-existent in the Charismatic church, or at least in our public conversation.

But according to Bill Johnson, we shouldn't criticise a man like Branham.

> For example, I am told that William Branham had over 10,000 open visions with 100 percent accuracy in his miracle ministry. This means I must give a place of great value in my heart for this kind of ministry if I want to experience it myself. This usually starts by valuing God's anointing on others who operate in word of knowledge, specifically through open visions. We must refuse the temptation to compare and critique. Rather we celebrate. For what we celebrate we will be much more likely to participate in.[18]

But I don't think we should participate in anything that Branham did.

THE REST OF THE HEALING REVIVAL

But perhaps we shouldn't reject the whole Healing Revival because of one man. What about the other healing evangelists? After all, they might have used similar methods, but their doctrine was much more sound. What if the problem was not the method but the man?

Apart from Branham, Oral Roberts was considered to be the main leader of the Healing Revival. What does his life and ministry tell about this "golden age" of healing?

In 1959, when the healing revival had waned, Oral told a reporter,

> I can't prove any person who ever came to me was healed, that is I can't prove it to the satisfaction of everyone.[19]

In 1956, Oral said, "I don't try to prove it, I just say, 'There's the person. Let him tell you.'"[20]

Oral's comment cuts to the heart of the fundamental weakness of the Healing Revival and most subsequent healing revivals. Verifying any healing medically has never been a major goal of the stage performance model.

Tommy Tyson, Oral's associate evangelist in the 1960s, estimated that two or three per cent of whom Roberts prayed for were healed instantly, like a miracle, although many others seemed to be gradually helped.[21] That is a low number. But even that assessment is based on what seemed to have taken place on stage and not on later medical verification. It is likely that the real numbers were much lower.

The Catholic Church verifies any alleged healings meticulously with the help of doctors, and they report far fewer healings, but they are all verified. The stage performance model inflates the number of healings and miracles by not inspecting them at all.

But healings are either verifiable or not. You can argue for the reason why someone got better, but they either get better or not. The reason might be a mystery, but the actual healing is a fact.

The Charismatic church has created a culture where the appearance of spiritual gifts is enough. It doesn't really matter whether they are real or not. In fact, many churches find that the illusion of gifts is a lot more manageable and tolerable than a genuine intervention from God. This is a direct result of the stage performance model.

But all this leaves Christians empty, weak and without a direct, intimate relationship with God.

In so many ways, our churches resemble the secular media environment.

The entertainment business is full of sets that are kept together by duct tape. If they hold together long enough for the camera to be switched off, that is perfectly acceptable. Not so with ministers whose righteous appearance is barely kept together until they leave the stage.

But from the perspective of stage management, it doesn't matter whether a miracle is real or not, as long as it looks real, as the emotional impact is the same.

The business model of healing evangelists was a travelling circus. It advertised miracle crusades or prophetic words, promising them even before the event had taken place. Then it tried to deliver the illusion or the fact of them to audiences before moving on to another city. Unlike with the circus, the entrance was free—but if you entered, you were often subject to holiday property type hard sales about giving.

You might object to my analysis, as somewhere in the back of your mind there is a picture of Jesus and the apostles performing signs and wonders. Aren't we supposed to do the same?

But the sequence of activities with Jesus and the apostles was different. They never advertised signs and wonders. It was the gospel that was the selling point, and signs and wonders followed them. But signs and wonders evangelists declare that they will have a show of signs and wonders, and then they will be under pressure to deliver them.

They might advertise an event as an 'evangelistic' crusade, but the whole event has been built for Christians. That becomes clear during the offering talk.

But Jesus never worked like that. Take the story in John 2:1-11 of the wedding in Cana, where water was turned into wine. It is remarkable how hidden the performance of this miracle was, as only the servants carrying the water would have *witnessed* to it turning into wine. It is clear in the story that even the master of the feast, who tasted the wine first, had no idea that a miracle had taken place. And the same applies to the five thousand people who were fed miraculously with five loaves of bread and two fish in Matthew 14:13-21. Only the disciples and the little boy offering his food to Jesus would have been immediately aware of the miracle.

Now, I am not saying that there are no public miracles—of course there are—but many successful ministers are no more than actors performing a role on stage. An actor 'believes' in their role whilst on stage, if for nothing else than the pay cheque.

It seems to me that we have taken something that was meant to be used as a tool for love and spreading the gospel, in obedience to the Great Commission, and attempted to repurpose it for entertainment, and as a result, it has lost its power, but instead of acknowledging that it has lost its power because of this repurposing, we keep on pretending that everything is fine.

But the Church needs more than that. We need more than a good show that is paid by passing the bucket around, like with any street performer. The Church needs the reality of the gifts.

Perhaps the greatest defect of the stage performance model, when it comes to using the gifts, is that it introduces a mediator between God and man, as the receiving of blessings becomes dependent on the performer.

But Paul says to Timothy,

> For there is one God and one Mediator between God and men, the Man Christ Jesus, who gave Himself a ransom for all (1 Timothy 2:5-6)

The stage performance culture of our churches introduces an implicit albeit unintentional aspect of idolatry into our churches. Often, there is very little difference between the demands and lifestyle of celebrities and successful Christian ministers, and we justify that with a certain level of celebrity logic.

It is fine that these people have the excesses of the superstars, because they *are* superstars, we say—but all it reveals is that we have embraced our idolatry to the point that we use it in our argumentation against the Bible.

If you haven't noticed yet, you will soon see that the Charismatic church is spiritually bankrupt, chasing viewership figures, larger congregations and external signs of success—by any means necessary.

But all this is slowly being destroyed in the new media environment, where it is becoming harder and harder to conceal what takes place off-stage, as there are no more media gatekeepers. Many churches will die when their congregation members, tired of hypocrisy, will spill the beans. Sometimes one tweet is enough.

Today's ministers aren't ready for the onslaught of scrutiny that will face us in the new media world. It is becoming impossible to hide the dirty linen.

But the Church will only reflect what is already happening in the world. Bill Clinton, for example, was a lot less 'qualified' as a womaniser than many of the US presidents before him. But the change of communication technology and media caught up with him.

In his illuminating book *All the Truth Is Out: The Week Politics Went Tabloid*, Matt Bai writes about "the moment when the worlds of public service and tabloid entertainment, which had been gradually orbiting closer to one another, finally collided."[22] That moment was when Gary Hart's presidential campaign collapsed in May 1987 because of an allegation of infidelity.

Bai says,

> That's largely because, beginning with Watergate and culminating in Gary Hart's unravelling, the cardinal objective of all political journalism had shifted, from a focus on agendas to a focus on narrow notions of character, from illuminating worldview to exposing falsehoods.[23]

Before Gary Hart, media had kept personal issues, such as potential sex scandals, out of the headlines, when it came to politicians. It was a sort of gentlemen's agreement to focus on what everyone considered real politics, rather than the politics of image.

In today's media world, media, the most hypocritical of all professions, exposes the hypocrisy and double standards of everyone else but themselves.

Never before have the words of Jesus rung more true:

> "What you have said in the dark will be heard in the daylight, and what you have whispered in the ear in the inner rooms will be proclaimed from the roofs." (Luke 12:3)

The biggest shocks are yet to come in the Church when it comes to exposing our hypocrisy. And for most of the time, to our shame, it will be the secular media rather than the Church exposing the fake.

3

WHAT IS SUPERNATURAL LOVE?

In our media driven culture, we have elevated what is fake, or at best superficial, on the pedestal. Media theorist Shani Orgad writes,

> Thus, a considerable part of the work of media representation is invested in the creation and perpetuation of a polished account of a world to which viewers are invited and given the impression that they can seamlessly inhabit.[1]

In the church environment, this polished account of the world often leads to hypocrisy. In our effort to present and communicate well, we often end up giving an account of things that is untruthful.

In itself, this is nothing new, as the apostle Paul writes in 1 Corinthians 2:1-5,

> And I, brethren, when I came to you, did not come with excellence of speech or of wisdom declaring to you the testimony of God. For I determined not to know anything among you except Jesus Christ and Him crucified.
>
> I was with you in weakness, in fear, and in much trembling. And my speech and my preaching were not with persuasive words of human wisdom, but in demonstration of the Spirit and of power, that your faith should not be in the wisdom of men but in the power of God.

Although Paul is probably the greatest theologian of all time and an excellent communicator, unlike the Corinthians, he wasn't interested in polishing his performance or in any verbal acrobatics. Instead, he was focused on preaching the gospel in the power of the Holy Spirit.

The apostle Paul took a very different route than we take when it comes to the use of spiritual gifts. Most of what we know about the gifts comes from Paul, who was instructing the Christians in Corinth on how to use them properly. The Corinthians seemed to have been enamoured with the ecstatic aspects of the gifts, and their favourite gift was speaking in tongues. And it seems that they liked to speak in tongues as publicly and loud as possible.

Much like the Christians of our stage performance driven church today, they were products of their environment and oblivious to many aspects of their behaviour, which they attributed to their faith but which, in reality, had pagan roots.

The Christians of Corinth had been influenced by the Greek emphasis on wisdom but also by the mystery religions. And when it comes to mystery religions and pagan understanding of prophecy, speaking in tongues was exciting, and it would have made Christianity to stand out attractively as a new 'mystery cult'. Speaking in tongues, which even many Pentecostals today consider to be embarrassing, wouldn't have been embarrassing at all in Corinth. The embarrassing part of Christian faith was belief in God who had been crucified.

The apostle Paul wrote:

> For Jews request a sign, and Greeks seek after wisdom; but we preach Christ crucified, to the Jews a stumbling block and to the Greeks foolishness, but to those who are called, both Jews and Greeks, Christ the power of God and the wisdom of God. (1 Corinthians 1:22-24)

Paul's letters to Corinthians are extremely relevant to us today. Paul had to deal with a sex-crazy culture that idolised man's wisdom, sex and carnal pleasures, and tried to smuggle them to the church. It seems that the church in Corinth had heard Paul's message of grace but hadn't quite got the essence of it. They tolerated sexual behaviour that even pagans found reprehensible. And whereas the church in Corinth had to learn how to help people who had come from a pre-Christian culture, we now have to learn how to help people that come from a post-Christian culture, and we can no more assume that new Christians know even the basics of our beliefs.

One thing the Corinthian Christians seemed to excel in was religious ecstasy. That was a reflection of what was valued in Corinth. But they seem to have embraced the gifts more than any other church in Asia, and because of them we have the longest list of gifts of the Spirit in the Bible.

It seems that the Corinthian Christians thought that because they had the gifts, they were doing well with God, and that the moral aspects of Christian teaching were redundant.

Because of the overall negative tone of 1 Corinthians, many readers misinterpret the letter and think that Paul had low view of the gifts, but, in fact, Paul's view of the gifts was very positive. He was simply giving correction on how to use the gifts, but he never wanted to quench their use.

As 1 Corinthians 12 ends with Paul writing that he will teach the church "a more excellent way", after he has been teaching about the gifts, many readers assume that the more excellent way that Paul is referring to is love, as Paul moves on to write about love. To them, it appears that Paul is saying that spiritual gifts have only little value in comparison to love.

1 Corinthians 13 says,

> Though I speak with the tongues of men and of angels, but have not love, I have become sounding brass or a clanging cymbal. And though I have the gift of prophecy, and understand all mysteries and all knowledge, and though I have all faith, so that I could remove mountains, but have not love, I am nothing. And though I bestow all my goods to feed the poor, and though I give my body to be burned, but have not love, it profits me nothing.
>
> Love suffers long and is kind; love does not envy; love does not parade itself, is not puffed up; does not behave rudely, does not seek its own, is not provoked, thinks no evil; does not rejoice in iniquity, but rejoices in the truth; bears all things, believes all things, hopes all things, endures all things.
>
> Love never fails. But whether there are prophecies, they

will fail; whether there are tongues, they will cease; whether there is knowledge, it will vanish away. For we know in part and we prophesy in part. But when that which is perfect has come, then that which is in part will be done away.

When I was a child, I spoke as a child, I understood as a child, I thought as a child; but when I became a man, I put away childish things. For now we see in a mirror, dimly, but then face to face. Now I know in part, but then I shall know just as I also am known. And now abide faith, hope, love, these three; but the greatest of these is love.

Yet Paul is not downplaying the value of spiritual gifts at all. Much of 1 Corinthians is about the spiritual gifts; it is the main text we have in the Bible about them. But love is the necessary prerequisite for using them. What many readers are missing is that Paul is still teaching about the gifts when he writes about love.

Unfortunately, the chapter and verse structure imposed later manages to obscure this. Many readers lose interest in the end of the thirteenth chapter—when the bit we read mostly at the weddings ends—and they miss the more excellent way altogether. And they miss that what Paul wrote wasn't meant mainly for the newlyweds, but for those who use the spiritual gifts.

Straight after the section on love, in 1 Corinthians 14:1, Paul writes,

> Pursue love, desire spiritual gifts but especially that you may prophesy.

The more excellent way isn't love alone, but love *and* spiritual gifts brought together. But, obviously, if we have to choose between them, we will have to put love first.

Without love, spiritual gifts never develop beyond their kernel stage, and that is one of the main reasons for the fact that, after over a hundred years of the beginning of the Pentecostal movement, we still know so very little about them.

Love is such an overused word. We all have our own definitions of it, and they can be contradictory to each other. And it seems like such a soft word that it has no edges, hardly a starting point for anything, and yet it must be the starting point for our journey into the gifts, as unless our gifts are energised by love, they have no value.

Referring to love, Paul uses the Greek word *agape* that appears in all its forms 320 times in the New Testament, but it has been found to be used only once outside the New Testament. It was one of the four words used for love, but it was seemingly used rather infrequently. It seems that Paul chose a rarely used word that didn't have any strong pagan connotations and invested it with a new meaning.

Agape simply meant honouring others, welcoming them, with the emphasis on giving rather than getting.

Paul gave the word *agape* new substance and repurposed it to be used as the word for God's love.

For years, I used to try to help people in different situations, in obedience to the Bible. But this kind of loving that was energised solely by my will to love often wore me out.

But *agape* brings along its power source, the Holy Spirit. *Agape* is God working in the world through His Spirit.

To live in *agape* means living in God, for God is love.

1 John 4:8 says,

> He who does not love does not know God, for God is love.

God is the *agape*, and someone who isn't full of *agape* doesn't know Him that well. The attributes of love the apostle Paul lists in 1 Corinthians 13 are really *God's* attributes.

In essence, Paul is saying that the Corinthians shouldn't use the gifts of the Spirit in a way that they did—without manifesting love. Instead, they should use them *full of God*—with love.

If you want to grow in spiritual gifts, you need to learn what *agape* means in practice.

Over the last decades we have had many revivals in the Western Church, but it seems we have learned very little new about the spiritual gifts.

Partially, it is because the parts of the Church excited about the gifts aren't the same parts that pursue practical love. Hence love and the gifts never meet and never get an opportunity to empower each other.

But the other part of the problem is that it takes a long time to really begin to understand the *dynamics* of the gifts, and most give up long before that.

It seems to me that God gives these gifts *freely* to people, but that they come in a seed form, not in fullness, and it is love, hope and faith that begin to mature them. Without love, the gifts will only puff you up, and your pride will cause your downfall.

The Pentecostal movement that reintroduced the spiritual gifts to the wider world was birthed out of the Holiness movement. Unfortunately, often the Christians who talk most about holiness are the ones the least interested in love.

Focusing on personal holiness is a very narcissistic activity, and it easily leads to self-obsession. You can witness this in every religion. The people focused on holiness often have the hardest of hearts. They see the faults of everyone else. Yes, holiness is important, but without love, it becomes an abomination. It leads you to think, deluded, that you are better than the rest, and hence makes you unable to give any genuine gifts to others. On the other hand, love leads to valuing other people and becoming able to truly bless others.

Only Jesus has successfully reconciled love and holiness with each other. Unconditional love and unmerited grace are the two radical ideas of Christianity. But if you replaced a Pharisee with an evangelical and a Sadducee with a liberal Christian in the Gospels, and wouldn't tell that you are reading from the Bible, most people wouldn't blink an eyelid; the evangelicals can often sound much like the Pharisee, and the liberal Christians much like the Sadducee.

The only shock we would experience would come from actually hearing the words of Jesus. It is embarrassing how little of Jesus' actual teaching is included in our teaching and our preaching in the Charismatic churches.

All sort of spiritual discipline, including prayer and fasting and trying to live a holy life, develops spiritual pride, unless you are firmly rooted in a desire to love. But our fleeting efforts to love will expose our selfish desires and the fact that we will never be able to become perfect on earth. It is noteworthy that the systems of thought that teach that it is possible to reach a sinless state on earth always focus on holiness but never on love. They are the systems of the Pharisees.

But the ultimate and biblical measure of holiness is how well we are able to love other people.

The spiritual gifts are meant to supercharge our love, so that in one moment God can achieve in the lives of other people more than through a lifetime of discipleship programmes.

Both the gifts and the fruit of the Spirit are side effects of God's presence in our lives. Hence we shouldn't be seeking the gifts as much as we seek to live in the presence of God.

It is love that keeps the presence of God. Supernatural love is *God's love*, and when we seek to love our neighbour, the spiritual gifts line up with God's nature and His will.

4

1 CORINTHIANS AND THE GIFTS

Many Protestant theologians assert the doctrine of *cessationism*—a belief that the gifts of the Spirit have ceased to operate. The central argument is that gifts of the Spirit were needed to authenticate the message of the original apostles but ceased with them, as they were no more needed after the New Testament was completed.

You have probably heard that argument and might think that there is some theological merit for it, especially, as it is often propagated by people who have a title of a professor in New Testament theology. But in fact the argument is nonsensical, as if miracles and the gifts of the Spirit were needed to authenticate the gospel in times of the early church, it will always need authentication with them.

Nothing has changed since Jesus' time, because people haven't changed, and today, they are still confronted with the same questions regarding the authenticity of the gospel. The reasoning behind cessationism seemed only rational when there was a state church that everyone was forced to attend. Cessationism was a doctrine created by the Reformation, and, at the time in Europe, nearly everyone, apart from the Jews, was at least nominally a Christian.

More importantly, the cessationist argument ignores the actual message and content of the Bible that testifies about the unchanging, miracle-working God.

It is evident that the apostle Paul never expected the working of the gifts to cease, but to remain an indispensable part of the Church's everyday life. And he didn't limit their use to the apostles.

Paul writes about the spiritual gifts in 1 Corinthians 12:7,

> But the manifestation of the Spirit is given to each one for
> the profit of all.

Spiritual gifts are for the benefit of individuals *and* the whole Christian community. There is not a single verse in the Bible predicting that the gifts would cease on earth. Paul does say in 1 Corinthians 13:12 that they will cease when we will see Jesus "face to face". The gifts are no more needed in heaven.

Paul adds in verse 17,

> If the whole body were an eye, where would be the hearing?

The Body of Christ needs many other things, but it also needs the gifts of the Spirit.

There is no biblical basis for cessationism. It might conform to many Christians' experience, but that doesn't make it biblical.

So where does cessationism come from?

It is a bad doctrine created by the Reformation in a quarrel between the Protestants and Catholics. So much poor theology has been generated through arguments between Christians, as different Christian groups have defended their corner rather than focused on the biblical truth!

When the Reformation began, the Roman Catholic Church demanded that the Protestant dissidents produce miracles as proofs that God approved their doctrines. Martin Luther and John Calvin said they needed no miracles, as theirs was no new doctrine but simply the gospel of Christianity. Luther said,

> Now that the apostles have preached the Word and have given
> their writings, and nothing more than that what they have
> written remains to be revealed, no new and special revelation
> or miracle is necessary.[1]

To argue for the absence of miracles, Calvin developed the doctrine of cessationism, claiming that they had ceased with the end of the biblical era, as they were no longer needed to confirm the gospel.[2]

What the reformers overlooked is that the same Bible they defended also testifies of miracles. Also, they discounted every miracle story from the early church to the Reformation, rejecting the testimony of church history as superstition. And certainly, not every miracle story should be believed, but there is enough evidence in church history to discount the doctrine of cessationism.

But because of that doctrine generated during a quarrel, many Protestants have looked at spiritual gifts suspiciously ever since. But sporadically, the gifts of the Spirit have returned back to the Protestant churches, although they have often been suppressed quickly.

Faith in the miracle-working God was an integral part of the early Methodism. Bishop of Gloucester remonstrated with John Wesley, the founder of Methodism, for having "laid claim to almost every apostolic gift, in as full and ample a manner as they were possessed of old."[3]

That was sarcasm not praise.

In his journal entry of 15th December 1741, John Wesley tells about praying for his travelling companion, who is about to die. The man recovers. It is clear that Wesley believed in the gifts of healings. But Wesley seemed hesitant to embrace the spiritual gifts fully, as he could see the potential for their abuse.

Much of what we know about gifts was written in response to them being abused in Corinth. I would love to see the letter Paul would have written about them, had the Corinthians used them in a mature way!

According to James D. G. Dunn, a British New Testament scholar, Paul's opponents in Corinth were heavily influenced by thought that would later on characterise Gnosticism.

Paul was confronting those who called themselves the pneumatics, the spiritual ones (*pneumatikoi*). Linked to this arrogant self-assessment was a high evaluation of what the pneumatics called wisdom (*sophia*). They despised the simplicity of Paul's teaching, and thought that they had already achieved Christian 'perfection'.[4]

A key feature of Gnosticism was that its followers thought that perfection was attainable through secret knowledge. Many features of Gnosticism, such as the disregard of the body, were already visible in Corinth.

Perhaps Paul preferred to call the spiritual gifts *charismata*—gifts of grace, or gifts of favour—to refute the pre-Gnostic understanding and arrogance that was related to the word *pneuma*. By his choice of words he told the pneumatics that they didn't understand even the basics about the gifts.

According to Paul, spiritual gifts were given free of charge, as God's favour, and there was nothing that the recipients had done or could do to earn them. Neither was there any *gnosis*—secret knowledge—needed to receive them.

Paul's definition of the gifts is still relevant to us today, as the Charismatic church today is full of teachers who claim to have attained some secret knowledge, by being raptured in heaven, through personal conversations with angels, or through some other mystical experience.

Paul writes in Colossians 2:18,

> Do not let anyone who delights in false humility and the worship of angels disqualify you. Such a person also goes into great detail about what they have seen; they are puffed up with idle notions by their unspiritual mind.

Unlike the Charismatics today, who warn against 'touching the Lord's anointed', Paul didn't hesitate to criticise false prophets and visions. Neither did he value visionary experiences on their own.

But regardless, Paul had a high view of the gifts. He writes in 1 Corinthians 1:4-9,

> I thank my God always concerning you for the grace of God which was given to you by Christ Jesus, that you were enriched in everything by Him in all utterance and all knowledge, even as the testimony of Christ was confirmed in you, so that you come short in no gift, eagerly waiting for the revelation of our Lord Jesus Christ, who will also confirm

you to the end, that you may be blameless in the day of our Lord Jesus Christ.

Paul never criticised Corinthians for having gifts. In fact, he praised them for that.

Paul writes in 1 Corinthians 2:6-15,

> However, we speak wisdom among those who are mature, yet not the wisdom of this age, nor of the rulers of this age, who are coming to nothing. But we speak the wisdom of God in a mystery, the hidden wisdom which God ordained before the ages for our glory, which none of the rulers of this age knew; for had they known, they would not have crucified the Lord of glory. But as it is written: "Eye has not seen, nor ear heard, nor have entered into the heart of man; the things which God has prepared for those who love Him."
>
> But God has revealed them to us through His Spirit. For the Spirit searches all things, yes, the deep things of God. For what man knows the things of a man except the spirit of the man which is in him? Even so no one knows the things of God except the Spirit of God. Now we have received, not the spirit of the world, but the Spirit who is from God, that we might know the things that have been freely given to us by God.
>
> These things we also speak, not in words which man's wisdom teaches but which the Holy Spirit teaches, comparing spiritual things with spiritual. But the natural man does not receive the things of the Spirit of God, for they are foolishness to him; nor can he know them, because they are spiritually discerned. But he who is spiritual judges all things, yet he himself is rightly judged by no one.

Paul disregarded the Greek understanding and respect of wisdom, and argued that the wisdom we should value is the wisdom that we can receive only through hearing the voice of the Holy Spirit.

Early into the letter, he is already building a case for the spiritual gifts, telling that true wisdom can only come from God.

But then, in 1 Corinthians 3:1-3, he says that he can't speak to the Corinthians as if they were spiritual, as they were carnal, due to their divisions.

> And I, brethren, could not speak to you as to spiritual people but as to carnal, as to babes in Christ. I fed you with milk and not with solid food; for until now you were not able to receive it, and even now you are still not able; for you are still carnal. For where there are envy, strife, and divisions among you, are you not carnal and behaving like mere men? For when one says, "I am of Paul," and another, "I am of Apollos," are you not carnal?

Disunity expresses a lack of love, and later on, Paul will detail his vision of how the Christians in Corinth should live—in demonstrating love.

Paul says in 1 Corinthians 3:16-17,

> Do you not know that you are the temple of God and that the Spirit of God dwells in you? If anyone defiles the temple of God, God will destroy him. For the temple of God is holy, which temple you are.

We can all possess the gifts of the Spirit, because we all are temples of the Holy Spirit. And if we are temples of the Holy Spirit, any theory of cessation ceases to make sense, as the presence of the Holy Spirit in us hasn't ceased.

But it is only in 1 Corinthians 12 where Paul really begins to delve deeper into the gifts, after he has dealt with the sexual sins, divisions and selfishness that plagued the church in Corinth.

Today, many in the Charismatic church are willing to ignore sin because of the gifts, but Paul never did that. He never looked up to people just because they had gifts.

He writes in 1 Corinthians 12:1-11,

> Now concerning spiritual gifts, brethren, I do not want you to be ignorant: You know that you were Gentiles, carried away to these dumb idols, however you were led.

> Therefore I make known to you that no one speaking by the Spirit of God calls Jesus accursed, and no one can say that Jesus is Lord except by the Holy Spirit. There are diversities of gifts, but the same Spirit. There are differences of ministries, but the same Lord. And there are diversities of activities, but it is the same God who works all in all.
>
> But the manifestation of the Spirit is given to each one for the profit of all: for to one is given the word of wisdom through the Spirit, to another the word of knowledge through the same Spirit, to another faith by the same Spirit, to another gifts of healings by the same Spirit, to another the working of miracles, to another prophecy, to another discerning of spirits, to another different kinds of tongues, to another the interpretation of tongues. But one and the same Spirit works all these things, distributing to each one individually as He wills.

In many ways, this is an interesting list. But what is especially interesting is that, apart from the gifts of speaking in tongues and their interpretation, all these gifts were already clearly present in the lives of the Old Testament prophets. The gifts themselves are nothing new. What is new is how widely and freely they are now available. Now, God isn't giving the gifts just to prophets like Samuel and Elisha, but to every Christian.

Then Paul adds,

> Are all apostles? Are all prophets? Are all teachers? Are all workers of miracles? Do all have gifts of healings? Do all speak with tongues? Do all interpret?

Paul isn't talking about himself but about the church in Corinth. It seems evident that he had the gift of prophecy, the gift of discerning spirits, the gift of speaking in tongues, the gift of faith, the gift of working miracles, and the gifts of healings. The Bible doesn't say explicitly that he had the gift of interpreting tongues, but he might have had that as well.

Paul isn't saying that all spiritual gifts couldn't operate through one person, only that not all the people seem to have all the gifts.

Jesus said that some have one talent, others five or ten talents; equally some Christians will have more gifts than the others.

Paul adds,

> But earnestly desire the best gifts. And yet I show you a more excellent way. (1 Corinthians 12:31)

According to Paul, we should desire the gifts. And we shouldn't assume any gift to be beyond our reach.

The gift list in 1 Corinthians 12 isn't the only list of spiritual gifts in the Bible. Later in the same chapter, Paul gives another list that starts with the offices of the apostles and prophets, includes administration and helping, and ends with the gift of speaking in tongues. This reminds us that the nine gifts of the Spirit don't exist in a vacuum, but they are only part of the larger work of the Holy Spirit in and through the Church.

Yet, it seems justified to inspect these nine gifts together, apart from the diversity of all the gifts, as they share a special dynamics. They are all linked to the *manifest* presence of God within us.

And just because the nine gifts are listed together only in 1 Corinthians 12, it doesn't mean that they only operated in Corinth. We can see glimpses of them all through the New Testament. Paul didn't invent the gifts; he only described them more precisely than any other New Testament writer.

In Matthew 14:22-33, Jesus walks on water:

> Immediately Jesus made His disciples get into the boat and go before Him to the other side, while He sent the multitudes away. And when He had sent the multitudes away, He went up on the mountain by Himself to pray. Now when evening came, He was alone there. But the boat was now in the middle of the sea, tossed by the waves, for the wind was contrary.
>
> Now in the fourth watch of the night Jesus went to them, walking on the sea. And when the disciples saw Him walking on the sea, they were troubled, saying, "It is a ghost!" And they cried out for fear. But immediately Jesus spoke to them, saying, "Be of good cheer! It is I; do not be afraid." And Peter

answered Him and said, "Lord, if it is You, command me to come to You on the water." So He said, "Come."

And when Peter had come down out of the boat, he walked on the water to go to Jesus. But when he saw that the wind was boisterous, he was afraid; and beginning to sink he cried out, saying, "Lord, save me!" And immediately Jesus stretched out His hand and caught him, and said to him, "O you of little faith, why did you doubt?" And when they got into the boat, the wind ceased. Then those who were in the boat came and worshiped Him, saying, "Truly You are the Son of God."

In this passage, we see the working of diverse gifts, and also how all the gifts flow from the person of God.

First, Jesus walking on water is clearly working a miracle. Jesus was anointed in the power of the Holy Spirit, and later on He would release the power of the Holy Spirit to His Church, and it is through the power of the Holy Spirit that He worked the miracles in the world.

The full divinity of the Son will be manifested in His return, but one reason that Jesus operated in the power of the Holy Spirit, rather than in the power of the Son, was to demonstrate to us how the Holy Spirit works in the world.

Jesus says in John 14:12,

> "Most assuredly, I say to you, he who believes in Me, the works that I do he will do also; and greater works than these he will do, because I go to My Father."

Some say that because of this we can become some sort of 'mini-Jesuses', able to perform the same works than Jesus did, and even more, but that is not what the Bible teaches. Jesus was fully divine when He walked on earth. He wasn't man who became God; but He

> who, being in the form of God, did not consider it robbery to be equal with God, but made Himself of no reputation, taking the form of a bondservant, and coming in the likeness of men. (Philippians 2:6-7)

Jesus ministered primarily in the power of the Holy Spirit, rather than in the power of the Son—the disciples saw only glimpses of His divinity before His resurrection—as His mission was to become one of us so fully that He would be able to take our punishment for sin as one of us and yet innocent.

But Jesus never had to deal with His own sin; instead He came in the likeness of men to set us free from our sin, and from the power of death. But even when we are anointed we will still struggle with our sinful nature, and the anointing of the Holy Spirit will never work as purely in our lives as in the life of Jesus.

So, Jesus commanded Peter to come to Him on water, demonstrating the power of a prophetic promise at its most extreme. Jesus promised Peter that if he stepped on water, he would make it to Jesus.

Jesus also released the gift of faith. Peter understood it well that faith is a gift, as he asked Jesus to command him to come. He understood that his faith was dependent on Jesus' word.

But in essence, the story is all about the unbreakable power of God's promises and His faithfulness. When Peter's faith wavered, Jesus reached out to him. That's how God's promises work. When we take a simple, small step of faith, His promises reach out and sustain us, even when our faith wavers.

When you read the Bible, you soon realise that, from beginning to end, it is full of stories about miracles, healings, prophecies, words of knowledge and wisdom, and spiritual discernment. Our God is supernatural and because of that, He works in a supernatural way.

THE GIFT-GIVER BRINGS THE GIFTS

It is vital that we understand that we are temples of the Holy Spirit before we begin to inspect the gifts more closely. Before we can embrace the gifts, we must embrace the understanding that the Holy Spirit works the gifts in us and through us in partnership with us. We are His temple, which means that He is the Lord of the temple, and partnering with Him means submitting to His will.

We are His temple *individually*, but we are also His temple *corporately*, as one Body of Christ.

John G. Lake was an early Pentecostal preacher who theorised that *pneumatology* was a "science of Spirit", by which one could uncover the laws of the Spirit. Lake described prayer as a dynamo that attracted the Holy Spirit—which Lake envisioned as a "tangible substance", much like electricity, which was powerful enough to control every "form of materiality". The Holy Spirit could literally "impregnate" any "material substance" which explained the healing properties of handkerchiefs.[5]

But this kind of thinking separates the gifts from the Gift-giver and makes them into some sort of impersonal powers that we can control and manipulate. Unfortunately, this magical understanding of the spiritual gifts is far too common in the Pentecostal and Charismatic movements. In this magical model of using the gifts, man is in control of the power of the Holy Spirit, rather than submitting to His will.

What Paul teaches is that when the Gift-giver comes, He will bring His gifts and they can never be separated from their Giver. Even when you experience the working of the Spirit as physical power, it is still the person of the Holy Spirit behind that power.

GIFTS FLOWING FROM WITHIN

Paradoxically, misapplying the Pentecostal symbolism of Acts 2 is one of the major reasons why so many Christians fail to live in the presence of God.

> When the Day of Pentecost had fully come, they were all with one accord in one place. And suddenly there came a sound from heaven, as of a rushing mighty wind, and it filled the whole house where they were sitting. Then there appeared to them divided tongues, as of fire, and one sat upon each of them. And they were all filled with the Holy Spirit and began to speak with other tongues, as the Spirit gave them utterance. (Acts 2:1-4)

Looking at the symbolism of the fire, it would seem that the anointing of the Holy Spirit, with the accompanying gifts, came from heaven as an external event. Hence many waitings of revivals have been based on expecting a move of God from above. How many times have you been praying for God to send His rain, believing that your refreshing could somehow be dependent on an external season of revival? How many times have you sung a song about the Holy Spirit sending His refreshing?

Countless Pentecostal preachers must have preached the sermon about the Holy Spirit being a sensitive dove—if you sin, He will flee. But nothing could be further from the truth!

According to Paul, we become a temple of the Holy Spirit the moment we accept Christ. No renovation work has been done on our soul, which remains as dark a place as the moment before we gave our life to Jesus. But that's the moment the Holy Spirit enters in. It is the Holy Spirit that does all the renovation work, not us, moving the sin and the dirt from our lives. He is the Holiness that will begin to flow from within.

There is an alternative version about the first giving of the Holy Spirit in the Gospel of John.

> Then, the same day at evening, being the first day of the week, when the doors were shut where the disciples were assembled, for fear of the Jews, Jesus came and stood in the midst, and said to them, "Peace be with you." When He had said this, He showed them His hands and His side.
>
> Then the disciples were glad when they saw the Lord. So Jesus said to them again, "Peace to you! As the Father has sent Me, I also send you." And when He had said this, He breathed on them, and said to them, "Receive the Holy Spirit. If you forgive the sins of any, they are forgiven them; if you retain the sins of any, they are retained." (John 20:19-23)

Pentecostal theology has chosen to focus on the Pentecost as the moment when the Holy Spirit entered the Church. This is probably because the moment was spectacular. But because of that we have missed the fact that, according to John, Jesus in fact gave the Holy Spirit to the Church between His resurrection and ascension.

John 7:37-39 says,

On the last day, that great day of the feast, Jesus stood and cried out, saying, "If anyone thirsts, let him come to Me and drink. He who believes in Me, as the Scripture has said, out of his heart will flow rivers of living water." But this He spoke concerning the Spirit, whom those believing in Him would receive; for the Holy Spirit was not yet given, because Jesus was not yet glorified.

As John doesn't mention the Ascension or the Pentecost in his Gospel, it remains unclear where he places glorification in the story. But according to John, the Holy Spirit was given to the disciples soon after His resurrection and before His ascension.

This event wasn't as dramatic as the First Pentecost, but the precursor of it. In John's Gospel, Jesus said that the fullness of the Holy Spirit flows from within us, so at least some of the disciples—the ones Jesus breathed over—were being filled from within at the Pentecost.

Being filled from within—not from the outside—is the fundamental *dynamics* of the Spirit-filled life. The Pentecostal movement has largely missed this biblical truth and the corresponding understanding of us as temples of the Holy Spirit, as it has emphasised the external manifestations of the Holy Spirit.

The same principle applies to the gifts. They will always flow from within. Many a deception would have been avoided had Christians understood this principle, rather than waiting for a move of God from the outside into within.

If whatever apparently supernatural happens around you doesn't resonate with the intimate relationship that you have with the Holy Spirit, stay clear of it. And if you don't have an intimate relationship with Him, get one! It is a lot more important than the gifts.

Paul writes in 1 Corinthians 14:29,

Let two or three prophets speak, and let the others judge.

It is not clear whether it is the other prophets judging, or the whole congregation doing the judging, but we are able to do the judging because we share the same Spirit. There might be instances when you need another prophet to judge. But we are able to judge because the Spirit of God within us witnesses if a prophecy is from God. Obviously, that demands sensitivity to hear the voice of the Holy Spirit. If you don't have an intimate fellowship with the Holy Spirit, it is unlikely that you will be able to judge prophecy on any other but theological, ethical and moral levels.

ONE GIFT FRAMEWORKS TOO COMMON

Many false doctrines have been birthed by misapplying individual gifts and overextending their reach. For example, many have tried to minister healing exclusively through the gift of faith. And although faith can possibly be used to release healing, it is not the primary healing gift. Others try to 'prophesy' through faith. You do need faith in God to prophesy, but if you try to prophesy through the gift of faith, you will easily walk into error.

Frequently, Christians seek to prophesy their word of knowledge, whereas others attempt to prophesy what they discern through their dormant gift of discerning spirits. But if you prophesy what you discern, you can easily end up prophesying a curse into people's lives. Misapplying gifts can be dangerous and destructive, and it often leads to deliberate or subconscious manipulation of people.

THE APOSTOLIC AND PROPHETIC CONTINUUM OF GIFTS

There are different ways to group the gifts. Some divide them in three groups: revelation gifts, communication or inspirational gifts, and power gifts. In this grouping power gifts are the gift of faith, healings, and working of miracles, the revelation gifts are discerning spirits, words of wisdom and knowledge, and prophecy, speaking in tongues and their interpretation form the communication or inspirational gifts.

But these categories aren't derived from the Bible, and to me, they are misleading. Listing prophecy as a communication or an inspirational gift is based on a low view of prophecy, and it also misses the primary function of prophecy—hearing from God.

The main function of prophecy isn't proclaiming but hearing. But this categorisation implies that every prophecy must be proclaimed publicly for it to be a prophecy, when in many cases a prophecy is meant to help intercession only. This poor understanding has caused many prophetically gifted people to share prophetic words immaturely.

The gift of prophecy is primarily a revelatory gift and only secondarily a gift for communication. This explains why Paul ranks the gift of prophecy the highest. It also helps to operate in all the other gifts properly, and gives birth to the gift of discerning spirits.

It is misleading to divide the gifts into these three groups, because all of them have to be used in partnership with the Holy Spirit, and hence they all demand some level of revelation from God and intimacy with Him.

As our teaching on the gifts has been largely based on our personal experiences when it comes to how they are used or received, the physical experience of the tangible power of God has misled our thinking. Yes, the "power" gifts are often experienced as tangible power, but they are energised by the person of the Holy Spirit—and He has a will—so the gifts can be used properly only under His guidance and control.

But if we remove the person of the Holy Spirit from the use of the gifts, His power becomes something that we can control—when the emphasis should be on us submitting to Him. At worst, this leads to a *magical* understanding of the gifts.

The gift of speaking in tongues is a revelatory gift, only we don't understand the revelation without the gift of interpretation. The gifts of words of wisdom, knowledge and prophecy are primarily revelatory gifts, but they also release power. The gifts of working miracles, faith and healings are powerful gifts but, ultimately, their operation is based on revelation.

John 5:19-20 says,

> Then Jesus answered and said to them, "Most assuredly, I say to you, the Son can do nothing of Himself, but what He sees the Father do; for whatever He does, the Son also does in like manner. For the Father loves the Son, and shows Him all things that He Himself does; and He will show Him greater works than these, that you may marvel."

At the heart of using the gifts should be a deep, tangible and intimate relationship with God, and life in His presence. If Jesus said that He only could do what He saw the Father do, it should be clear to us that the working of miracles in our lives should also be based on an intimate relationship with the Holy Spirit.

It is much better to perceive the gifts from the perspective of an apostolic and prophetic continuum, rather than dividing them arbitrarily based on some contemporary categories.

Paul writes in Ephesians 2:19-20,

> Consequently, you are no longer foreigners and aliens, but fellow citizens with God's people and members of God's household, built on the foundation of the apostles and prophets, with Christ Jesus himself as the chief cornerstone.

To Paul, it is the apostles and prophets that lay the foundation for the Church. He writes 1 Corinthians 12:28,

> And God has appointed these in the church: first apostles, second prophets, third teachers, after that miracles, then gifts of healings, helps, administrations, varieties of tongues.

He writes in 2 Corinthians 12:12,

> Truly the signs of an apostle were accomplished among you with all perseverance, in signs and wonders and mighty deeds.

Paul refers to signs, wonders and mighty deeds as "the signs of an apostle", but he also lists miracles as a separate gift. Although miracles can be a sign that someone is an apostle, and an apostle should perform miracles, there is a lot more to apostleship than miracles. And performing miracles doesn't automatically mean that someone is an apostle.

But the gifts of healings and the working of miracles are in the apostolic end of the continuum, as their emphasis is on the power of God released now.

The gifts of prophecy, discerning spirits, word of knowledge, word of wisdom, and tongues and their interpretation have a distinctly prophetic nature. But that doesn't mean they don't have immense power. In fact, they have plenty of power, and their impact can often be greater and more long lasting than the use of gifts that manifest immediate results.

The prophecy of Isaiah 53 about the suffering servant predicts the death of Jesus on the cross for our sins. It was proclaimed around seven hundred years before it actually happened. This would have been an open challenge to the devil. In Isaiah 53, God tells exactly how He is planning to bring deliverance to mankind, and gives the devil hundreds of years to scheme against it.

Why do you think King Herod asked to kill all the firstborn of Bethlehem? Powers much greater than his paranoia and jealousy were working behind that.

And yet everything happened *exactly* as Isaiah foretold.

How much spiritual power does it take to give the devil a 700-year challenge and still to deliver the promise exactly as prophesied?

We can see how the apostolic power is released immediately, whereas the release of prophetic power often takes *time*—but it doesn't make the prophetic gift any less powerful.

The gift of faith falls somewhere halfway in the apostolic and prophetic continuum. As we will see, it depends nearly as much on revelation as it does on power. And often, faith takes some time to work its way through. But it is important to understand that, in the Kingdom, there is no power without revelation and no revelation without power. That is why we can see the prophets in the Old Testament working miracles, and modern-day prophets also work miracles.

OTHER GIFT LISTS IN THE NEW TESTAMENT

Paul writes in Romans 12:4-8,

> For as we have many members in one body, but all the members do not have the same function, so we, being many, are one body in Christ, and individually members of one

> another. Having then gifts differing according to the
> grace that is given to us, let us use them: if prophecy, let
> us prophesy in proportion to our faith; or ministry, let us
> use it in our ministering; he who teaches, in teaching; he
> who exhorts, in exhortation; he who gives, with liberality;
> he who leads, with diligence; he who shows mercy, with
> cheerfulness. (Romans 12:4-8)

In this gift list, Paul presents prophecy with teaching, leading and giving—all as gifts from God. He lists the equipping gifts that are often called the fivefold ministry in Ephesians 4:11-16.

> And He Himself gave some to be apostles, some prophets,
> some evangelists, and some pastors and teachers, for the
> equipping of the saints for the work of ministry, for the
> edifying of the body of Christ, till we all come to the unity
> of the faith and of the knowledge of the Son of God, to a
> perfect man, to the measure of the stature of the fullness
> of Christ; that we should no longer be children, tossed to
> and fro and carried about with every wind of doctrine, by
> the trickery of men, in the cunning craftiness of deceitful
> plotting, but, speaking the truth in love, may grow up in all
> things into Him who is the head—Christ—from whom the
> whole body, joined and knit together by what every joint
> supplies, according to the effective working by which every
> part does its share, causes growth of the body for the edifying
> of itself in love.

Often, these gifts are seen as ministry offices, but Paul's focus is on their purpose—the *equipping* of the saints. But gifts aren't only in Paul's theology, as Peter writes in 1 Peter 4:10-11,

> As each one has received a gift, minister it to one another,
> as good stewards of the manifold grace of God. If anyone
> speaks, let him speak as the oracles of God. If anyone
> ministers, let him do it as with the ability which God supplies,
> that in all things God may be glorified through Jesus Christ,
> to whom belong the glory and the dominion forever and
> ever. Amen.

EXTINGUISHING THE GIFTS THROUGH CONTROL

I once visited a church where all gifts given to staff members by suppliers and ministry partners were confiscated by the leaders with a pretext that they should be shared with the rest of the organisation.

The 'teaching' point seemed to be that the gifts were supposed to be shared with everybody. But the real motivation behind this was that the leaders wanted to be in control over who gets which gift. As far as they were concerned, it was them and not the ministry partners who should control the flow of the gifts in their organisation.

In their minds, these leaders were the guardians of favour, and it was in their power to give favour or withhold it. They had tried to create a closed system where all favour in the organisation would depend on them, and any free gifts from outside the system disrupted that control. They saw gifts as a threat, and their response was to try to bring them under their control.

How often do we do that in churches when it comes to spiritual gifts? How often do we 'feel' that God has given the spiritual gifts—His favour—to the 'wrong' members of the church? And do we seek to extinguish them when they are operating through a person we dislike?

Spiritual gifts introduce a level of unpredictability to the finely managed performance and manipulation systems of many churches. As a result, any use of the gifts becomes carefully choreographed and, for example, only prophecies that clearly promote the leadership position of senior leaders are approved.

To these people, Paul writes in Galatians 3:3,

> Are you so foolish? Having begun in the Spirit, are you now being made perfect by the flesh? Have you suffered so many things in vain—if indeed it was in vain?

The context for this is freedom. Pauls writes in Galatians 5:1,

> Stand fast therefore in the liberty by which Christ has made us free, and do not be entangled again with a yoke of bondage.

For spiritual gifts to operate, there must be an atmosphere of freedom and not an atmosphere of control. This doesn't exclude training or correction, or that just anyone can use them publicly. But we need to be clear on the fact that, ultimately, it is God who is the Lord over the gifts and not the church leadership.

Cultivating this kind of culture of freedom, whilst still having safeguards, isn't easy. But in many churches, spiritual gifts lay unused on the leaders' table. They have been offered to the church leadership but rejected.

Yes, there is a level of unpredictability about the gifts, and yes, some people seek to operate through the gifts simply because they haven't been allocated a time to preach. It is amazing how many Christians who allegedly have a 'prophetic word' turn out to be frustrated preachers!

But instead of quenching the gifts, Christians should be trained on how to use them. These gifts have been given by God and can't be controlled by the leadership.

God is the God of order, but He gave us the gifts, which means that they are part of how He brings His order.

5

WAR BETWEEN TWO KINGDOMS

Using the spiritual gifts will, inevitably, lead to a conflict with the kingdom of the devil, and that is why they are not for the double-minded or fainthearted.

Jesus says in Luke 9:62,

> No one, having put his hand to the plow, and looking back,
> is fit for the kingdom of God.

There is a serious side to the Kingdom that is often missing from our teaching in the Charismatic movement that often sees gifts merely as entertainment. If the stage performance 'revivalists' do talk about the war between two kingdoms, it is reduced to a story in which the 'revivalist' is usually the hero, but which gives the audience an opportunity to join him on the hero's journey to victory.

So, some tell wild tales about angels that appear anywhere they go, others boast about their authority over demonic forces, but to me, much of it sounds more like playing a video game than engaging in real war with real costs. In reality, this war is serious, with real damage inflicted on us.

According to the Bible, there are four types of spiritual beings: God, angels, fallen angels i.e. demons, and human beings.

Some call the interaction between spiritual beings—both positive and negative—the spiritual realm, or spiritual dimension.

Whether the spiritual dimension is an actual dimension or not, or simply our ability to engage with other spiritual beings, we don't really know, but that doesn't really matter, when it comes to us.

In many ways, the concept of a spiritual dimension is problematic, as it implies some sort of impersonal, spatial realm, which might or might not exist, not at least the way we normally think about realms. To our purposes, it is adequate to limit our conversation to interaction and relationships between different spiritual beings, and use the concept of the spiritual realm, world or dimension metaphorically, as it can be helpful, when explaining the nature of spiritual war.

Human beings are in the middle of a war between two kingdoms—God and Satan's. And there is no no-man's-land. It is through the spiritual gifts that we begin to participate in this battle perhaps more deeply than in any other way, affecting it in a profound way. The simple reason for that is that when we operate in the spiritual gifts, we operate in the Spirit of God. And this applies to all spiritual gifts, not just the nine gifts.

God could win this war in an instant, but that would lead to major human casualties for eternity. The apostle Peter writes,

> The Lord is not slack concerning His promise, as some count slackness, but is longsuffering toward us, not willing that any should perish but that all should come to repentance. (2 Peter 3:9)

It is important to understand that there are only two spiritual kingdoms. One is the pure, unbroken and holy Kingdom of God. The other one is the twisted kingdom of Satan who has never created anything else but chaos and destruction. Satan has dark spiritual power, and that power is a corrupted version of the power God once gave to the angels, spiritual beings He created before He created us.

Jesus says,

> "When an unclean spirit goes out of a man, he goes through dry places, seeking rest; and finding none, he says, 'I will return to my house from which I came.' And when he comes, he finds it swept and put in order. Then he goes and takes

with him seven other spirits more wicked than himself, and they enter and dwell there; and the last state of that man is worse than the first." (Luke 11:24-26)

As Jesus said, there is no spiritual vacuum in our lives. Obviously, that doesn't mean people around Christians are demon-possessed, only that our lives are influenced by invisible, spiritual forces. But much of the humankind lives mainly in the area of the soul, blind to the spiritual forces but deeply affected by them.

Hebrews 1:14 says that angels are ministering spirits, sent to serve us. It follows that demons, the fallen angels, are also spirits.

The Holy Spirit is a spirit, but unlike demonic spirits and angels, He is omnipotent and omniscient. But no matter how mighty He is, we are still unable to see Him. He fills us, yet we are unable to see Him, but we can experience His presence and fullness in our inner being.

Angels and demons are also invisible to us, most of the time, although there are times when they can appear to people, as we can see in the Bible, and Christians with the gift of discerning spirits can often discern their operation and presence.

The people who are involved in the occult also have some level of spiritual discernment, but it has mainly to do with sensing the magnitude of spiritual power. It is not the discernment God gives, but false knowledge of spiritual powers that comes from being in the wrong side of the battle.

When I was at the university, I had a friend who was a Satanist. He was a genuine, well-educated, young man, who didn't believe that Satan is a real person, but he believed in the existence of life forces that he wanted to be filled with. He saw Satanism as a positive creed, affirming the value of human life, and in opposition to Christianity that he perceived as a negative, restrictive and condemning religion.

The spiritual beings he didn't believe in had deceived him, so that he even denied their existence.

We had some genuine and meaningful conversations about faith. I remember once sitting with him at the reception area of the largest newspaper in Finland with our professor and fellow students, discussing the finer points of how to interpret the book of Revelation, with everyone else eavesdropping in the conversation.

One day, I went to see him at his home, and I was surprised to see that he had a large collection of gospel music.

I asked him, "Why do you listen to the gospel music if you don't believe in God?"

"I can feel the energy in this music", he responded.

This Satanist was able to discern the 'high energy level' of this music that had been anointed by God, but he was unable to discern the difference between the two sources of spiritual energy—darkness and light. That takes discernment by the Holy Spirit, and he was lacking in it.

In Acts 8, Simon, who used to be a sorcerer and had become a Christian, saw the apostles praying for people who received the Holy Spirit.

> Simon offered the apostles money, saying, "Give me this power also, that anyone on whom I lay hands may receive the Holy Spirit." (Acts 8:18-19)

Peter rebuked Simon, and he repented, but what caused this issue is that although Simon had become a Christian, he perceived the Holy Spirit merely as a force that was more powerful than the occult forces he had been deceived by in the past.

He still had a magical understanding of the Holy Spirit, and he saw the power of the Holy Spirit as something he could control, rather than seeing the Holy Spirit as the Lord, someone he should submit to.

But how many Charismatic and Pentecostal ministers today would have been happy to sell Simon the programme that would 'release the authority' of the Holy Spirit in his life? A typical Charismatic conference advert guarantees an impartation of the Holy Spirit for anyone attending.

But one thing Simon could see clearly and it was that the Holy Spirit has more power than demons. And in this he was right. Both God's angels and demons have only limited spiritual power and no creative power. The angels of God use their spiritual power in total obedience to God, but demons use their power for rebellion.

I don't know if you have ever seen a demonic being manifest, but if you have, you will know where rebellion against God leads to—a dark place where there might be plenty of spiritual power but no God. And you will know something of what hell feels like.

The angels aren't a source of life. God is. It is important to emphasise that, as some of the Charismatic veneration of angels is close to angel worship. Only God's spiritual power is unlimited.

The demonic spirits are able to perform supernatural manifestations; yet they don't have creative but only destructive power. Their power is the power of rage and destruction of what God has created—but their favourite tool is deception. The devil delights in deceiving even his followers!

But God is full of love, and when He fills us up, He restores our strength.

All of the time, we are surrounded by angelic and demonic beings. When there is a sighting of them, it doesn't mean that these spiritual beings have suddenly materialised. What it means is that, for a moment, we can see into the spiritual reality around us. But what we see can also be deceitful, so we must be careful in accepting anything we see.

Demons don't respect angels. They fight against them. They don't respect God either. They fight against His plans and purposes. But they can't stop or even delay God.

This war will have one winner—God. But God is restraining His power, as He has more important objectives than defeating His enemies immediately. He is in the business of raising sons and daughters for Himself, and it is this process and plan the enemy is targeting.

God's strategy is not to release His full power on earth yet. First and foremost, He is raising His children, and He uses both empowering and discipline to raise us.

But the devil and his demonic army are not restraining their power, as their only goal is destruction. Revelation 12:12 says,

> For the devil has come down to you, having great wrath, because he knows that he has a short time.

The devil is full of rage, and he will target his rage mainly at the people who genuinely seek for God's Kingdom to come. He will also target his fury at people who seek to love and begin to operate in the spiritual gifts, as they can greatly advance the Kingdom of God if they learn to use these gifts in maturity.

Beware of teachers who teach about spiritual gifts with a sense of triumphalism and no reference to the battle against darkness!

Jesus warns against triumphalism in Luke 10:17-20,

> Then the seventy returned with joy, saying, "Lord, even the demons are subject to us in Your name." And He said to them, "I saw Satan fall like lightning from heaven. Behold, I give you the authority to trample on serpents and scorpions, and over all the power of the enemy, and nothing shall by any means hurt you. Nevertheless do not rejoice in this, that the spirits are subject to you, but rather rejoice because your names are written in heaven."

The name of Jesus has so much more power than any demon, including Satan, but we are so easily deceived. These demonic powers and principalities can affect us in so many ways, even building traps on our way today, activating them decades later, long after we have already forgotten that they have been set. The demons submit to us in Jesus' name, but it doesn't mean that the battle is over. The battle will only be over in heaven.

No matter if you want it or not, you are in this battle. And in Galatians Paul gives us a glimpse of an important principle that reveals our position in this war.

> Now I say that the heir, as long as he is a child, does not differ at all from a slave, though he is master of all, but is under guardians and stewards until the time appointed by the father. Even so we, when we were children, were in bondage under the elements of the world. But when the fullness of the time had come, God sent forth His Son, born of a woman,

born under the law, to redeem those who were under the law, that we might receive the adoption as sons. And because you are sons, God has sent forth the Spirit of His Son into your hearts, crying out, "Abba, Father!" Therefore you are no longer a slave but a son, and if a son, then an heir of God through Christ. (Galatians 4:1-7)

This is astonishing! We are in war, but it is God Himself who has let us be subjected under the tutorship of these forces. And it is through the Holy Spirit that we can begin to be liberated from the power of "the elements of the world"—also translated as *spiritual powers*. But it is the hostility from these demonic forces that disciplines us to increase in maturity, so that we can begin to live as His sons and daughters—the princes and princesses in His Kingdom.

What is also noteworthy is that, in Paul's view, submitting to the Law also brings you back under bondage to these spiritual powers.

Paul continues,

But then, indeed, when you did not know God, you served those which by nature are not gods. But now after you have known God, or rather are known by God, how is it that you turn again to the weak and beggarly elements, to which you desire again to be in bondage? You observe days and months and seasons and years. I am afraid for you, lest I have labored for you in vain. (Galatians 4:8-10)

The only way to stand up against the evil spiritual powers and win is to walk in the Spirit. But that automatically sets us on collision course with the enemy—again and again.

As we begin to rise up in our gifting and calling, it will automatically mean that we will begin to engage with the enemy's kingdom, for the simple reason that there is no spiritual vacuum on earth. There is no no-man's-land.

When I pray for people, I often feel how energy flows out of me into the lives of the people. This is the power of the Holy Spirit. That energy has the power to transform people's lives in a split second.

But it isn't just energy. It is also God's *love* condensed. It is His *presence*. It has a shape and a *direction*.

But it must be emphasised that here we talk exclusively of God's Spirit. No other spirit has such power.

When you use the spiritual gifts, you are operating in the power of God and His authority. This always has an effect on the devil's kingdom.

In Matthew 12:22-29, Jesus refers to Satan's kingdom, and how God deals with it violently.

> Then one was brought to Him who was demon-possessed, blind and mute; and He healed him, so that the blind and mute man both spoke and saw. And all the multitudes were amazed and said, "Could this be the Son of David?" Now when the Pharisees heard it they said, "This fellow does not cast out demons except by Beelzebub, the ruler of the demons."
>
> But Jesus knew their thoughts, and said to them: "Every kingdom divided against itself is brought to desolation, and every city or house divided against itself will not stand. If Satan casts out Satan, he is divided against himself. How then will his kingdom stand? And if I cast out demons by Beelzebub, by whom do your sons cast them out? Therefore they shall be your judges. But if I cast out demons by the Spirit of God, surely the kingdom of God has come upon you. Or how can one enter a strong man's house and plunder his goods, unless he first binds the strong man? And then he will plunder his house."

If you want to use spiritual gifts, it is imperative that you take everything that Jesus said about the Kingdom seriously. And most things He said about the Kingdom concern your inner being.

God wants to ensure that your inner being can be a dwelling place for His Spirit—a temple of the Holy Spirit—so that He can flow from your inner being, and that is why He is so focused on renewing it.

We care for external expressions of religion, but God cares for our inner being, as He knows that without the Holy Spirit dwelling in our inner being and guarding it, we will be an easy prey to the enemy.

Jesus says in Mark 4:24-25,

> "Take heed what you hear. With the same measure you use, it will be measured to you; and to you who hear, more will be given. For whoever has, to him more will be given; but whoever does not have, even what he has will be taken away from him."

This principle of increase applies to spiritual gifts. If you have them and you use them in love, God will give you *more*. But if you aren't willing to love and to give, even the gift you have will wither.

But many protest and refer to Romans 11:29,

> For the gifts and the calling of God are irrevocable.

Here Paul is writing about Israel and says that, regardless of their disobedience, God is always willing to graft them back into the vine if they repent. Many have taken this to mean that you can't lose any of the gifts God has given to you, but if you apply the logic of Paul's argument correctly, it would mean that God is always willing to give the gifts back to you if you begin to follow Jesus again.

You see, God is always calling us, but following Jesus happens on His terms and not on our terms.

I know many ministers who once operated in the Kingdom authority, but as their capacity to love didn't increase, many of their gifts were gradually taken away from them.

I once gave a prophetic word to a minister who operated in a blatant disregard of compassion. I told him, "God won't take away your healing gift." And gradually, he was stripped away from all his gifts, which he had many, until what was left was the gifts of healings that operated occasionally, as he ministered internationally.

But when he occasionally ministers in compassion, some of the other gifts return.

So many ministers operate like King Saul. Under anointing and submission to God, many victories came to them effortlessly, but now these victories have become impossible to attain. They are in the game of ever-diminishing returns.

I know someone who used to pray for hours and work a lot less, to now work sixteen to eighteen hours per day in a vain effort to maintain what he had received effortlessly through the gifts!

And the use of spiritual gifts can't protect us on the Judgment Day. Jesus said,

> "Not everyone who says to Me, 'Lord, Lord,' shall enter the kingdom of heaven, but he who does the will of My Father in heaven. Many will say to Me in that day, 'Lord, Lord, have we not prophesied in Your name, cast out demons in Your name, and done many wonders in Your name?' And then I will declare to them, 'I never knew you; depart from Me, you who practice lawlessness!'" (Matthew 7:21-23)

Jesus doesn't deny that these people operated in His power, but He says that He never knew them.

If there could be a clearer warning regarding giving excuses to leaders who operate in gifts but live in blatant sin, I don't know what it could be.

The way gifts work reflects the two commandments to love precisely. Loving your God with all your heart, mind and being leads to living in the fullness of the Holy Spirit. When you love God you will end up being full of Him. But the flow of the gifts is toward others. Unless you love others and are willing to bless them, the flow of God's love through your life will be blocked, and the presence and operation of the Holy Spirit in you will begin to wither.

There are many dangers in using the gifts, and the enemy will attempt to use our every weakness—and strength—against us.

Frequent use of gifts increases our spiritual authority and elevates the perception of others about us. This brings emotional satisfaction and feeds the ego.

Consequently, many people begin to manufacture 'an aura' of the gifts, projecting their giftedness into every situation. For example, prophetic people don't make it clear when they are not operating under the prophetic anointing, but use the 'halo effect' that comes from the gift to manipulate people, so that they can achieve selfish and carnal goals.

Psychologically, the borderlines between the work of God's Spirit and their own mind become blurred, so that soon the ministers no more discern if they are operating in the gift or not. They will begin to confuse their ego and adrenaline flow with the work of God's Spirit.

There are four main ways to combat the psychological blurring of the lines:

1. Daily Bible study for your spiritual development rather than studying for sermons.
2. Prayer life that is not satisfied for anything less than experiencing God's presence on a daily basis
3. Deliberate avoiding of religious and charismatic mannerisms
4. Focusing on the fruit of the Spirit rather than the gifts.

FOCUS ON THE FRUIT OF THE SPIRIT

Paul writes in Galatians 5:22-23,

> But the fruit of the Spirit is love, joy, peace, longsuffering, kindness, goodness, faithfulness, gentleness, self-control. Against such there is no law.

He also writes in Philippians 1:9-11,

> And this I pray, that your love may abound still more and more in knowledge and all discernment, that you may approve the things that are excellent, that you may be sincere and without offense till the day of Christ, being filled with the fruits of righteousness which are by Jesus Christ, to the glory and praise of God.

In the Charismatic movement we have a terrible habit of ignoring sound principles of Bible interpretation and make the Bible say what we want it to say.

For example, Randy Clark explains what he believes Philippians 1:9-11 to mean,

> This fruit is both the moral fruit of Galatians 5 and the fruit of the power of God for signs, wonders, working of miracles, healings, prophecy, words of knowledge, words of wisdom, discerning of spirits, gifts of faith, tongues and interpretation of tongues.[1]

He continues,

> "Fruit of righteousness" does not refer to righteousness itself or imputed righteousness. Nor does it refer to what happened to us at salvation. Another way of seeing the fruit of righteousness and glory verse talks about is to see that glory equals power and fruit equals both the fruit of supernatural deeds Jesus mentions in John 15 and the moral fruit Paul lists in Galatians 5:22-23.[2]

He adds,

> We also need to think of fruit as dealing with power gifts and works.[3]

But reading the context, there is absolutely no justification for this interpretation. Jesus says in John 15:1-17,

> "I am the true vine, and My Father is the vinedresser. Every branch in Me that does not bear fruit He takes away; and every branch that bears fruit He prunes, that it may bear more fruit. You are already clean because of the word which I have spoken to you. Abide in Me, and I in you. As the branch cannot bear fruit of itself, unless it abides in the vine, neither can you, unless you abide in Me.
>
> I am the vine, you are the branches. He who abides in Me, and I in him, bears much fruit; for without Me you can do nothing. If anyone does not abide in Me, he is cast out as a branch and is withered; and they gather them and throw them into the fire, and they are burned. If you abide in

Me, and My words abide in you, you will ask what you desire, and it shall be done for you. By this My Father is glorified, that you bear much fruit; so you will be My disciples.

As the Father loved Me, I also have loved you; abide in My love. If you keep My commandments, you will abide in My love, just as I have kept My Father's commandments and abide in His love. These things I have spoken to you, that My joy may remain in you, and that your joy may be full. This is My commandment, that you love one another as I have loved you. Greater love has no one than this, than to lay down one's life for his friends.

You are My friends if you do whatever I command you. No longer do I call you servants, for a servant does not know what his master is doing; but I have called you friends, for all things that I heard from My Father I have made known to you. You did not choose Me, but I chose you and appointed you that you should go and bear fruit, and that your fruit should remain, that whatever you ask the Father in My name He may give you. These things I command you, that you love one another."

There is no singular reference to signs and wonders, apart from the promise that the Father will give us what we ask. The emphasis of the whole chapter is on us bearing fruit by loving each other.

So, according to John, our aim should be to love each other, and that will bring fruit. According to Paul, we should pursue love when we use the gifts. Can you see how Paul and John are remarkably in agreement: loving each other releases many other gifts and blessings?

I have come to realise that our ability to ignore and redefine the most important practical commandment Jesus gave us—to love each other—is tremendous. We keep on explaining it away and avoiding it in so many ways.

According to Randy Clark, we haven't fully proclaimed the gospel if signs and wonders are not accompanying the preaching.

There is a simple reason why I am labouring this point. This model leads to a different destination than Jesus directed us to, and to eventual disappointment and disillusionment. This presentation of fruit as signs and wonders is part of a larger theological framework of Dominion theology. According to Bill Johnson, God's Plan A was dominion.

> Jesus then gave His authority to those who would follow Him. He basically announced that we were back to Plan A: taking back the dominion of a planet, now as redeemed humankind.[4]

To make this even clearer, he says, "Jesus our Savior came with dominion in mind."[5] According to him,

> While Jesus is eternally God, He emptied Himself of His divinity and became a man. (See Philippians 2:7) It is vital to note that He did all His miracles as a man, not as God.[6]

According to this way of thinking, this compels us to work miracles like Jesus did, as He worked them as man.

In the model Bill Johnson and Randy Clark propose, redefinition of fruit as miracles and wonders also leads Christians to try to reach an unattainable goal, performing miracles and wonders at the level of Jesus. Yes, Jesus said that we would do greater things than He did, but He spoke to us collectively as His Church. But all this redefinition is based on an understanding of the Kingdom coming through the Church, so that we will have dominion over the world, and supposedly, we need signs and wonders for that.

In the New Testament, signs and wonders were there to testify of the Lordship of Jesus, so that as many people as possible would be saved; now they have been repurposed to usher in the dominion of the Church over the world.

The Catholic Church achieved far greater dominion over the world than we could ever imagine to gain today, but spiritually, it didn't do it much good.

But as Jesus said, we should not rejoice because of power, but because our names have been written in heaven.

GIFTS BRING NIMBLENESS

General Stanley McChrystal, who led the Joint Operations Task Force from 2004 in Iraq, found the US forces completely unprepared for the new kind of warfare Al Qaeda waged.

He writes,

> The environment in which we found ourselves, a convergence of twenty-first-century factors and more timeless human interactions, demanded a dynamic, constantly adapting approach. For a soldier trained at West Point as an engineer, the idea that a problem has different solutions on different days was fundamentally disturbing. Yet that was the case.[7]

Much of the ministry of the Church is following well-established and tested methods, which we are increasingly finding to be ineffective, as the world and the cultural preferences of our populations are rapidly changing. Some people apply a methodical approach to gifts, but like the US soldiers in Iraq, they find that a problem has different solutions on different days. But that is why God has given us a diversity of gifts, and by stepping into that diversity we are able to apply them to different problems.

Every person you meet or pass on the street is facing different problems, and the gifts of the Spirit are there to solve unique problems—not methodically but uniquely—each time.

Once, I prayed for around twenty or thirty youth in one session. I had a word for each one of them. For some it was a prophecy, for others a word of knowledge that unlocked their inner being, but for the rest, it was a word of wisdom. But there was one individual whose problem was approached through the gift of discerning spirits.

Having more than one gift is useful, as you will be able to meet the needs of more people through your ministry.

6

GIFTS OF HEALINGS

We begin inspecting the individual gifts with the gifts of healings. This isn't my preferred order, as I don't consider myself to have the gifts of healings, but it is necessary, mainly as belief in healing unites most Christians, especially the Pentecostals and the Charismatics, and it is also where the failure of the stage performance model is at its most paramount and measurable.

In a 1996 Gallup Poll, 77% of respondents in America agreed that "God sometimes intervenes to cure people who have a serious illness" and 82% affirmed "the healing power of personal prayer." In 2003, 72% of those polled attested that "praying to God can cure someone—even if science says that the person doesn't stand a chance." A 2007 survey concluded that 23% of Americans believe that they have personally "witnessed a miraculous, physical healing."[1]

So, clearly belief in healing is common spread, and you don't have to be a Charismatic American to practise a prayer of healing, as prayer for healing is common even in traditional and liberal churches. Nearly all Christian traditions practise the prayer for healing.

And you don't even need to be a Christian to believe in this gift, as many people who don't believe in God at all are often happy to receive prayers for their healing.

Interestingly, participant accounts from the Azusa Street Revival indicate that healing, rather than speaking in tongues, was the primary attraction to outsiders.[2] This had much to do with California as a whole becoming the destination for health tourists and residents because of the favourable climate by the end the 19th century.

Los Angeles, the birthplace of Pentecostalism and Hollywood, had a disproportionate number of sick people, who had travelled to the West Coast to look for healing from a better climate. The reality of the late 19th century was that hardly any of the medicines we know today existed, so often doctors could do very little. For example, aspirin was first synthesised only in 1897.

Los Angeles became a centre especially for anyone suffering from lung diseases. One physician in 1873 remarked that he had never seen in any other state so many suffering from lung diseases. A tuberculosis patient described Los Angeles in the end of the 19th century:

> At every street corner I met a poor fellow croaking like myself. I strolled into the Plaza, there to imbibe the exhilarating effects of a community with broken lungs in all stages[3]

In 1906, when the Azusa Street Revival started, Los Angeles also had the highest level of religious diversity in the country. Ethnically, it was also the most mixed place on earth. But because of so many sick people living there, it is no wonder that healing became a major emphasis in the Pentecostal movement that believed in miracles.

But the modern Christian interest in healing had begun much earlier. In 1830-1835, Britain experienced a revival that predated the Pentecostal movement by more than seventy years and also birthed the Catholic Apostolic Church in 1832.

On 28th March 1830, a young woman, Mary Campbell, lay dying of tuberculosis in Scotland. While praying with her sister, she began to speak in an unknown tongue. The following month, James MacDonald, in Port Glasgow, also had an experience that he construed as the baptism in the Holy Spirit. He prayed for his dying sister in the name of Jesus, and his sister recovered. He then wrote to Mary Campbell who began to recover after she read the letter. Some days later James and his brother spoke in tongues for the first time, and the following night they also interpreted them.

Edward Irving, a Scottish clergyman in London, heard about these events and was greatly impacted by them.

Albury Conferences had gathered from 1826 to 1830 at the Surrey Estate of Henry Drummond to study biblical prophecy. At the final conference, Irvin encouraged the participants to pray for a renewal of the spiritual gifts. This happened around nine months before they appeared in his church in April 1831.

The conference resolved that "it is our duty to pray for the revival of those manifested in the primitive church—healing, miracles, prophecy, kinds of tongues and interpretation of tongues and that a responsibility lies on us to enquire into the state of those gifts said to be now present in the west of Scotland."[4]

It is interesting to see how Edward Irving and his fellow Christians began to pray for the gifts based on simply studying the Bible and not because of any supernatural experiences. It was their firm belief that the Church needed these gifts, even when they didn't see them operational. They might also have been the first proponents of the latter rain theology—the belief that the Holy Spirit would be poured out again like at the Pentecost in the End Times.

One of the verified healings in London was the healing of Elizabeth Fancourt. She was visited by Pierrepoint Greaves. She had been crippled and suffered pain for eight years. She was able to walk one and a quarter miles the following Sunday to demonstrate healing.

This movement encountered enormous resistance from the rationalist Christians with cessasionist views. According to them, the uniformity and universality of the laws of nature were paramount.[5] They simply couldn't not be broken.

Unfortunately, many of the theologians today still hold the cessasionist view, even when natural science has shifted to see the universe in a lot less mechanical terms, with quantum physics creating space for uncertainty and mere probabilities at the core of the physical particles, thus creating the needed 'scientific' space for miracles.

Cessationism has never affected Catholicism to the same extent than the Protestant churches, especially when it comes to healing.

The emphasis on divine healing increased both in the USA and UK from the 1880s. One of the major figures promoting divine healing was J.A. Dowie, who might have begun with genuine healings but soon degenerated into a cult leader.

Unfortunately, J.A. Dowie has made a significant, negative contribution to Charismatic theology through his demonisation of all sickness. According to Dowie,

> All disease is the oppression of the Devil, but there are some which are possessions by the Devil, or by Devils.[6]

Dowie demonised sickness, and the Pentecostal and Charismatic movements have suffered from this false doctrine ever since. In the Bible, there are a few instances where a demon possession had side effects that resembled sickness, for example when Jesus cast out a "mute spirit" in Mark 9:14-27, but these were instances of demon possession, and not sicknesses; in only a few occasions they had been misidentified as sicknesses, and mostly correctly identified as demon possession.

But Dowie popularised the idea that sickness itself was directly demonic and a result of demonic influence.

Often, we perceive the rise of spiritual healing within Protestant Christianity in America as a Pentecostal phenomenon, but in fact that was not the case. For example, the Episcopal Church embraced divine healing. But unlike the Episcopal Church, the Pentecostals viewed medical institutions with indifference and even suspicion.

> The value placed on medical science by the Episcopal Commission greatly separated it from the common attitude held by most Pentecostals toward the medical community. Pentecostals, more in keeping with folk religion, viewed the medical community as well as most institutions of high learning with a benign indifference. Healing for the vast majority of them was theological in nature.[7]

The concept of attributing specific illnesses to identifiable demonic forces was advanced further in sizeable sections of the successor Pentecostal movement. Charles Parham, one of the founding figures of Pentecostalism, believed that there were "demonised torments that feed upon the body in various diseases". One demon, he maintained, lived in a Chicago woman's cancer and "ate or absorbed over a pound of raw beef steak laid upon it each day."[8]

The demonisation of illness has plagued Pentecostalism and the Charismatic movement until this very day. But it has been a very 'useful' doctrine for many healing evangelists, as it works well with the theatrics of stage performance. Combining the fact that all demonic forces must submit to the name of Jesus with the false belief that all illness is demonic meant that there really wasn't any need for a doctor's certificate to prove any healing.

Pentecostalism has rarely confronted the difficult issues related to the birth of the movement, including Parham's belief in white superiority and in eight-day creation. These issues have mainly been silenced. According to Parham, the Adamic race was created on the 8th day. Intermarriage between the two races, he believed, brought the trouble to earth in Noah's time, Noah was saved, as he had a "pedigree without mixed blood". Miscegenation could, according to him, cause similar distress in America by introducing many diseases and wiping "the mixed bloods off the face of the earth."[9]

These were clearly racist ideas, even according to the standards of the time, and they elevated the white supremacist ideology above the revelation of the Bible.

Divine healing was always an integral part of the Azusa Street Revival, but it was further emphasised because of the influenza epidemic of 1918, which served as an impetus for wide acceptance of divine healing in global Christianity. World War 1 claimed 16 million lives; 50 million lives were claimed by influenza in 1918. In October 1918 alone, the flu claimed 200,000 lives in the USA.[10]

It seems clear that when millions of people died of influenza, which didn't have a cure at the time, millions of people also turned to God in desperate search for healing. We can see clearly how the influenza epidemic of 1918 has left its marks in Pentecostal and Charismatic understanding of healing. This emphasis has continued, even when the medical science has greatly improved in the last hundred years.

EXTRAPOLATING FROM PERSONAL HEALING EXPERIENCE

It seems clear that in the Pentecostal understanding of healing, which later on spread into the Charismatic movement, three factors have come together.

1. Selective reading of the Bible from the perspective of the latter rain doctrine
2. An understanding that the ministry of Jesus as described in the Gospels is attainable to an individual filled with the Holy Spirit rather than the total Body of Christ
3. Generalisation from personal experience of healing.

If we read the New Testament in totality, we soon realise that although healing was a real part of the early church ministry, the healing ministry of Jesus was entirely unique, and that stories about healings become less commonplace as the story of the early church advances. But stories about healings never completely disappear.

At the heart of many healing ministries has been an attempt to reproduce a personally experienced healing on a mass scale, thus building a ministry model based on one experience of success. For example, when Oral Roberts, the other leading evangelist alongside William Branham of the Healing Revival, was a teenager, he caught tuberculosis. Four months into the sickness, he made the personal decision to follow Jesus. Before that, his family had been praying a long time for his healing. Later on, Oral's brother Elmer took him to a tent revival where flamboyant "divine healer" and evangelist George W. Moncey preached.

In 1982, Oral Roberts remembered this healing experience of his youth.

> Brother Moncey said words I think I can quote . . . Pretty accurately . . . Because they were so different and they were so penetrating. He did not pray, "O Lord, heal this boy." . . . He spoke to another power and he said, "You foul tormenting disease, I command you in the name of Jesus Christ of

Nazareth, come out of this boy. Loose him and let him go free!" Now, you see, nobody was praying prayers like that . . . I felt the healing power of the Lord. It was like your hand striking me, like electricity going through me. It went into my lungs, went into my tongue, and all at once I could breathe. I could breathe all the way down. Before that when I tried to breathe all the way down I would haemorrhage.[11]

Many in the audience knew Oral and were praising God for healing him, but they fell silent when he was told to speak, as he stuttered when under pressure. But Oral jumped up on the platform, shouting, "I'm healed! I'm healed!" Then he ran back and forth across the stage for several minutes.

Although according to the story, the healing seems instantaneous, Oral's actual recovery took months. But this personal experience of real healing undoubtedly both guided him forward and led him astray. Oral recalls a particular scene in Jacksonville in 1951.

The miracle started and all of the sudden I cried out that my right hand was like it was on fire. My hand was hurting like you were sticking it with a thousand pins . . . Suddenly I jumped to my feet. I didn't say anything and the crowd jumped up and here they came and completely engulfed the platform and me.[12]

Oral came to use prayer line as the "method" for healing. And when he pioneered with nationwide TV broadcasts, it was Roberts who asked people to touch the screen to claim their healing. For Roberts, the secret behind healing was the power of the touch—although Roberts didn't claim that he could heal anyone, he believed that he was the channel of God's power.

Through the Healing Revival, Oral simply attempted to multiply his unique healing experience, believing that what God did for him, He could do to others en masse.

DID THE HEALING REVIVAL WORK?

The stories of the healing evangelists sound impressive, but we need to look at the actual evidence for healings to gain an understanding regarding the real effectiveness of these ministries.

Rev. Mr. Shuler was an early critic of healing evangelists, and he criticised the healing crusades of Charles Price, who modelled his ministry on Aimee McPherson's. Price ministered in the decades before the Healing Revival.

He writes,

> Dr. Price has become an evangelist of almost as startling pretensions as those assumed by the woman [Mrs. McPherson] who discovered him. Several months ago he conducted a great campaign in Vancouver, B.C. Following this campaign, the Christian forces of that city met and appointed a commission to investigate the results. That report is before us as we write. The commission was composed of eleven ministers, eight Christian physicians, among whom were the most prominent specialists in Vancouver, three university professors and one eminent member of the legal fraternity. Several months of painstaking investigation, and several investigators working constantly, finally produced the facts, and they are most startling.[13]

According to the report, 350 cases of healing were claimed, but 39 of the cases died within six months of the diseases they were supposed to be cured of, and 5 went insane. Altogether, 301 of the 350 cases were found at the end of six months to have received no benefit, many acknowledging that it was so. But 5 were reported to have been cured from functional ailments.

Now, it is not actually reported, whether or not Dr. Price's ministry had anything to do with these lasting improvements of health or not.

Rarely do healing evangelists ever mention the backlash after a healing crusade. According to Rev. Mr. Shuler,

Scores of people who went for healing, professed absolute faith, but were not healed, and are now bitterly antagonistic to the Christian religion. Indeed it was discovered that the campaign upset and overturned the faith of literally hundreds of Christian people, whose expectations for their poor mortal bodies were not met.[14]

Now, Rev. Mr. Schuler probably wasn't an unbiased observer, as he campaigned against healing evangelists, so we must look for testimonies from more sympathetic observers.

Roberta Salter, Aimee's daughter, told it was commonly understood that not all healings lasted. Aimee, as quoted in one of her posthumous autobiographies, stated that there was usually a reason for this, and that it was very foolish to ask God to heal you, only to go back to doing the "usual things."[15]

But if healings don't last, are they still healings? Genuine healings should last, although, if someone's high blood pressure is caused by a poor diet, it will probably go up again after a healing if they don't improve the diet. But a real healing should be a physical, verifiable fact.

The Pentecostal belief that all will be healed if there is enough faith has always been based on selective reading of evidence. And it has never worked even in the lives of the Pentecostal pioneers who professed it most loudly.

William Durham, the early Pentecostal pioneer, prayed for Aimee McPherson's broken ankle, and Aimee testified:

> I suddenly felt as if a shock of electricity had struck my foot. It flowed through my whole body, causing me to shake and tremble under the power of God. Instantaneously, my foot was perfectly healed.[16]

But then some time after, Aimee's first husband, Robert J. Semple, died in Hong Kong, after two years of marriage, of haemorrhagic dysentery and exhaustion.[17] And on 7th July 1912 William H. Durham himself, secretly suffering from pulmonary tuberculosis, died, aged under forty.[18]

Looking at the historical evidence, it is instructive to realise that the preachers of divine healing have been rarely protected from sickness themselves. Why did William H. Durham die of tuberculosis? Surely, if total healing was the manifestation of the Holy Spirit when He worked, William H. Durham should have been the first one protected from tuberculosis.

As we can see, extrapolating total healing for everyone is contrary to the evidence of the real life of the early Pentecostals. It is necessary to say this, as many in the Charismatic movement point to the early Pentecostals and the Healing Revival as the gold standard of healing ministry we should all aspire to. But their experience of healing was no better than ours.

The contemporary critics described Oral Roberts as overeager to confirm a healing, pronouncing a healing solely based on the excited testimony of a person that he felt better.[19]

For example, writer John Kobler interviewed two individuals recommended by Roberts himself, and reported that while both believed they had been healed, one had never visited a physician and the other had subsequently undergone a cancer surgery.[20]

The reality is that there were no accurate records of healings. In 1981, Evelyn Roberts, Oral's wife, confessed, "We never even kept count of those who were healed. I have no idea of how many people were healed."[21]

It is noteworthy that a ministry that was publicly focused on healing kept no records of actual healings.

Tommy Tyson, Oral's associate evangelist in the 1960s, estimated that 2%-3% of for whom Roberts prayed were healed instantly, although many others seemed to be gradually helped.[22] But that number is based on a visual assessment on the events and not on follow-up, so even this figure is probably rather inflated.

Roberts often referred to the "point of contact" as the greatest discovery he had ever made. In his early years he believed that all could be healed.[23] But at least Oral Roberts was a lot more honest than many other healing evangelists, as later on, he acknowledged the failure of the model, although he still believed that the era of healing evangelists had been beneficial.

The healing evangelism model was originally based on hiring a large venue that was acceptable to an interdenominational crowd.

What happens in that environment is that we move from a congregation, where most people are known to each other, to a large crowd, where hardly anyone knows each other. There is very little you can do immediately to verify anyone's healing if anything that looks like healing happens. And many healing evangelists manipulate this crowd. They don't really care whether someone has genuinely been healed or not. What they care about is whether it *looks* like someone has been healed.

If you believe in healing, you might feel that I am overtly critical of healing ministries. But this is necessary, as much of today's healing ministry is based on the examples set by the Healing Revival, and more specifically, the ministries of William Branham and Oral Roberts. Or, rather they are based on their legends. But as we have seen, the reality is far different from the legend.

HEALING ON STAGE

One of the main traits of the Charismatic healing practice has been public prayer for the sick. This model originates from the misapplication of Jesus' public healing ministry. Jesus often healed publicly, but His emphasis was not on demonstrating His power to the crowds, but the healing of an individual. Also, in most cases, only a few people would have seen the actual moment of healing, but the whole village or town would have seen the effect, as the life of the healed was totally transformed.

John 9:8-11 illustrates this well.

> Therefore the neighbors and those who previously had seen that he was blind said, "Is not this he who sat and begged?" Some said, "This is he." Others *said*, "He is like him." He said, "I am *he*." Therefore they said to him, "How were your eyes opened?" He answered and said, "A Man called Jesus made clay and anointed my eyes and said to me, 'Go to the pool of Siloam and wash.' So I went and washed, and I received sight."

We can see how Jesus rarely focused on demonstrating the moment of healing, as He knew that the true demonstration of healing was that it lasted. But when the healing revivalists took the healing on stage, they also brought the need for demonstrations on stage. This needed more theatrics, but as everything happened on stage, there was no time or 'need' to verify the permanency of healing.

B.J. Morris the director of religious education at Trinity Methodist Church in Berkeley, described an Aimee meeting in the *Pacific Christian Advocate* in 1923:

> As the patient approaches, Mrs. McPherson takes the card and reads the written diagnosis of the ailment. This diagnosis is usually given by the patient, and is not the diagnosis of a physician. After it is read Mrs. McPherson dips her fingers into a silver vessel containing oil and anoints the patient.
>
> She then prays, using formulas as follows: "Oh Lord Jesus, in Thy name we command this paralysis, (or deafness, or blindness, or whatever it may be) to be gone. Let it fall from our brother like a mantle that is worn and old. Pour in Thy own life giving virtue and strength, in Jesus' name. Amen." After a brief prayer of this kind, Mrs. McPherson asks, "Have you faith to believe that Jesus heals you now?"
>
> Usually the patient who has passed through the long period of training answers "I have." "Then in the name of Jesus," Mrs. McPherson says, in the case of one suffering with paralysis, "Lift up your arm." The patient usually tries and then Mrs. McPherson says, "Now, lift it again." This is repeated until the patient exerts his utmost to lift the arm which frequently results in some considerable degree of success.[24]

All this happened on stage. We saw in an earlier chapter how William Branham developed Aimee's methodology by probably memorising the prayer cards rather than displaying them openly. This enabled him to present the information from the prayer cards as "words of knowledge", which made it easier to believe that a healing was taking place when it was declared.

Healing ministry was more prominent in Aimee's early years, but it waned after she built Angelus Temple and began to utilise complex theatrical stages that resembled sets from Broadway and West End musicals.

So, healing revivalists made the prayer for healing into a theatrical act on stage, where what happened before and after the stage performance didn't really matter. The large auditoriums, where the audience members didn't really know each other, facilitated this, as most people wouldn't have known what the actual condition of the sick was—before or after.

One of the most dramatic demonstrations of this was when someone got up from a wheelchair. It would look like an amazing miracle, but in most cases, the audiences had no information about how serious the condition of the sick person sitting in a wheelchair was. Most audiences would have assumed that the person was fully paralysed, even if that was not the case, as many people in wheelchair still have a limited mobility.

This doesn't mean that there haven't been any genuine healings in healing revivals, only that we need to wait for a while to discover whether anything resembling a genuine healing has actually taken place on stage. But in most cases, healing revivalists would declare a healing with no attempt to verify it.

With healings by Jesus and His apostles, the healings were a permanent fact; in many modern healing revivals, the healing effect of the revival is often soon lost, indicating that no genuine physical healing has ever taken place.

FAITH, HEALING AND DEMONS

In his sermon 'Gifts of Healings and Miracles', Smith Wigglesworth said,

> There are some times when you pray for the sick and you are apparently rough. But you are not dealing with a person, you are dealing with the Satanic forces that are binding the person . . . When you deal with a cancer case, recognize that it is a living evil spirit that is destroying the body.

Smith Wigglesworth believed that cancer was caused by demonisation or demon-possession. This is clearly not the case, as we know from modern medicine. But this doctrine made it a lot more convenient to declare a healing on stage, as most of the audience would have automatically believed that the preacher had the spiritual authority to cast out a demon on the spot.

William Branham also believed that Satan was the author of all sickness. To him, diseases were simply the physical form of beings called demons. According to him, what doctors called "a cancer, God calls it a devil."[25]

And it was never Branham's fault if someone didn't get healed. If a sick person didn't receive healing in a Branham service, the problem was either some unconfessed sin or the presence of a demon.[26]

Branham used a lot of scare tactics to force the audiences to believe that a healing had taken place. He claimed that when a demon was cast out, it would be looking for a new habitat, and asked the sceptics to go away before the healing part of the service. He said once,

> "Epilepsy is the one thing that gets away from me. Twenty-eight people in the audience got it one night."[27]

We can see demonisation of sickness everywhere in Branham's theology and ministry. F.F. Bosworth, who ministered with Branham, said about the "gift of discernment" that Branham presumable had,

> When the afflicting spirit comes into contact with the gift it sets up such a physical commotion that it becomes visible on Brother Branham's hand, and so real that it will stop his wristwatch instantly. This feels to Brother Branham like taking hold of a live wire with too much electric current in it.[28]

As we can see, Branham's methodology of healing was inseparable from his theology of healing. Borrowing the methodology from him, many healing evangelists still resort to the demonisation of sickness. The problem with this approach is that it completely denies the power of the Holy Spirit in us and the truth that all Christians are temples of the Holy Spirit. And looking at the audiences in meetings such as held by Smith Wigglesworth and William Branham, it seems clear that most people they prayed for were Christians. This leads to an unbiblical theology, in which the Holy Spirit doesn't have the power to keep demons out of His temple.

FAITH AND UNBELIEF

Healing revivalists are often called faith healers, and for a good reason, as the prevalent theory amongst them seems to be that any sickness can be healed if only people have enough faith. Unfortunately, this leads to the psychologizing of faith, seeing it as some sort of mental ability.

According to Branham, the "only thing that keeps you from being healed is a lack of faith."[29]

But this is based on misunderstanding of Jesus' teaching about faith and taking it out of context.

In Mark 5:34, Jesus says to the woman who has suffered from bleeding for twelve years,

> "Daughter, your faith has made you well. Go in peace, and be healed of your affliction."

This might make it look like our faith has healing power, but this isn't the case, as the verse 30 says,

> And Jesus, immediately knowing in Himself that power had gone out of Him, turned around in the crowd and said, "Who touched My clothes?"

It was the power of God that healed her, not her faith, but it was her faith that caused her to defy social and religious conventions, and approach and touch Jesus. She was not supposed to touch Jesus, as according to the Mosaic Law, she was impure because of her bleeding.

We can see the same in the story about the blind Bartimaeus who called Jesus to have mercy on him. Mark 10:51-52 says,

So Jesus answered and said to him, "What do you want Me to do for you?"

The blind man said to Him, "Rabboni, that I may receive my sight."

Then Jesus said to him, "Go your way; your faith has made you well." And immediately he received his sight and followed Jesus on the road.

So, we can see that it was the persistency of Bartimaeus that got him to the situation that Jesus was able to pay attention to him, but it was the power of God in Jesus that brought him healing.

Many faith teachers have taken the story about Jesus in Nazareth in Mark 6:1-6 as evidence that people's unbelief will stop healings from happening. In their view, an atmosphere where people don't have faith in the healing power of God can stop God from working. But this is based on a complete misreading of the passage.

It is clear that the people of Nazareth had no trouble of believing that Jesus could heal people. They never doubted His healing gift. What they had trouble in believing was that He might be the Messiah or a prophet. They didn't believe His message, and they were suspicious of His power source. But even in Nazareth, Jesus still laid His hands on a few people and healed them.

In Matthew 11:23, Jesus says that if the mighty works that had been done in Capernaum had taken place in Sodom, the city of Sodom would never have been destroyed.

In Nazareth and Capernaum, miracles failed to produce repentance, because the people weren't open to the possibility that it was God who had sent Jesus.

In the chapter on the gift of faith we will see that the American healing evangelists were not just influenced by the Bible but also by New Thought that elevated psychological faith to become a mind-bending force.

F.F. Bosworth, an early Pentecostal healing revivalist who later on worked with Branham, writes,

Jesus said, "The Word is the seed." It is the seed of the divine life. Until the person seeking healing is sure from God's Word that it is God's will to heal him, he is trying to reap a harvest where there is no seed planted. It would be impossible for a farmer to have faith for a harvest before he was sure the seed had been planted. It is not God's will that there shall be a harvest without the planting of the seed—without His will being known and acted on.[30]

Bosworth seems to put the responsibility for healing firmly on the faith of the person who needs healing. He adds,

> Praying for healing with the faith-destroying words, "if it be Thy will," is not planting the "seed"; it is destroying the seed."[31]

Bosworth continues,

> After being sufficiently enlightened, our attitude toward sickness should be the same as our attitude toward sin. Our purpose to have our body healed should be as definite as our purpose to have our soul healed. We should not ignore any part of the Gospel.[32]

Much has been made in the Pentecostal circles about Isaiah 53:5, "And by His stripes we are healed." And certainly, many Pentecostals saw and still see physical healing as something that is an integral part of salvation. But like our freedom from sin, our freedom from disease is incomplete, until we die and reach eternity.

Paul writes in 1 Corinthians 15:35-36:

> But someone will say, "How are the dead raised up? And with what body do they come?" Foolish one, what you sow is not made alive unless it dies.

Paul adds,

> For this corruptible must put on incorruption, and this mortal must put on immortality. So when this corruptible has put on incorruption, and this mortal has put on immortality, then

shall be brought to pass the saying that is written: "Death is swallowed up in victory." (1 Corinthians 15:53-54)

The fullness of Jesus' accomplishment in our lives will only be visible in eternity. But according to Bosworth, this is bad theology. Bosworth writes,

> The reason why many of the sick in our day have not returned to their physical possessions is that they have not heard the trumpet sound concerning healing. "Faith cometh by hearing", and they have not heard because many ministers had their Gospel trumpet put out of order while in the theological seminary.[33]

The Pentecostals and Charismatics have often openly despised the apostle Paul who seemed to delight in weakness a bit too much to their liking. When Paul recounts his visit to Corinth, he writes,

> For I determined not to know anything among you except Jesus Christ and Him crucified. I was with you in weakness, in fear, and in much trembling. (1 Corinthians 2:2-3)

Later on, he speaks about his predicament:

> You are already full! You are already rich! You have reigned as kings without us—and indeed I could wish you did reign, that we also might reign with you! For I think that God has displayed us, the apostles, last, as men condemned to death; for we have been made a spectacle to the world, both to angels and to men.
>
> We are fools for Christ's sake, but you are wise in Christ! We are weak, but you are strong! You are distinguished, but we are dishonored! To the present hour we both hunger and thirst, and we are poorly clothed, and beaten, and homeless. And we labor, working with our own hands. Being reviled, we bless; being persecuted, we endure; being defamed, we entreat. We have been made as the filth of the world, the offscouring of all things until now. (1 Corinthians 4:8-13)

Paul writes in Galatians 4:13-15,

> You know that because of physical infirmity I preached the gospel to you at the first. And my trial which was in my flesh you did not despise or reject, but you received me as an angel of God, even as Christ Jesus. What then was the blessing you enjoyed? For I bear you witness that, if possible, you would have plucked out your own eyes and given them to me.

Both in Corinth and Galatia some seemed to look down on Paul, focusing exclusively on the kingly position that God has given to us and completely ignoring the rest of the Bible—and even their own daily experience.

It is the same with the healing and prosperity teachers. Their basic argument is: God is good hence sickness can't be His will. So, God must be willing to give us 100% healing 100% of the time. And they refer to the stories of healing evangelists and the early Pentecostals to argue for their view. The main reason for this is that what they preach is not the present-day experience of their own congregations, and they are making an argument from the legends of the past.

So, they say, "Perhaps we don't have the experience of 100% healing 100% of the time now, but the pioneers of the healing movement had. So, it is attainable." Only the pioneers of the healing movement didn't have this experience of 100% healing 100% of the time. Their real experience was far from it.

MISLED BY A SENSATION OF POWER

There is an issue that must be looked at in more detail, and it is the experience of power that many of the healing evangelists and also the people prayed for have testified about. Both Branham and Roberts talked about vibration in hand that they took as a sign that God was healing the people they prayed for.

By and large, most healing evangelists take power 'leaving them' as a sign of God's healing activity. But the fact that God's Spirit is moving isn't an automatic indication that God is healing, not even when you are praying for the sick.

One of the key lessons I have learned when I have prayed for the sick, or for people's needs, is that the presence of power doesn't automatically mean that someone will be healed. God often works in many levels through prayer, and the most obvious need often isn't the greatest need. We need to resist inferring anything from any sensation of power, unless the Holy Spirit speaks to us.

MISLED BY PAIN AND DISCOMFORT

The son of Oral Roberts, Richard, says that his gift of healing operates through a word of knowledge.

> Here is how it operates in me. Many times I will feel something in my own body. Now when it first started happening I didn't know what it was . . . All of a sudden I will get a pop or a ringing or something in my ear . . . And I learned over a period of time that that was the Lord giving me an indication that someone was receiving a healing.[34]

Many preachers take pain or a sensation in any part of their body to indicate that God is healing someone with an issue in that part of the body. It might be that God is using these bodily sensations to communicate to some people in some instances, but the *proof* of healing should be a real healing rather than a preacher's bodily sensation. This methodology has some major issues—with a large crowd and a number of diseases in the Western world, it is likely that no matter what part of your body starts itching or hurting, there will always be someone in the crowd with an issue in that part of the body. So, in real terms, the proof of this methodology should be in a lasting healing of someone in the audience. Unfortunately, most 'healing evangelists' will be happy for anyone to stand up, so that they can declare a healing. And many people will take this as healing, as they will assume that it was a word of knowledge for healing.

Now I am not saying that the Holy Spirit has never used this method of communicating to us, only that we must be extremely careful with any bodily sensations, especially if they aren't accompanied with the presence of God. As I get older, I feel that all sorts of bodily sensations only increase with more pains in my body!

Does it mean my healing gift is increasing? I think not.

Some time ago I suffered from a sport injury and my hurt shoulder seriously limited my workouts. One day, I came from the gym and a Bible college student I met on the way prayed for it. He declared healing, as he could feel the warmth of the Holy Spirit spreading into my body as he prayed. I experienced the same sensation.

But two weeks later, my shoulder was still unhealed—yet the experience of the anointing was real. That day, God wanted me to get a refilling of the Spirit rather than to heal me.

MANIPULATING PEOPLE'S FAITH

How does manipulating the faith of the sick work? It is rather simple. Many Christians have been exposed to faith teaching, and they genuinely believe that a way to claim their healing is to testify about it publicly. So, they approach a preacher and tell him or her that they have been healed, and more often than not, the preacher is delighted of their testimony. So, they get on stage, declaring that they have been healed, believing that their public confession of faith could somehow release their healing.

Another way an illusion of healing is being created is when a preacher declares that the person they are praying for is healed in the name of Jesus. This creates an appearance that the person has been healed, when nothing has in fact taken place. Surely, if someone is declared healed "in the name of Jesus", that person has been healed, especially as there are no further updates afterwards!

It is common to see someone who is partially deaf or blind to go on stage, or they have an issue with mobility. So when a partially deaf person goes on stage, he is likely to say that he is deaf, when in fact he has partial hearing. Then a preacher prays for them and claps their hand. He asks if the person prayed for can hear the clapping. Of course he can, for he never had an issue with hearing the clapping, only with hearing properly. Or they still can't hear anything, but they can interpret the movement of hands, and answer affirmatively.

Our sensory experiences can be quite deceiving.

Did you know that the main reason you might not like the taste of instant coffee is not the poor ingredients, but the lack of scent? What you perceive as taste of freshness is in fact the sensory experience from scent.

In a similar way, the taste of airplane food often feels quite bland, when in fact, it is the dry air and the altitude that reduce our ability to smell and taste—and the ability to smell scents is reduced first.[35]

And just because you cover the hearing ear of a partially deaf person, it doesn't make much difference. Or someone has a partial mobility issue, and they arrive on a wheelchair. Of course they will be able to get up momentarily on stage, especially as they are on a very motivated mental state.

In these scenarios, no healing has in fact taken place.

In healing meetings, it is common to see people testify on stage that they used to suffer from chronic pain, but that it is now gone. This is often taken as a sign that a healing has taken place. But the human mind has an amazing ability to block pain temporarily because of an adrenalin rush, so in reality, we will know only later if a real healing has taken place.

I have seen all these scenarios too many times. And they are repeated every day around the world in healing meetings and crusades. But the truth is that a real healing is lasting.

Regardless, I don't think that all healing meetings should be closed down, only we need to get a lot more honest about these issues.

ARE THERE REAL, MIRACULOUS HEALINGS?

I believe that there are gifts of healings operating in the Church simply because the Bible says so. I also believe in healing by praying to God simply because the Bible teaches us to do that. I also believe that healing prayer isn't some sort of mind trick based on increasing our level of psychological faith. Although it might be difficult to ascertain if anyone's healing is attributable to prayer alone, the actual healing should still be verifiable medically.

And, certainly, modern biomedical science must mostly be seen as part of the healing work God has brought into the world.

But that doesn't shut out the need for healing prayer, and there are many illnesses we don't yet know the cure for.

Candy Gunther Brown, Associate Professor, Department of Religious Studies, and Adjunct Associate Professor, American Studies Program, at Indiana University, Bloomington, has authored an excellent book, *Testing Prayer*, that looks at the verification of healings medically.

According to Brown, certain modern scientists worry that studies on the effects of prayer might seem as validating religious healing claims, and propel a return to a superstitious past.[36] Because of that, the research papers on testing the effect of prayer aren't as numerous as you would think they should be, and some of them seem counterintuitive.

For example, the Harvard researcher Herbert Benson challenged the idea that prayer is good for someone's health in his study. Heart patients that received distant intercessory prayer fared no better, but actually worse, if they knew they were objects of special prayer.[37]

We can see the weaknesses of this study, but also warnings, when we look at the groups that prayed for the people more closely. One of the prayer groups consisted of members of a "Protestant" church, but when you look at their teachings, you realise that they have very little to do with Christianity. What the study demonstrates is that prayer by people who aren't followers of Christ can in fact often be harmful.

Whereas many studies that have produced positive results have been based on using "born-again" Christians in praying, this study used a group that doesn't even necessarily pray to God in a traditional Christian sense.

It matters who you pray *to*, and who is praying, not that you pray.

The setup of many of these studies is distant and randomised intercessory prayer, trying to isolate prayer from factors such as compassion. But obviously, that is not how prayer works in real life when it comes to healing prayer. You mostly pray for someone you care deeply about, so isolating empathy from the research arrangements makes little sense.

According to Brown, there are natural factors that affect results in real life—empathy effects, observer effects, short-term improvements resulting from the motivational effect of attention paid to subjects, hold-back effects, tendency to unconsciously perform worse at first to demonstrate improvement later, demand effects, subject performing better after the test in order to meet the presumed expectation of those conducting the study, practice effects, and the tendency of subjects to perform tasks better when they have more experience.[38]

Brown writes,

> Scientific investigation protects against the post hoc, ergo propter hoc fallacy to which healing practitioners are susceptible—that people who receive prayer for healing and then recover can attribute their newfound health to prayer. There is empirical evidence that as many as 90 percent of sick people recover regardless of treatment, as long as the healer does not do something actively to make the patient worse. Even diseases of unknown causation, especially infections, are often self-limiting once the body's immune system kicks into gear. And cancers, which are poorly understood, may grow or stop growing or even regress without any clear explanation. It is often by chance that the last practitioner who treats the patients before recovery gets the credit.[39]

The body's capacity to self-heal is amazing, and it is a God-given gift. But that often works autonomously from divine healing as we would normally define it. But regardless, Christians will often attribute their healing to prayer.

The issue of medical documentation is more complicated than it seems at first, and not just because the healing ministries are not usually actively looking for medical proof to validate their claims, often relying on personal testimonies. But although medical records can probably never prove a healing miracle, as that is a matter of interpretation, they should be able to document improvements.

Brown writes,

> Medical records can indicate that a problem was at one point diagnosed by a credentialed professional and that on subsequent examination the condition appeared better or

resolved, and that there is no obvious medical or natural explanation. Despite the apparent objectivity of x-rays, laboratory reports, and doctors' notes, the significance of such documents requires subjective interpretation. Medical documentation cannot prove that prayer accounts for a recovery or that a divine or other suprahuman agent or force is responsible, or even that a condition has been permanently cured.[40]

Trials on the efficiency of healing prayer are challenging both to believers and unbelievers, but in different ways. For Christians, it shows we need more truthfulness and factuality; for unbelievers, the possibility that divine healing can be real.

When Brown performed tests in rural Mozambique, they measured highly significant improvements in hearing and statistically significant improvements in vision across the tested population linked to Heidi Baker's ministry. According to her, potential confounds such as inadvertent hypnosis or suggestion do not account for these findings. The survey respondents typically perceived improvement along a continuum. They measured improved hearing and vision thresholds rather than generally finding a change from total deafness or blindness to a clinical standard of perfection. The team managed also to get statistically significant improvements in visual thresholds in urban Brazil. Similar tests in the USA produced inconclusive results.[41]

These were real results, tested scientifically, but although they showed a real improvement, they weren't tested long-term. It seems clear that many healing testimonies are exaggerated but also that they can be real.

Many people attribute the alleged higher number of healings in the developing countries to lack of faith in the developed countries.

But Brown's findings seem to support two assumptions: the gifts of healings seem to operate better in places with most need, and they occur more in places where the gospel is being preached. That is very much in line with what Jesus promises in the Great Commission—signs and wonders will follow them who take the gospel to the nations.

Yet, in *Testing Prayer*, there are also many stories of permanent healings in the West, so it illustrates the fact that God moves wherever there is need.

According to Brown, although the overall percentages of people reporting healing at the conferences in America were relatively small, such a finding would not surprise many Pentecostals. Often, Pentecostals and Charismatics receive prayer on multiple occasions for a given problem before claiming complete healing, believing that the healing process usually occurs over time. The model of persevering prayer contrasts with another influential Pentecostal model, the Word of Faith view that prayer should be offered only once for any one problem before claiming healing by faith, lest repeated prayer denote lack of faith and thus block healing.[42]

The practice of soaking prayer was popularised by the Catholic Francis MacNutt. For MacNutt, prayer is comparable to radiation therapy in its cumulative effects, because there are presumably levels of "more" and "less" anointing, difficulty and healing.[43]

According to MacNutt's Christian Healing Ministries,

> Soaking Prayer is coming into the Presence of God in a posture of receiving, allowing Him to minister to you directly in body, mind, soul and spirit. It involves either sitting or lying in stillness, relaxed and inwardly turning toward Jesus. Often gentle worship music in the background helps to focus on God and experience His presence, for He dwells in our praise (Psalm 22:3). Soaking prayer is available on Day of Healing Prayer and Generational Healing Service.[44]

I am sure that the presence of God is beneficial to us all. But it is important to understand that God's presence doesn't automatically lead to healing.

Personally, I don't consider Christ-centred meditation or contemplation to be harmful to anyone. But interestingly, this sort of contemplation isn't mentioned in the Bible as a source for healing.

LOOKING FOR BIBLICAL HEALING MODEL

I am indebted to George Jeffreys, the founder of the Elim Pentecostal Church in the United Kingdom, when it comes to understanding healing better. His book *Healing Rays*, published first in 1932, a year after he opened Kensington Temple, the church where I have served on staff over sixteen years, is an invaluable contribution to our understanding, mainly as it is balanced and still trying to formulate a theology for healing relying on the Bible nearly exclusively, rather than theories by other Pentecostals.

And based on the documentary evidence compiled by R. E. Darragh in book *In Defence of His Word. Being a number of selected testimonies of dire suffering, healed by the power of Christ, under the ministry of Principal George Jeffreys*, published by Elim Publishing Co., 1932, it is hard to explain many of the healings in Jeffreys' ministry in any other way than as miraculous healings.

Jeffreys divided the operation of the healing gift in three dispensations—the times of the Old Testament, times of Jesus, and the time of the Church—or healing by the Father, the Son and then by the Holy Spirit. And he saw Jesus' healing ministry as unique.

Many people in the Charismatic church seem to believe that the ministry of Jesus is somehow fully repeatable in the life of one person. Yes, Jesus is still working in a mighty way, but He is doing that through His Body—through all Christians in all times and ages. But Jesus was and is the Son of God. In a much lesser way, we can be called sons and daughters of God, as we have been adopted into His family. But that doesn't make us into gods. Jesus is God. We have the privilege of being carriers of God's presence, but we are not gods.

Also, the dispensation of the Son is different from the dispensation of the Holy Spirit. We don't need to become cessationists to affirm the unique nature of the ministry of Jesus.

What is also noteworthy in the Bible is that there are a lot less healing stories linked to the apostles than to Jesus. It is clear to me that the healing ministry of Jesus was something we will never see again in the world.

Preachers like Kathryn Kuhlman said that they believe that, one day, everyone will get healed. It is a sincere wish, but it doesn't seem that 100% healing all of the time is in fact a biblical doctrine.

Yet, there are gifts of healing and they operate today, bringing a diversity of healings to diverse sicknesses. And yes, even the dead can be raised. But not even in the lives of the apostles, or in the life of Jesus, did it seem to bring 100% healing to everyone.

Think about the man who was healed at the Pool of Bethesda in John 5. Jesus healed one man on Sabbath, and yet the pool was surrounded by a "great multitude of sick people."

Yet Jesus healed only *one*.

What does it tell about the importance of the gifts of healings? The least we must admit is that the biblical evidence is not for wholesale healing of every sick person in Israel, not even when Jesus was around. And yet Jesus healed a lot of people.

The concept of the "gifts of healings" implies that every healing is an individual gift—a unique miracle—and can't be multiplied through any method.

Jeffreys defined healing as a gradual recovery.

> The word healing suggests a gradual recovery, and many are restored in this way. Another among the nine gifts is the working of miracles, which suggests an immediate Divine interposition, so that a person is instantaneously healed. In our Lord's own ministry there were these two kinds of healings.[45]

Looked at this way, the gifts of healings are probably quite common in the Church, but the gift of working miracles, when it comes to healings, might be rarer than we think.

Jeffreys preferred to use the term divine healing rather than faith healing as it

> implies bodily healing as it is exclusively taught in the Scriptures, whereas the latter might mean healing by faith along the many lines of psychology. The former denotes acceptance of the Bible as the Word of God in its entirety, and

healing through the Lord Jesus Christ. The latter can imply believing in any kind of faith healing that might be taught in books that are decidedly anti-Christian.[46]

Also, Jeffreys taught that healing can be obtained in two realms, namely natural and supernatural, and that it is a huge mistake to ignore natural healing. He made three statements:

> Firstly. There must have been a beginning to sickness and disease just as there was a beginning to sin. Secondly. There is no scripture to show the sickness and disease can be traced back to God . . . Thirdly. There is no definite scripture to show that sickness and disease can be traced back to Satan.[47]

From here, he concludes that it is reasonable to assume that because sin and death can be traced back to Satan, sickness can be indirectly traced to Satan. But the indirectness of that relationship means that sickness is a result of the Fall and not demonisation or demon possession.

METHODS OF HEALING

It is clear in the Bible that there isn't one method of healing. Jeffreys lists the following "modes of healing."

1. The direct appeal on the part of an individual (Matthew 8:2)
2. The cooperation and fellowship of practical sympathisers (Mark 2:4, 5)
3. The cooperation and mutual fellowship of prayer warriors (Matthew 18:19)
4. The laying of hands (Mark 16:18)
5. The anointing of oil (James 5:14)
6. The going forth of God's Word (Psalm 107:20)
7. The ministry of prayer in the Church (Acts 4:30).[48]

George Jeffreys testifies of his own healing.

I was first convinced of the Spirit's quickening power when, as a frail youth, I received the experience in my own body. My weak state began to manifest itself in a facial paralysis, and I was heavily burdened, for I felt the creepiness of paralysis down one whole side . . . When my mouth began to be affected, the one thing that distressed me greatly was the possibility of my not realising the one call and ambition of life, the Christian ministry . . . We were kneeling in prayer one Sunday morning and were interceding on the subject of the services that day. It was exactly nine o'clock when the power of God came upon me, and I received such an inflow of Divine life that I can only liken the experience to being charged with electricity. It seemed as if my head were connected to a most powerful electric battery. My whole body from head to foot was quickened by the Spirit of God, and I was healed. From that day I have never had the least symptoms of the old trouble.[49]

Apart from healing, Jeffreys came to depend on this quickening power of God in ministry.

All who conduct prolonged evangelistic campaigns will admit that a great deal of physical strength is necessary. This in many cases could never be found if it were not for Divine strength that is given. The body, tired and weakened by constant labour, needs a special inflow of Divine life. Sometimes towards the end of a campaign I have been confronted by monster congregations, and if it were not for the frequent quickening of the body I would have been helpless. Even the voice is charged and changed as the result of the body being quickened by the Spirit. The difficulty with opposers to this truth generally is that they consult people about these experiences who have never known them.[50]

It is interesting to see the contrast between George Jeffreys, who was energised by the Holy Spirit, and William Branham, who was paralysed and exhausted by his 'angel', when ministering healing on stage.

Like many ministers, Jeffreys was criticised a lot during his lifetime, and it is clear that not all people were healed in his meetings. A.J. Pollock, a contemporary of George Jeffreys, criticised the large meetings:

> What do we find today? Pentecostal healing meetings are conducted pretty much as follows. The service is begun by the singing of catchy lilting jazz-like choruses accompanied by piano, violin, guitars, as the case may be. In the case of Principal Jeffreys' Easter meetings in the Royal Albert Hall, London, there was a choir of nearly 2,000 voices. Is this like the methods employed by the early disciples, who HAD the pentecostal gifts without a doubt? . . . The singing goes on, the catchy choruses are repeated again and again, till the audience is excited, and emotional. Such methods go down with the crowds. Mass-suggestion is a well-known psychological modus operandi . . . No wonder the crowds flock. The entertainment is equal to the music hall and cinema without having to pay for the seats.
>
> When the audience has been whipped up to a state of red-hot emotion, the sick and crippled are invited to come to the healer. The emotional singing is kept up. No one can hear what the healer says to the sick. Hallelujahs go strong. Is this like sending for the elders of the church to the home of the sick person, and quiet, fervent prayer, the prayer of faith being offered up? It is just this spectacle of healing that constitutes a great draw to the services.[51]

Yet, Jeffreys' ministry had a real impact, and hundreds of churches were planted around Britain in the first twenty years of his ministry. Many people were saved, and for example, during the Easter services in the Royal Albert Hall in 1928, over a thousand believers were baptised.

That group would have included Christians that were 'converted' from child baptism to adult baptism. With the birth of every new denomination, there is always an influx of Christians from the already established denominations into the new one. But these campaigns had a large number of verified healings from serious illnesses as well, and like the healing of Jeffreys himself, they were long-lasting, and not just lasting for the duration of the services.

HEALING AND OTHER GIFTS

The gifts of healings can operate in harmony with other spiritual gifts. Once, I sat in a car with my friend and listened to him. His family had gone to their favourite restaurant a few days earlier. One of their kids had caught a tropical bug, and it was eating his stomach and intestines from the inside. He was vomiting nearly twenty times a day, and they were concerned, as there was no known cure for this bug.

As I sat in the car, I began to sense strongly that this bug was somehow an attack from the enemy. The bug was a tropical bug, but only one of the children had caught it. So, the illness wasn't a demonic curse as such. The rest of the family were fine, and they had been going to this restaurant regularly for years, so this child seemed to have been particularly unlucky.

Still, I felt as if it was the enemy who had sent the bug, perhaps through manipulating the circumstances. As I spoke with his dad, I felt a strong demonic presence. I cursed the bug and felt how the Spirit of God moved through me, as I prayed for him.

When the little boy woke up the next morning, he vomited twice. That was it. The bug had vanished without a trace.

Cursing a bug might not be standard in these kinds of situations, but it seemed to do the trick. It was the one thing the Holy Spirit had anointed me to do.

Is it biblical to curse a sickness? In this case, the sickness had been caused by a living bug, and cursing the bug seemed to kill it, at least that's the way I see the event.

But it is impossible to tell whether the ending of the vomiting and his recovery was the result of me cursing the bug, like Jesus once cursed the fig tree, or the result of his parents' fervent prayers. Or perhaps the illness had simply run its course. But I do believe that the gift of discerning spirits at least contributed to his recovery.

Like with any other gift, you will find that the gifts of healings will often work in partnership with another gift, such as the word of knowledge, faith or prophecy. Once, I was working out in the gym when my gym buddy had a phone call about his brother having taken an overdose. He had no idea about what his condition was. Without prayer, I could say nothing, but after a little time spent in prayer I felt that he would make it through, and that my friend would play a key part in his recovery and return to Jesus.

I heard the next day that the police unit responding to the emergency call had practically been in front of their house at the time, which was miraculous timing, as the doctor said that even five minutes' delay would have made the difference between life and death. And it was my friend who got to pray for his brother when he came back to church and rededicated his life to Jesus a few weeks later!

There have been times when I have been asked to pray for someone who was about to die, and as I've tried to pray for them, I have sensed that it is their time to go. At those times, no prayer has made any difference. At other times, I have sensed that it's not their time to die yet, and prayed with boldness, and without exception, those people have all recovered. Now, I'm not saying that it has been my prayer that has made them recover, as often the whole church has been praying, only that because of my prophetic gift, I have known the outcome long before the actual recovery, and also that another person would pass away, regardless of our prayers.

HOW GIFTS OF HEALINGS OPERATE

I have had an opportunity to spend some time with leaders who actually have the gifts of healings. The interesting thing is that these people don't need to claim healing by faith, and they don't need to rely on a word of knowledge either. Often, they only say a simple prayer, and with a lot higher number of the sick than usual, healing follows.

I believe that this is the gifts of healings at its purest. Nothing else but a simple prayer is needed.

The gifts of healings aren't for show business, but they flow out of compassion and deep love for people.

In James 5:14-15, there is perhaps the most all-encompassing reference to wholesale healing.

> Is anyone among you sick? Let him call for the elders of the church, and let them pray over him, anointing him with oil in the name of the Lord. And the prayer of faith will save the one who is sick, and the Lord will raise him up. And if he has committed sins, he will be forgiven.

It is clearly the prayer of faith by the elders, not the faith of the sick, that will heal the sick. Also, what is noteworthy is that this seems like a rather private affair. But even this text doesn't seem to actually support 100% healing, as it is a clever play of words.

It seems clear that these verses have a double meaning, and that is why they have been translated in two different ways. First, the Greek word *sosei* means both "save" and "heal", and the Greek word *egerei*, translated here as "will raise up", is also used for resurrection in 2 Corinthians 4:14.

So, what James seems to say is that the sick will either be healed, or pass away, but if they will pass away, the Church and the persons in question can have the assurance that they will be resurrected and their sins have been forgiven.

So, James is not claiming that someone's sins might have caused the sickness at all. And he is not promising 100% healing to all sick, if only the elders make it to their house, only that they will make it to heaven, if they die, no matter what sins they have committed on earth.

> Jesus said, "Those who are well have no need of a physician, but those who are sick." (Mark 2:17)

Until now, our healing paradigm has come largely from the faith movement. And faith movement often asks you to confess things as if they were, even when they are clearly not.

But when it comes to healings, God has never asked us to be nothing less than completely truthful. It brings no glory to God to claim a healing when it hasn't taken place.

Each 'faith claim' and 'prophetic promise' that doesn't bring healing can bring unrepairable damage to people's lives, wrecking their faith. And there is a genuine mystery about who God heals and why. Why would God use John Wimber, the leader of the Vineyard movement, to heal many sick, let him recover from cancer, and then let him die as a result of a fall that caused a fatal brain haemorrhage?

It is good to pray for people for healing, and see what happens. You can leave the rest to God.

I believe that a paradigm shift from 'faith healing' to gifts of healings will liberate the gifts of healings into the body of Christ. Then we will be able to pray for healing with no anxiety. We will not fear what will happen if a healing won't take place, but, instead, we will be eager to see what God will do!

There is no showmanship needed, as the prayer for healing can take place in any church. But we must begin to recognise who those Christians are in our midst that God has given the gifts of healings to, and ask these people to be the ones who mainly pray for the sick.

John Wimber writes,

> A principle that guides me in divine healing: obedience to God's word is the fundamental reason why I pray for the sick, even when I don't see healing as a result of my prayers. I decided a long ago that if I pray for one hundred people and only one is healed, it is better than if I never pray at all and no one is healed. [52]

He adds,

> Faith is the medium through which God releases his healing power. Most divine healing comes as a result of someone's faith in God ... But it would be a mistake to assume that faith exercised by the person being prayed for is always required for healing. In fact, scripture is full of examples of people other than the person being prayed for that are sources of healing power. [53]

He also writes,

The prayers, as I have already noted, may vary greatly: intercession, words of command, words of pronouncement, even getting the person himself or herself to pray. As I pray I listen to God for specific instructions or words of knowledge that might be occasions for releasing healing power.[54]

It is good for us to pray for the sick as individuals and together in church. And it is also good for us to begin to discern those in our midst to whom God has given the gifts of healing. But there is absolutely no reason to claim healings if they clearly haven't taken place. And the healing ministry is certainly the one area where the evidence should be demonstrable.

In Matthew 8, Jesus heals a leper. He says to him,

> "See that you tell no one; but go your way, show yourself to the priest, and offer the gift that Moses commanded, as a testimony to them." (Matthew 8:4)

In the ancient Israel, the priest was the one who could inspect a former leper and declare that he had been cleansed and able to re-join the community. His report was as close to the doctor's certificate you could get. His declaration wouldn't necessarily have told the reason why someone's condition had improved, but it would have verified that improvement.

Perhaps, in a similar way, the healings in our midst should become a testimony to the doctors—even when the doctors wouldn't be willing to attribute the reason for healing to a miracle.

7

PROPHECY

Much of our current understanding about the gift of prophecy comes from a movement that was influential in the 1980s and was known as the Kansas City Prophets.

Many of those who shaped what is called the Apostolic-Prophetic Movement in the United States today were based in Kansas City, Missouri and became known as the Kansas City Prophets.

One of the Kansas City Prophets, Paul Cain, had participated in the Healing Revival and worked with William Branham,[1] so there was a clear continuity with the Healing Revival.

Unfortunately, not all of their influence has been good. This is not a judgement on individuals or churches, as we live in an imperfect world and the Church will remain imperfect on earth, at least as long as I am a member. But as this is one of the most influential streams when it comes to our understanding of how prophecy works, we must dissect it here.

In the early days of the Kansas City Prophets, the two main prophets were Bob Jones and Paul Cain, and their work was linked to what later on became the IHOP, led by Mike Bickle.

Many years ago I read an influential book, *Some Say It Thundered* and, writing this book, I decided to read it again, as it concerns the origins of the Kansas City Prophets.

Time has not been kind to the book, as it starts with a prophecy given in August 1989 at a conference by Bob Jones to James Irwin, the eighth astronaut to walk on Moon.

"Well", said the prophet, "it's strange, since you should not really be here, but I saw you in a vision last night. Another strange thing is that you are not a prophet either and yet you have seen the earth from the heavenlies! What is more you have been searching for the remnants of Noah Ark on Mount Ararat but you have been looking for it in the wrong place. And you are going to find it."[2]

At the time, everyone was excited, but James Irwin passed away many years ago without finding the ark.

Neither has the Internet been kind to the book, as nowadays it is rather effortless to fact-check past prophecies that made specific statements.

When I read the book many years ago, one of the most impressive stories in the book was about Bob Jones declaring in May 1983 that there would be three months of drought in Kansas City, ending on 23rd August.

In this city everything will be withheld. For three months, there will be a drought. That's a sign! God has spoken! The drought for three months is because the people have rejected the call to fast—they have mocked God. But for three months there will be no rain—not till 23 August.[3]

The author quotes Mike Bickle who tells the story:

For the whole of June there was no rain! It was terrible! For the whole of July there was no rain! It was terrible! No rain still during the first week of August or the second of the third. It was terrible! Bob Jones said that the Lord had told him it would come on 23 August. We had all been poised since early dawn that day but by 1 p.m. there was still no rain. By six o'clock we were just resigned to wait for another day when suddenly it began. And did it rain? It poured! No man could have manipulated that. It just had to be God![4]

It is a wonderful story. The only problem is that it doesn't seem to be true.

According to the historical weather data from Kansas City International Airport, around 15 miles from central Kansas City, the rainiest day of the year was 18th June.

> The day with the *largest quantity* of precipitation was June 18. That day saw 59.7 mm of liquid (or liquid equivalent) precipitation, compared to a median value of 5.2 mm.[5]

The driest month of the year was July, but it still rained in July.

> The month with the largest fraction of dry days was July, with 87% of days reporting no measured precipitation at all.[6]

But even in July it rained. It did rain on 23rd August [7], as Mike said, but it also rained on three other days in August before the 23rd, and on 23rd August it rained only 6.6mm, nothing like the torrential rain of 18th June when it was not supposed to be raining.

But according to the story, Kansas City suffered from drought for three months!

This is one of the stories that cemented Bob Jones' reputation as an 'Elijah-level' prophet, capable of moving in the level of prophetic authority that the Old Testament prophets carried.

Many leaders in the Apostolic-Prophetic movement tell that Bob Jones was one of the most accurate prophets of all time. Unfortunately, the accuracy isn't real but invented.

In later re-tellings of the story, it has been significantly modified. But in the minds of many Americans, this story would have easily got mixed up with the US Drought of 1983 that affected many other states harder than Kansas, so in the mind of many people, the story could have rung true. But that year, the driest season in Kansas City was from 16th February to 4th March, and not the summer.

So, what do we make of it all? Did Bob Jones and the Kansas City Prophets simply hand out a few bad prophecies? If that were the case, they wouldn't be worth majoring on in our exploration of the gift of prophecy.

No. The Kansas City Prophets redefined what prophecy is.

The Kansas City Fellowship—now IHOP—has what they call a prophetic history, and in 1988, Mike Bickle and Bob Jones recorded around five hours of informal dialogue entitled *Visions and Revelations*. These recordings and their transcription are still available on their website as part of their prophetic history. In the recordings, Mike Bickle asks Bob Jones about his prophecies:

"So there has been errors. There has been a number of errors."

Bob Jones says, "Oh, hundreds of them."

Mike Bickle asks: "The Lord will correct them?" to which Bob Jones responds, "Absolutely."[8]

According to Mike Bickle, the way to test the prophecies is when the other prophets are in agreement. Those are the *right* prophecies.

But this is a radical redefinition of prophecy, and not what the Bible teaches. According to this teaching, it doesn't really matter if you get hundreds of prophecies wrong, as long as a few prophets can agree with a few.

This teaching has led to the practice of prophetic roundtables, where dozens of prophets gather regularly to synthesise a word from the words of many prophets, and their consensus becomes 'God's word'.

This is misapplying 1 Corinthians 14:29, which says,

> Let two or three prophets speak, and let the others judge.

The consensus principle here isn't about the consensus of the prophets on any other thing than whether the word is from the Lord or not. But the prophet that gets the word doesn't get it through conversation with other prophets, but through listening to the Lord.

Jeremiah 23:18 says,

> For who has stood in the counsel of the Lord, and has perceived and heard His word? Who has marked His word and heard it?

Jeremiah 20:9 says,

Then I said, "I will not make mention of Him, nor speak anymore in His name." But *His word* was in my heart like a burning fire shut up in my bones; I was weary of holding it back, and I could not.

Jeremiah was weary of prophesying, but the prophetic word was stronger than him. And Jeremiah's prophecies weren't a series of guesses that might be proven right or wrong. Jeremiah's system of prophecy wasn't trying to get one right out of ten, and celebrating if that actually happened.

Habakkuk 2:3 says,

> For the vision *is* yet for an appointed time; but at the end it will speak, and it will not lie. Though it tarries, wait for it; because it will surely come, it will not tarry.

These verses outline the prophetic process clearly. All prophecy refers to the *future*. We receive prophecies in the presence of the Lord. They are not some random words, but like a burning fire, and in the end, we will have to proclaim them either privately or publicly, to be released of our burden, and they will come to pass, even when it might take a lot of time.

Generally, false prophets give false prophecies, and genuine prophets give genuine prophecies. But Bob Jones has reduced the gift of prophecy to some kind of weather report—it might or might not rain, but the important thing is that the prophet is prophesying.

I suspect that it is because of the high failure rate that the Apostolic-Prophetic Movement began to emphasise the office of the prophet and the idea that we should all be in an apostolic-prophetic alignment with the prophets and apostles. If the prophet has authority because of his office, we should still obey and follow him or her because of their office, regardless of how inaccurate their words turn out to be. But that is not what the Bible teaches.

Deuteronomy 18:21-22 says,

> And if you say in your heart, "How shall we know the word which the Lord has not spoken?"— when a prophet speaks

in the name of the Lord, if the thing does not happen or come to pass, that is the thing which the Lord has not spoken; the prophet has spoken it presumptuously; you shall not be afraid of him.

According to the Bible, the first measure of the prophet is the reliability of his or her word.

Teaching that we should respect the prophets because of their office has led to 'prophetic' and 'apostolic' leaders endorsing each other through all sorts of 'anointings' and 'impartations' in order to gain that office. But these endorsements have very little value, as the only endorsement a prophet needs is a reliable prophecy that comes from God—accompanied by a lifestyle that displays the nine fruit of the Spirit, and a sound doctrine.

Also, many ministers proclaim 'prophetic' callings and anointings over people's lives to get them to submit to their control, as you are likely to follow someone who promises blessings to you and gives you a sense of importance.

In this new world of prophecy, prophets need to feel no sorrow for any false words, as long as the prophetic consensus supports their office.

In 1 Kings 22, four hundred prophets advise the kings of Israel and Judah to go to war, with only Micaiah disagreeing. He says,

> "Therefore hear the word of the Lord: I saw the Lord sitting on His throne, and all the host of heaven standing by, on His right hand and on His left. And the Lord said, 'Who will persuade Ahab to go up, that he may fall at Ramoth Gilead?' So one spoke in this manner, and another spoke in that manner. Then a spirit came forward and stood before the Lord, and said, 'I will persuade him.'
>
> The Lord said to him, 'In what way?' So he said, 'I will go out and be a lying spirit in the mouth of all his prophets.' And the Lord said, 'You shall persuade him, and also prevail. Go out and do so.' Therefore look! The Lord has put a lying spirit in the mouth of all these prophets of yours, and the Lord has declared disaster against you." (1 Kings 22:19-23)

A prophet should never seek comfort in the agreement with other prophets but in the presence of God. In the same conversation, Bob Jones and Mike Bickle talk about "the new breed" that will walk in a higher level of miracles than any other generation. Bob Jones says,

> They will move into things of the supernatural that no one has ever moved in before. Every miracle, sign and wonder that are seen in the Bible—they will move in it consistently, they will move in the power that Christ did. Every sign and wonder that's ever been will be many times in the last days.[9]

Mike Bickle then paraphrases a vision Bob Jones allegedly saw:

> He looked back. Those were the leaders of the past generations like John Wesley, Charles Finney, Martin Luther, who thought their generation is the chosen generation. And every time they pulled their hand they came up empty-handed. Because there is one generation that will enter into that which is beyond all others. The chosen generation of history that will go beyond all the others in power. They thought it was theirs. It is not . . . So he sees the 300,000 and the Lord looks at Bob and says: "From out of the sands of time I have called the best of every bloodline in the earth unto this generation." He said, "Even the bloodline of David, the bloodline of Peter, James and John. The best of their seed unto this generation. They will be even superior to them in hearts, stature and love for me[10]

Bob Jones adds,

> First he will bring the fivefold, but there is a ministry after the fivefold called the ministry of perfection—the Melchizedek priesthood. You are that are here now, you'll be moving into the fivefold ministries, but your children will be moving into the ministries of perfection. Coming to that characteristic—coming into the divine nature of Jesus Christ.[11]

This is going way beyond what we call the fullness of the Holy Spirit, so that this new generation will operate in the priesthood of Melchizedek—like Jesus did—the ministry of perfection.

At this point, we have gone away from what we consider to be the orthodox teaching of Christianity, way beyond what the Bible teaches, and into similar doctrines that some Gnostics taught. It is teachings like this the apostle Paul fought against when he said that some people in Corinth had "already become kings".

Continuing the same conversation, Mike Bickle paraphrases Bob Jones,

> So he told me that the healing angels that were used in the great outpouring in the 40s and 50s, that the Lord Himself would call it, the chief angel is Dominus, and he is the angel of the Presence, I mean, the Lord isn't an angel, so don't misinterpret that, but he's the chief of the angels.[12]

Then he tells how Jesus allegedly spoke to Bob Jones.

> And so He said that, "I'm going to have a healing revival", and I'm sure that those angels are going to gather in other places, not just here, but He said, "I'm gonna have a healing reunion of those healing angels." Remember Emma?"[13]

This is the continuation of the healing angel heresy of William Branham. For example, Todd Bentley and the Lakeland Revival referred to this same 'healing angel' called Emma. But nowhere in the Bible does it say that angels have healing powers, although John 5:4 refers to a Jewish myth about an angel stirring the waters of the pool of Bethesda for healing.

Paul writes in Colossians 2:18-19,

> Let no one cheat you of your reward, taking delight in *false* humility and worship of angels, intruding into those things which he has not seen, vainly puffed up by his fleshly mind, and not holding fast to the Head, from whom all the body, nourished and knit together by joints and ligaments, grows with the increase *that is* from God.

Later on, in the same conversation, Mike Bickle tells how Bob Jones said he was taken to heaven.

> Bob, one thing that I want you to add to that. That's the accountability factor, but there's another factor—that Paul was anxious—because he said that he came running up to him and he said, "You're Paul." And he said, "But you are a prophet from the end time generation, you have far surpassed, your generation, mine." And he says, "And I have a right to hear you first." Because Paul was anxious to talk to the end time apostle and prophet more than the end-time apostle and prophet would have been to talk to Paul. He said, "Because what they would do would go far greater in the glory of God."[14]

So, according to Bob Jones, even the apostle Paul has recognised that Bob Jones' ministry will be far more important and impactful than his own!

It is vital to know the theological lens of the prophets, as they prophesy in line with their doctrines.

According to Bob Jones, there will be an End-Time superhuman army led by 35 apostles. Undoubtedly, prophecies about you being a leader in the End Time army will feed your ego. But these kind of teachings have led to spiritual elitism, which is clearly against the New Testament teaching.

These are the 'founding fathers' of the most influential stream in the modern-day prophetic movement. As you can see, it is important to look at the roots and beginnings of movements.

PROTECTING YOUR DISCERNMENT

The prophetic gift and the word of knowledge need a spiritually safe space to operate. That is why the prophets hear God in His counsel—in the presence of the Lord.

The apostolic gifts, on the other hand, are less dependent on a safe spiritual environment, but they are able to operate in hostile spiritual environments more aggressively. This doesn't mean that prophets can't operate in hostile spiritual spaces, only that they often have to rely on the gifts in the apostolic end of the continuum. And at minimum, they will have to be able to create a safe spiritual space immediately around them.

Psalm 23:5 says that God prepares "a table before me in the presence of my enemies". We are temples of the Holy Spirit wherever we go!

But the spirit of deception attacks anyone operating with the prophetic gifts, and one of the grave mistakes is to attempt to rely on everything you 'hear' or 'see' in a disturbed spiritual environment. It is best to rely only on the flow of the Holy Spirit from within in those kinds of circumstances.

In many situations, I have discerned a strong resistance in the Spirit, when I have gone to minister. In those situations, I am very reluctant to operate in the gifts of knowledge or prophecy. Instead, I'd 'hammer' through with the Word of God, until I feel a release. What often follows is a flow of prophetic words to individuals or to the church.

It is a mistake to assume that a church would be automatically a safe spiritual environment just because it is a church. The devil is not scared at all to enter our churches. I don't think that our worship makes the devil flee as such, only the power and a strong presence of the Holy Spirit does that.

That is why the prophets must cultivate the lifestyle of God's presence more than most.

FIVE PRINCIPLES FOR KNOWING IF IT IS GOD

Prophecies come to us verbally either through hearing an inner voice, or when we pray aloud, through the proclamation of our mouth.

It takes time to mature in the prophetic gift, and I have a lot more to say about the gift of prophecy than I can fit in this book. I recommend my book *Five Movements: Winning the Battle for Your Prophetic Gift* if you want to go more in-depth with the gift of prophecy.

Nevertheless, I want to share five principles that help you discern if a word is from the Lord.

1. Prophecy comes with a strong presence of God

Unless a prophecy that you receive in your inner being comes with a strong presence of God, you shouldn't automatically accept it as a word from God, or share it immediately.

Instead, you should pray over it, until you are certain that it indeed is a word from God. The gift of prophecy is primarily a gift of hearing; if you aren't sure that you're hearing from God, you are not operating in the gift.

In many cases, there is no rush, and as you keep on praying over the word, God will reveal more to you, until there is a sense that you have received the word in fullness. If you practise your gift in a community, it often means that releasing a prophetic word to the church or an individual can wait for a few weeks or even months.

Often, the sense of urgency we have about sharing a prophecy is created by the stage performance model that forces prophetic people to try to fit their word into a performance schedule. But if you understand that, mostly, there is no need to share the word to the whole church at all, you are released from the pressure of the schedule.

Prophecy is not public performance but private hearing from the Lord.

I have often spent a month or two seeking God before sharing a major word to church leaders.

But if the word is accompanied with a strong presence of God, and the person the word is meant for is present, you can usually share it immediately.

2. Prophecy should never contradict the Bible

A prophetic word should never contradict the Bible, although it can challenge your Bible interpretation. One of the fun things about my prophetic hearing is that often God challenges me to read a particular section of the Bible, and as I do, deep revelation that I have previously ignored begins to flow out from the Word. I'm not adding anything to it, but reading the book with the Author helps you to see meanings that you might have missed. But these are not some esoteric readings of Scripture, but easy to communicate to others, as they are clearly in the Word—once you see them.

This happened with Jesus, and the Jews wondered where He had accumulated all that learning. The Pharisees couldn't really argue with Him, as most teaching Jesus did was simply to explain the Scripture, not adding anything to it. Much of Jesus' teaching can be found in the Old Testament, but He seemed to be able to communicate it with irresistible clarity.

God often speaks to you to illuminate a biblical truth you might not be aware of. If a revelatory word challenges your Bible interpretation, but you discover through your Bible study that it is in fact consistent with the Bible truth, the chances are that God is dealing with your imperfect understanding of the Word.

3. God's words are always enveloped in His presence

The Holy Spirit never speaks a word that isn't enveloped in His presence. The devil can camouflage as the angel of light, but he can't manufacture God's presence. Words spoken by the enemy to your mind are either full of poison, or when he masquerades as the angel of light, like empty shells, devoid of life. They have an aura of restlessness about them. The enemy might recite the Bible, as he did to Jesus when He was tempted, but he can never manufacture the unique mix of peace and energy that accompanies the presence of God. Jesus said,

> "Most assuredly, I say to you, he who does not enter the sheepfold by the door, but climbs up some other way, the same is a thief and a robber. But he who enters by the door is the shepherd of the sheep. To him the doorkeeper opens, and the sheep hear his voice; and he calls his own sheep by name and leads them out. And when he brings out his own sheep, he goes before them; and the sheep follow him, for they know his voice. Yet they will by no means follow a stranger, but will flee from him, for they do not know the voice of strangers." (John 10:1-5)

4. *God will give you enough time to test the prophecy*
The Holy Spirit knows you intimately, and He has already factored in the time it will take for you to discover whether the word is from Him or not. This is another problem caused by the stage performance model. The meetings last only a few hours at most, and if you see your main job as a proclaimer rather than hearer of the prophetic word, you will be easily compelled to share a prophetic word you might not be that certain about.

But a prophetic word is like a fire that you find unable to contain. There is no hesitance in that. God will never ask you to proclaim or act on a word if you aren't certain of its origin. Some people don't want to be certain about a prophecy, because they don't like its content, but that is not what we are talking about here.

5. *God's focus is on your relationship with Him*
Sometimes, discerning the origin of a revelatory word takes a lot of time. I have spent months in seeking clarity regarding certain prophetic words, with the Holy Spirit never answering to me clearly but drawing me deeper into His presence. This is God's way of luring you to spend more time with Him!

HOW TO DELIVER A PROPHETIC WORD

If you learn to deliver a prophetic word in a mature way, your ministry will be constructive rather than destructive. What many prophetically gifted people fail to understand is that the way you deliver the word is an integral part of the message, and that a genuine word delivered inappropriately can be harmful.

1. *Who should hear the word?*
Most prophetic words aren't meant to be shared publicly, not even when they concern the whole church. Most words for the church should be shared with the church leaders first. It is their decision to go public with them—or not. Often, the leaders choose to bring the prophetic theme to the church through teaching rather than prophecy. For example, you might receive a prophetic word about

a coming season of refreshing and take it to the leaders, but rather than letting you proclaim it from the pulpit, they might introduce the new theme through a Bible study.

If you love your church, you shouldn't feel bad about that, as this approach is often more beneficial to the church. Always pray to God to give you the right person to give the word, even when the recipient seems obvious. Just because you receive a clear word about specific people, it doesn't mean that you should share it with them, as the word might be for intercession only.

2. When should you share the word?

Prophetic words aren't always meant to be shared immediately. If the word comes with a strong presence of God and the person in question is present, there is a high probability that you should share the word on the spot, but that doesn't mean that everyone else in the room will have to hear it. It is mostly better to give a word privately rather than publicly.

If you receive a word in a meeting and you are in the congregation, you should perhaps wait until the end of the service. That will also give you the opportunity to pray over the word, and God might reveal more. If you meet the person or people in question regularly, it might make sense to be quiet about it and take the word home to pray over it, until you have full assurance about every aspect of it. I have often prayed over a prophetic word for at least a month before sharing it with church leaders.

3. How should you share the word?

Many words can be given verbally, but it is wise to share any lengthier word in a recorded or written form. This will give the recipient an opportunity to assess the prophetic word in detail. You can also proclaim the prophetic word aloud and send its main content to the recipient later.

4. What is your attitude?

If you don't have compassion in your heart for the recipients, you shouldn't deliver the word at all. Instead, pray for them, until their best interest is in your heart.

Always share the word with humility and never ask anyone to obey any directional words. Instead, ask the recipients to pray over them. If the recipient sincerely seeks God regarding the word, God will confirm it. The purpose of the prophetic ministry is to bring people into an intimate relationship with God and produce disciples of Jesus, not disciples of you. It is up to the people what they do with the prophetic word, not up to you. Unless prophetic words lead to deeper intimacy with God, they can often be destructive, as the only way to apply them properly is with the guidance of the Spirit.

HOW DO YOU KNOW IF A DREAM IS FROM GOD?

The prophetic gift includes seeing dreams and visions. In fact, the first Old Testament words for a prophet were *hozeh* and *ro'eh*, which both mean a seer.

Joel 2:28-29 prophesies,

> And it shall come to pass afterward that I will pour out My Spirit on all flesh; your sons and your daughters shall prophesy, your old men shall dream dreams, your young men shall see visions. And also on My menservants and on My maidservants I will pour out My Spirit in those days.

We rarely need to minister based on a dream straight away after seeing it, so there is usually time for reflection.

Here are some principles that help you discern the origin of a dream.

1. Can you remember the dream?

If you can't remember a dream when you wake up, it wasn't from God. If God chooses to communicate to you through a dream, He will ensure that you remember it.

You should write down any dream that you believe might originate from God straight away, as that will help you remember it later.

When you do that, you should describe the main plot, characters and elements such as colours, objects and the atmosphere.

Daniel 7:1 says,

> In the first year of Belshazzar king of Babylon, Daniel had
> a dream and visions of his head while on his bed. Then he
> wrote down the dream, telling the main facts.

2. Is it clearly structured or confusing?

God brings order into chaos and clear focus into confusion. You might not understand a God-given dream fully, but if a dream is confusing, it is never from God. Paul told Timothy,

> For God has not given us a spirit of fear, but of power and of
> love and of a sound mind. (2 Timothy 7:1)

Others translate the spirit of fear as 'the spirit of confusion'. When God speaks, He will always communicate with clarity—even when you don't understand what He says.

3. Is the dream dealing with what you are processing in your mind?

If a dream deals with something you worry or think about a lot, it is probably a result of your subconscious mind attempting to resolve what your conscious mind can't. Also, if you watch a movie late at night, you might see a sequel to it at night—with you playing the hero!

Unless the dream gives an unexpected solution to your problem, you should disregard it.

4. What is the emotional atmosphere?

Most dreams filled with anxiety or despair come from the subconscious, which functions as an overpressure valve for our fears. If you suppress your fears and anxieties, they will appear in your dreams.

But God never adds fear to your life; He always reduces it. You might see a dream that shows you the cause of your fear, but then provides a solution. This kind of dream is often from God.

The emotional atmosphere is often the key to the interpretation.

5. *Is the dream linked to something God has already revealed to you?*
God often adds or brings depth to what He has already revealed to you through a dream. It is yet another channel for Him to reveal His purposes and perspective.

6. *Is there biblical symbolism?*
Distrust any dream dictionaries, as symbols often have different meanings in different cultures. If God uses symbols, He chooses them based on what they mean to you rather than someone else. On the other hand, biblical symbols often point to a dream coming from God.

7. *Is it a 'realistic' dream?*
If so, it might refer to a real-life future situation, unless it clearly refers to the past. You might not be sure whether the dream was from God, until you face that situation, and then it will help you to act the right way.

8. *Is there a demonic element in the dream?*
Just because there is a demonic element, it doesn't automatically mean that the dream originated from the enemy, as it might be the gift of discerning spirits in you reacting to an unseen demonic influence.

You should always pray over these dreams, and the Holy Spirit will either give you more understanding about them, or ask you to reject them outright.

9. *Are you doing something wrong in the dream?*
If you see a dream in which you are doing something wrong, it is never from God—unless it is something you are doing or in danger of doing in real life, and God is convicting or warning you.

These dreams might be the product of your subconscious or originate from the enemy.

10. Do you wake up into God's presence?
Sometimes, I wake up with a distinct sense that a dream was from God. At other times, I wake up into a strong presence of God, and that can be a sign that it is a God-given dream.

At other times, God is present, as He is dealing with a demonic attack that took place through a dream. It is usually easy to tell the difference.

11. What happens when you pray over the dream?
You should always pray over a dream you think might have come from God. When you do that, the Holy Spirit will often reveal you more and begin to explain its elements.

INTERPRETING DREAMS

We can learn from the lives of Daniel and Joseph that prophetically gifted people often have the ability to interpret dreams.

In Genesis 41, Joseph is brought from the dungeon to see the Pharaoh, as his chief butler knows that Joseph has the gift of dream interpretation. Both the butler and the Pharaoh worshipped the Egyptian gods. Perhaps the Pharaoh was used to seeing demonic dreams.

But this dream had been given by God. That is why none of the magicians of Egypt could interpret it.

Here are five principles that can help you interpret God-given dreams.

1. Ask God for the interpretation
Many often miss this first step. Remember that if God gave you the dream, He can also give you the interpretation.

2. Consider the symbols
Are there any symbols in the dream that have personal significance to you? Be careful with dream dictionaries, unless they focus on

biblical symbols. In the ancient Babylon, a black cat was the bearer of good fortune, but in the Middle Ages it was linked to witchcraft. There are no references to black cats in the Bible. What does a black cat mean to you?

3. What is the emotional atmosphere?
The emotional atmosphere of a dream is important, and it often helps you interpret it. For example, a dream might show a challenging situation, but the atmosphere is faith-filled. This usually means that God is showing that you will be able to overcome your challenges.

4. Does the dream feel realistic?
There are dreams that appear realistic, and they can refer to past real events or future events. If they come from God, they usually bring their own interpretation.

5. Is the dream meant to be understood immediately?
Dreams often refer to distant future. It took years before Joseph's dream about the Sun, Moon and the eleven stars bowing down to him came to pass. When he saw the dream, he had no real understanding of its meaning.

If you don't understand a dream, put it aside, but don't disregard it. Later on, it can give you great confidence, as when it comes to pass, you will know that you are walking in the will of God. Joseph knew that it was God who had raised him to rule Egypt because He wanted to save Joseph's family, so he blessed his brothers, rather than revenged their treachery.

6. Is the dream meant to be shared immediately?
Don't assume automatically that a dream should be shared immediately. Instead, pray over it, and God will give you wisdom regarding sharing the dream at the right moment. Often, a God-given dream is meant to guide you only. Often, God will give you more understanding when you wait patiently for him to give it an explanation.

SEEING VISIONS

A vision can be an image, a series of images or an animated image, a kind of mini-movie that God shows to you when you are awake. Your eyes can be open or closed. They can take over your whole sight, or you can stay aware of your environment. Like dreams, they can be symbolic, realistic, or a mixture of both.

The process of interpreting visions is fairly similar to interpreting dreams. You might see them and experience a strong presence of God; at other times they might enter your consciousness abruptly, without a clear sense of God's presence but with a sense of revelatory significance.

There is an issue with seeing visions that is particularly applicable to ministry situations. When you see a dream, you are rarely in a situation where you are about to minister to someone, but when you are ministering to people, you can often see visual symbols. The problem is to know whether it is your gift of prophecy, word of knowledge, or the gift of discerning spirits that is operating.

If there is a disturbing presence when you see any visual images, it is often the gift of discerning spirits that is operating. In that case, God is showing you the nature of demonic influences you are dealing with.

But it could also be that the enemy is seeking to mislead you. Hence you shouldn't verbalise what you see, but rather ask diagnostic questions that don't assume too much, but get to the heart of the matter. For example, you might see pornographic images around someone. This could mean either that the person is being tempted by the enemy in this area, or he or she might have a serious sexual sin in their lives. The best way to approach this is simply to ask if they are feeling oppressed by the enemy in this area, and see how they answer.

1. *Ask God for the interpretation*

If you ask God, He will often give you the interpretation straight away. At other times, He will begin to explain the vision even without asking. He might explain the vision partially or completely.

Always listen to a sense of completeness in His voice—or the absence of it.

2. Consider the symbols
Are there symbols in the vision that have personal significance to you? Are there any biblical symbols? Considering the meaning of these symbols will often open up the vision.

3. Is it a realistic or symbolic vision?
Most visions are symbolic, but they can have some realistic elements. Realistic visions usually bring their own interpretation, but you can interpret symbolic visions through the symbols.

4. Is the vision meant to be understood immediately?
Like dreams, visions often refer to distant future. That is why you should never try to force an interpretation, as at worst that can have disastrous consequences, if you act based on a false interpretation. In Daniel 8:26, an angel tells Daniel to "seal up the vision, for it refers to many days in the future." The meaning of most visions will unfold over time.

5. Is the vision meant to be shared immediately?
You might comprehend a vision straight away, but that doesn't mean that you should share it immediately. Always pray over the vision, and God will give you wisdom when and to whom to share it.

8

TONGUES AND THEIR INTERPRETATION

Jesus tells His disciples after His resurrection in Mark 16:15-18,

> "Go into all the world and preach the gospel to every creature. He who believes and is baptized will be saved; but he who does not believe will be condemned. And these signs will follow those who believe: In My name they will cast out demons; they will speak with new tongues; they will take up serpents; and if they drink anything deadly, it will by no means hurt them; they will lay hands on the sick, and they will recover."

According to Jesus, speaking in tongues is one of the miraculous signs that will define the Church, and in many ways, apart from the emphasis on healing, speaking in tongues has come to define the Pentecostal movement specifically. This doesn't necessarily mean that the Pentecostals of today would pray in tongues much more than any other Christian group, but they have emphasised the gift since the Azusa Street Revival.

Nowhere is the division between the Charismatic and Pentecostal churches and the rest as visible as with speaking in tongues. The other gifts are so clearly discernible in both the Old and the New Testament that explaining them away means discrediting the Bible—which liberal theology has done—but because of the Bible stories, even the most traditional churches are more open to the other gifts, such as the gift of faith and even the gift of prophecy, although their nature and use has often been redefined.

But praying in tongues is by no means merely a Pentecostal phenomenon. Tom Wright, the former Bishop of Durham, said, speaking at St Paul's Cathedral on 20th October 2015, that he prays "with the Jesus Prayer which I also do, and praying in tongues, which I also do. I am fairly eclectic, a typical Anglican."[1]

So, we can see how the gift of praying in tongues has travelled from Pentecostalism via the Charismatic movement into the traditional churches, and even to theological academies.

The classic Pentecostal experience is described in Acts 2:1-4,

> When the Day of Pentecost had fully come, they were all with one accord in one place. And suddenly there came a sound from heaven, as of a rushing mighty wind, and it filled the whole house where they were sitting. Then there appeared to them divided tongues, as of fire, and one sat upon each of them. And they were all filled with the Holy Spirit and began to speak with other tongues, as the Spirit gave them utterance.

The classic Pentecostal version of church history goes much like this: there was the first Pentecost, and then the Church grew exponentially for the first few hundred years, but gradually, she lost her way, and the anointing of the Holy Spirit, for at least a millennia and a half, until, abruptly, in 1906, the Holy Spirit returned to the Church. That is the version of church history, focused on the former and the latter rain, that I kept on hearing in my youth. What bothered me then was that, according to this history, the Holy Spirit had deserted His Church for most of her existence. That didn't sound right to me. But God has worked through His Church in all times.

Yet, in the early church, it was the baptism by the Holy Spirit with the sign of speaking in tongues that convinced Peter and the apostles that the Gentiles could also be saved.

Acts 10: 44-46 says,

> While Peter was still speaking these words, the Holy Spirit fell upon all those who heard the word. And those of the circumcision who believed were astonished, as many as

came with Peter, because the gift of the Holy Spirit had been poured out on the Gentiles also. For they heard them speak with tongues and magnify God.

In the early church, the baptism of the Holy Spirit, with speaking in tongues and prophesying, seemed to mark that the Christians—both Jews and Gentiles—had received the gospel message in all its fullness.

> And it happened, while Apollos was at Corinth, that Paul, having passed through the upper regions, came to Ephesus. And finding some disciples he said to them, "Did you receive the Holy Spirit when you believed?" So they said to him, "We have not so much as heard whether there is a Holy Spirit." And he said to them, "Into what then were you baptized?" So they said, "Into John's baptism."
> Then Paul said, "John indeed baptized with a baptism of repentance, saying to the people that they should believe on Him who would come after him, that is, on Christ Jesus." When they heard this, they were baptized in the name of the Lord Jesus. And when Paul had laid hands on them, the Holy Spirit came upon them, and they spoke with tongues and prophesied. Now the men were about twelve in all. (Acts 19:1-7)

So, faith in Jesus and the baptism of the Holy Spirit marked the key differences between the disciples of John the Baptist and the disciples of Jesus.

It is because of Bible passages like this that many Pentecostals tend to think that praying in tongues is the sign of Spirit baptism, and that it is impossible to be filled with the Spirit without speaking in tongues. But if that was the case, every Spirit-filled Christian should also be able to prophesy, as in most of these passages the believers both speak in tongues and prophesy.

When I was fifteen, I responded to an altar call at a Pentecostal tent meeting, where a minister tried to get me to speak in tongues, convinced that if I spoke in tongues, that would mean that I was being filled with the Holy Spirit. I managed to utter a few unintelligible words, and he seemed satisfied. But that wasn't a filling of the Holy Spirit, although I do think I actually spoke in tongues. But I thought, mistakenly, that I might have been filled with the Holy Spirit, and, consequently, it took five years longer before I was actually filled with Him. And it was only then when I realised that through all that time, I hadn't actually been filled with Him at all. And when I was actually filled with the Holy Spirit, I didn't speak with tongues at all in the moment of filling, although I began to speak with tongues a few weeks later.

Speaking in tongues is a gift of the Spirit, but it seems to me that you can actually speak in tongues without being filled with the Holy Spirit, if you are a believer.

Paul clearly didn't think that speaking in tongues would have been the only sign of being filled with the Holy Spirit. He says in 1 Corinthians 12:30,

> All do not have gifts of healings, do they? All do not speak with tongues, do they? All do not interpret, do they?

In Paul's argument, there is no sense that he was expecting everyone who had been filled with the Holy Spirit to speak in tongues.

When I was filled with the Holy Spirit, the experience was very powerful and tangible, as the person who prayed for me and I were both thrown on the ground by an invisible force, as if we had been struck by a lightning. When I got up, my life had been completely transformed. I had suffered from deep depression for months, and it had been lifted in an instant.

But that evening I didn't speak in tongues at all. Instead, that night the sign of my baptism in the Spirit was uncontainable joy. When I went on to the streets to evangelise, this time without any sense of intimidation, many kept on asking where they could get the drugs I had taken, as they said they had never seen anyone as happy as I.

There are three key events recorded in Acts that were unique moments in the history of the Church: the beginning of the Church, the beginning of the Gentile mission, and the bringing of some of John's disciples into the Church.

They were moments of birth and new beginnings, to give the apostles a clear sense of direction regarding God's plan for mankind, but it doesn't mean that the baptism of the Holy Spirit would happen to us all in an identical way.

In my own ministry, the other sign of the Spirit baptism mentioned in Acts, prophesying, has been far more prominent and important. And yes, I speak in tongues nearly on a daily basis, but in my life, the continual anointing of the Holy Spirit is not dependent on speaking in tongues. I mostly use speaking I tongues when I need a spiritual breakthrough, and in spiritual warfare.

TONGUES IN CORINTH

Unlike in any other churches the apostle Paul worked with, speaking in tongues became a problem in Corinth, and it is only because of the scale of that problem that we have any sort of biblical understanding about the gift.

Paul writes,

> But now, brethren, if I come to you speaking with tongues, what shall I profit you unless I speak to you either by revelation, by knowledge, by prophesying, or by teaching? Even things without life, whether flute or harp, when they make a sound, unless they make a distinction in the sounds, how will it be known what is piped or played? For if the trumpet makes an uncertain sound, who will prepare for battle? So likewise you, unless you utter by the tongue words easy to understand, how will it be known what is spoken? For you will be speaking into the air.
>
> There are, it may be, so many kinds of languages in the world, and none of them is without significance. Therefore, if I do not know the meaning of the language, I shall be a foreigner to him who speaks, and he who speaks will be a foreigner to me. Even so you, since you are zealous for spiritual gifts, let it be for the edification of the church that you seek to excel. (1 Corinthians 14:6-12)

As in 1 Corinthians 14:13 Paul says, "The one who speaks in a tongue should pray that they may interpret what they say", it might appear that Paul devalued the gift of speaking in tongues, but in fact he was eager to see the Corinthians go deeper in other forms of prayer with the Spirit.

Paul continues,

> For if I pray in a tongue, my spirit prays, but my mind is unfruitful. So what shall I do? I will pray with my spirit, but I will also pray with my understanding; I will sing with my spirit, but I will also sing with my understanding. Otherwise when you are praising God in the Spirit, how can someone else, who is now put in the position of an inquirer, say "Amen" to your thanksgiving, since they do not know what you are saying? (1 Corinthians 14:14-16)

Some Christians use these verses to belittle the speaking in tongues, but Paul isn't belittling them at all. It is clear that he is trying to restore order in public meetings, as in the verse 18 he says,

> I thank my God I speak with tongues more than you all

But in verse 19 he says,

> Yet in the church I would rather speak five words with my understanding, that I may teach others also, than ten thousand words in a tongue.

In verses 20-21 he continues,

> Brethren, do not be children in understanding; however, in malice be babes, but in understanding be mature. In the law it is written: "With men of other tongues and other lips I will speak to this people; and yet, for all that, they will not hear Me," says the Lord.

Here Paul is referring to Isaiah 28:11,

> For with stammering lips and another tongue, he will speak
> to this people

The Assyrian language, though a Semitic idiom nearly allied to Hebrew, was different enough to sound in the ears of a Jew like his own tongue mispronounced. What Paul is saying is that hearing the Assyrian language that brought destruction nevertheless failed to bring the people of Israel to repentance, so the Corinthian Christians shouldn't expect speaking in tongues to bring anyone to God either.

Then he continues in verses 22-25,

> Therefore tongues are for a sign, not to those who believe but to unbelievers; but prophesying is not for unbelievers but for those who believe. Therefore if the whole church comes together in one place, and all speak with tongues, and there come in *those who are* uninformed or unbelievers, will they not say that you are out of your mind?
>
> But if all prophesy, and an unbeliever or an uninformed person comes in, he is convinced by all, he is convicted by all. And thus the secrets of his heart are revealed; and so, falling down on his face, he will worship God and report that God is truly among you.

It seems that the Corinthian Christians looked to the first Pentecost and the story about many foreigners in Jerusalem hearing their own language spoken miraculously by the disciples in order to validate their speaking in tongues.

But Paul's argument was that this wasn't the case in Corinth; it was more like the Israelis hearing the Assyrians but not quite understanding them. The first Pentecost was a special case, as the people visiting Jerusalem could actually understand the foreign tongues and could hear God being praised; in Corinth no one could understand what the Corinthian Christians were saying.

Unfortunately, 1 Corinthians is the only text in the New Testament that gives a more detailed teaching on speaking in tongues. Thankfully, looking at the historical context is helpful in getting more out of the text.

Corinth was a centre of idol worship and it had many temples, and it is in this same letter that we can see multiple references to the believers of Corinth bringing pagan practices to the church. And their understanding of what speaking in tongues is seems more connected to their pagan culture than being filled with the Holy Spirit.

In Paul's letters to the Corinthians, we can see many references to early forms of Gnosticism. Gnosticism was the mixing of pagan ideas with Christianity.

James D. G. Dunn writes,

> To sum up, the root of the trouble facing Paul at Corinth was almost certainly the strong influence of gnostic (or pre-Gnostic) ideas on large section of the Christian community. [2]

In his argumentation in 1 Corinthians, Paul often chooses words used by his opponents, as he confronts those who called themselves pneumatics, the spiritual ones (*pneumatikoi*), that held 'wisdom' (*sophia*) in high esteem. [3]

The parallels of what Paul faces in Corinth with Gnosticism are striking. Paul writes in 1 Corinthians 2:6-8,

> However, we speak wisdom among those who are mature, yet not the wisdom of this age, nor of the rulers of this age, who are coming to nothing. But we speak the wisdom of God in a mystery, the hidden *wisdom* which God ordained before the ages for our glory, which none of the rulers of this age knew; for had they known, they would not have crucified the Lord of glory.

Paul is writing against the pre-Gnostic heresies affecting the Christian community of Corinth. As Gnosticism developed, it would be the right knowledge that would bring salvation, rather than the finished work of Jesus on the cross.

Paul also mocks the teachings of the Corinthian 'prosperity gospel'.

You are already full! You are already rich! You have reigned as kings without us—and indeed I could wish you did reign, that we also might reign with you! (1 Corinthians 4:8)

Dunn writes,

> A striking feature of the later Gnosticism was their conviction that having been given knowledge of the true state of things and of themselves they were already 'perfect'. Analogously we see in the Corinthian faction opposing Paul an overemphasis on the 'already' and a neglect of the 'not yet' of eschatological salvation.[4]

The more you study 1 Corinthians, the clearer it becomes that Paul is dealing with the early days of a Gnostic heresy.

He writes,

> Do you not know that you are the temple of God and that the Spirit of God dwells in you? If anyone defiles the temple of God, God will destroy him. For the temple of God is holy, which temple you are. (1 Corinthians 3:16-17)

The Gnostics believed in total separation between the body and spirit, which led either to asceticism or immorality. If body was seen evil, it needed to be deprived of pleasure, or alternatively, it didn't really matter what you did with it. It seems clear that in Corinth it had led the second option and to immorality, as Paul referred to some Corinthian Christians sleeping with prostitutes.

> Or do you not know that he who is joined to a harlot is one body with her? For "the two," He says, "shall become one flesh." (1 Corinthians 6:16)

This matters to us, when it comes to speaking in tongues, as it makes it clear that the speaking in tongues in Corinth was probably pre-Gnostic and pagan in nature. This seems evident, as the Corinthians seemed very interested in the 'heavenly knowledge', and speaking in tongues was speaking the language of 'angels'—that no one could understand you was the whole point and evidence for speaking the language of heaven. It seems that they believed that heavenly language had magical powers.

The Egyptian ideas and magic were quite popular in the Roman world. My friend Claudio Ferro has written a fascinating book: *Angels and Demons: Ancient and Modern Spiritual Warfare*, in which he maps the Egyptian influences in the architecture of Rome.

The obelisks weren't brought to Rome just because of the many Roman victories, but also because many Romans believed in the Egyptian ideas of occultism. It seems that both the ancient Greeks and Romans were fascinated by Egyptian magic.

The Greek Magical Papyri is the name given by scholars to a body of papyri from Greco-Roman Egypt, which each contain a number of magical spells, formulae, hymns and rituals. The materials in the papyri date from the 2nd century BC to the 5th century AD. One of the best known of these texts is the Mithras Liturgy.

In Book IV of the Greek Magical Papyri in which the Mithras Liturgy occurs, lines 1-25 are a spell calling on Egyptian and Jewish powers in order to obtain information. Lines 1127-64 are a spell for exorcising a demon, using Coptic words of Christian origin, with instructions for preparing an amulet. Lines 1716-1870 are headed "Sword of Dardanos" and they are a love spell.

The Mithras Liturgy shares several elements found widely in magic as practised in the Greco-Roman world, which drew on or claimed the authority of Egyptian religion and magic. These include the preparation of amulets and ointments, the timing of rituals based on astronomical phenomena or horoscopes, and the manipulation of breath and speech. Vocalisations include popping and hissing sounds for onomatopoeia—the imitation of sounds—variations on the sequence of Greek vowels, speaking in tongues, and words that are untranslatable, but seem to derive from or are intended to sound like Egyptian, Hebrew and other languages.[5]

Origen, a scholar and early Christian theologian, who was born and spent the first half of his career in Alexandria, cites analogous views among Egyptian experts in magic.

One of their doctrines is that names acquire, or are able to unleash, their power, if they are repeated in an imbricated or complex sequence, another that each language disposes of words which are the names of daemonic powers which have the power to perform certain highly specific tasks: the Egyptian language for example contains words which are the names of powers specific to Egypt, the Persian language powers specific to Persia and so on.[6]

Put simply, there was a strong belief in the magical power of languages, which was lost when they were translated. In the magical use of languages, you recited certain words, and it didn't really matter whether you understood their meaning or not, as long as you pronounced them correctly.

Origen writes,

> Thus, if we were to translate the name "Israel" into Greek or another language, we would effect nothing. But if we keep it as it is, linking it on those words with which experts in these matters have thought fit to connect it, then something would happen in accordance with the power which such invocations are said to possess when a formula of this kind is pronounced.[7]

Now we get to the heart of the matter—the "heavenly language" remained heavenly *only* if it was *not* translated.

Iamblichus, a Syrian Neoplatonist philosopher, defended the use of the 'heavenly' language.

> First, he claims that there are two classes of "meaningless names", those whose meanings have been revealed, and those which have not. The gods know the true meaning of all "meaningless names".[8]

Neoplatonism and Gnosticism were interrelated but separate movements, and here Iamblichus effectively tells that when you are reciting "meaningless names", you are speaking the language of gods, which only they understand. Iamblichus had a positive view of magic, so he would have believed that reciting meaningless names would have special power.

It seems clear that many Corinthian Christians believed that speaking in tongues, especially when no one could understand them, had some sort of magical power, as they imagined speaking the language of God or angels, and that speaking in tongues would lose its power if translated.

But Paul argues that speaking in tongues publicly has no value, unless someone interprets it, and makes it intelligible.

So, the Corinthians despised prophecy, or preferred tongues to prophecy, as intelligible words were not perceived to have as much spiritual power as the unintelligible words.

This was paganism and belief in magic, and the apostle Paul argued that the words themselves had no magical power, but that their power lay in clear communication.

HOW DO TONGUES EDIFY?

Paul writes in 1 Corinthians 14:4, "He who speaks in a tongue edifies himself". He also writes,

> For he who speaks in a tongue does not speak to men but to God, for no one understands him; however, in the spirit he speaks mysteries. (1 Corinthians 14:2)

Paul says that you speak to God in the Spirit, and that is always beneficial, even if you don't understand what you are saying. The added benefit is that you don't pray with your mind but in the power of God.

To me, although I don't speak in tongues as much as I used to do, mainly as I tend to pray prophetically, speaking in tongues is one of the most meaningful gifts you can have.

The gift of speaking in tongues is firmly linked with the experience of the baptism of the Spirit, although it is not the sign for it.

FROM TONGUES TO INTERPRETATION

Whether you are praying in tongues or not, Paul writes,

> Pursue love, and desire spiritual gifts, but especially that you
> may prophesy. For he who speaks in a tongue does not speak
> to men but to God, for no one understands him; however, in
> the spirit he speaks mysteries. But he who prophesies speaks
> edification and exhortation and comfort to men. He who
> speaks in a tongue edifies himself, but he who prophesies
> edifies the church.
>
> I wish you all spoke with tongues, but even more that
> you prophesied; for he who prophesies is greater than he
> who speaks with tongues, unless indeed he interprets, that
> the church may receive edification. (1 Corinthians 14:1-5)

We don't have quite as a magical view of speaking in tongues as
the Gnostics had, but many Pentecostals do use tongues in a nearly
magical way, not unlike they use the phrase: "In the name of Jesus!"

But by and large, most Christians today don't understand the value
of tongues at all, as we approach them from a completely opposite
direction than the Christians in Corinth. We are the products of
rationalism, and anything unintelligible seems to us like a waste of
time.

Paradoxically, most Pentecostals who have championed the gift
have also missed its primary purpose as a gateway into other gifts,
such as the gift of prophecy.

It is not the only gateway into prophecy, but a major one, and that
explains why so many Christians, when they are filled with the Holy
Spirit, also receive the gift of speaking in tongues, as God is opening
their ability to hear from Him.

In 2006, University of Pennsylvania School of Medicine
constructed the first ever neuroimaging study of speaking in tongues.
The study demonstrated changes in cerebral activity during prayer.
The frontal lobes, parietal lobes and left caudate were most affected.
The frontal lobes are the area of the brain associated with being in
control of one's self. The images of the brain taken during praying

in tongues showed that the subjects weren't in control of the usual language centres.[9]

To me, this points to the Holy Spirit being actively involved in speaking with tongues. We might be able to control the flow, but it is the Holy Spirit who energises it.

You might have seen abuses of the gift and perceive it more as an embarrassment than a blessing. But God has a lot more grace and patience with us than we have with other Christians. If you see your toddling son trying to learn to walk and see him fall, you will encourage him rather than ask him never to attempt to walk again!

Praying in tongues takes faith. You must trust that the Holy Spirit is working in you. When you pray in tongues, you will gradually lose control over your physical tongue and give it to God. The fact that you must practise faith, and that you don't understand what you are saying, will gradually detach your praying from your rational mind. In this instance, the confession of your faith—which you don't understand—will take control over your mind, even when your mind can't grasp what you are uttering. When you are speaking in tongues, you are learning to speak in the Spirit.

Prophetic prayer and proclamation are other forms of speaking in the Spirit, but it is a lot harder to move directly from intelligible mind-generated prayer to intelligible Spirit-generated prayer than through the 'irrational' gateway of speaking in tongues. Praying in tongues disconnects your prayer life from the limitations of your rational mind and reconnects it with prayer in the Spirit.

In 1 Corinthians 14:13, Paul asks the one who speaks in tongues to pray for their interpretation. It seems to me that Paul perceived speaking in tongues as a step toward prophetic speaking through the gift of interpretation.

Prayer in tongues connects your mouth with the Spirit who resides in your inner being. Initiating the flow with speaking in tongues brings the presence and power of the Spirit. You will learn to trust in the flow of the Spirit rather than your intellect.

As the flow of the Spirit will begin to bring intelligible words, you will rely on the flow, as it carries the presence of God. Your mind will understand what you are saying, but rather than your mind controlling your prayer, through the gateway of speaking in tongues, you will have shifted from intelligible mind-generated prayer to Spirit-generated prayer.

Learning to prophesy with the 'training wheels' of speaking in tongues is perhaps the safest way to develop the gift. It is safer to let the Spirit take control over your mouth through speaking in tongues and release the flow of the Spirit from your inner core into your mouth rather than attempt to listen to God's inaudible voice. This way, you can move directly from receiving to proclamation, rather than seek God for months in an attempt to figure out whether it was God that spoke to you or not.

According to 1 Corinthians 14:27, there is another way to interpret tongues rather than the speaker interpreting himself or herself, and that is someone else interpreting the tongues. What is slightly unclear is whether Paul expected the interpreters to understand the speaking in tongues naturally or supernaturally.

In the first Pentecost, the people who interpreted the tongues interpreted them naturally, as they knew the languages spoken. I have come across many credible stories in how this has happened today.

Also, I have spoken in tongues, using the same words repeatedly, words that I have not understood, and as I have looked for their meaning, I have found it.

But most of the time, I have no idea about what I am actually saying, although, in intercession, names of people I know often pop up. This gives me some ideas about what I might be praying for.

TONGUES OF ANGELS

Many believe that speaking in tongues can be speaking a human language unknown to the speaker, or a language of heaven. Fascinatingly, we can find only two references to the content of speaking in tongues and actual languages used in the Bible.

The first one is in Acts 2:5-13, which describes the first Pentecost and the baptism by the Holy Spirit in the Upper Room.

And there were dwelling in Jerusalem Jews, devout men, from every nation under heaven. And when this sound occurred, the multitude came together, and were confused, because everyone heard them speak in his own language. Then they were all amazed and marveled, saying to one another,

"Look, are not all these who speak Galileans? And how *is it that* we hear, each in our own language in which we were born? Parthians and Medes and Elamites, those dwelling in Mesopotamia, Judea and Cappadocia, Pontus and Asia, Phrygia and Pamphylia, Egypt and the parts of Libya adjoining Cyrene, visitors from Rome, both Jews and proselytes, Cretans and Arabs—we hear them speaking in our own tongues the wonderful works of God." So they were all amazed and perplexed, saying to one another, "Whatever could this mean?" Others mocking said, "They are full of new wine."

It seems clear that the writer's understanding was that speaking in tongues was mainly speaking in human languages unknown to the speaker.

But there is another reference in 1 Corinthians 13:1:

Though I speak with the tongues of men and of angels, but have not love, I have become sounding brass or a clanging cymbal. (1 Corinthians 13:1)

Now, the question must arise whether we actually speak with the tongues of angels or not, as it seems clear that Paul is critiquing the Corinthian understanding of tongues—the belief that speaking in tongues gave you the authority inherent in the language—hence if you spoke with tongues of angels, you released the spiritual authority of the angels, as you spoke their language.

There is a similar type of reference in 1 Corinthians 15:29.

Otherwise, what will they do who are baptized for the dead, if the dead do not rise at all? Why then are they baptized for the dead?

This is a reference to the practice of some Greek mystery religions of being baptised on behalf of the dead, and because of this verse, Mormons practise it. But Paul doesn't condone the practice. It remains unclear what Paul's actual belief was regarding whether we could actually be speaking in tongues of angels. Unfortunately, the Bible is silent on this matter.

So, biblically, we know very little about tongues, and what follows now is mostly based on my observations after over twenty-five years of praying in tongues.

In principle, I believe that tongues can be used for any type of prayer.

TONGUES IN INTERCESSION

I often find myself praying in tongues with the only *recognisable* words being names of some people I know. Often, this happens when I don't really know how to pray for them.

I believe that, often, when I pray in tongues for people, I pray for things that might not be that useful for me to know about. I have a passion for these people, but, perhaps, the information in these prayers might be damaging to our relationship, or, perhaps, in my heart I might not be ready to pray these prayers.

So, you can certainly intercede for others with praying in tongues, and this can also happen spontaneously when you are praying for someone.

TONGUES IN SPIRITUAL WARFARE

I am certain that praying in tongues can be used in spiritual warfare. In fact, I probably pray with tongues more in the context of spiritual warfare than in any other way.

Often I feel a level of depression or anxiety, and as I begin to pray, I begin to speak in tongues. After a little while, I feel how the presence of the Holy Spirit begins to flow in me, and the depression and anxiety begins to lift. Often, I shift into an intelligible language and begin to command the forces of darkness to depart.

KICK-STARTING ANY OTHER FORM OF PRAYER

I don't usually speak in tongues for hours, but only for a few minutes, enough to kick-start another form of prayer.

Paul writes in Romans 8:26,

> Likewise the Spirit also helps in our weaknesses. For we do not know what we should pray for as we ought, but the Spirit Himself makes intercession for us with groanings which cannot be uttered.

Now, this is not even praying in tongues, but these groanings—and also speaking in tongues—begin to direct our prayers, so that after a little later we will know how to pray.

EMPTY SPEAKING IN TONGUES

There are times when I begin to speak in tongues, but after a few minutes, it just feels empty and meaningless. Normally, when I pray in tongues, soon I will begin to feel the energising presence of the Holy Spirit, and I either continue to speak in tongues, or the Holy Spirit directs my mind to intelligible prayer. If I continue to feel empty, I will stop praying in tongues and perhaps begin to seek God's presence through stillness, as I get grasp that I am trying to exercise the gift when God is not that interested in me operating in it.

In churches, you can often hear empty speaking in tongues, as many Christians approach speaking in tongues as a method of prayer, rather than something that reconnects them with the Holy Spirit.

It is common in Pentecostal churches for a preacher to ask everyone to speak together in tongues, when he or she wants to take the prayer 'to a higher level'. There are times when this is perhaps advisable, although in most cases this is a waste of time, especially if we approach this as a method or as if it were some kind of magic.

It is also one of the tricks of the stage performance model to get the congregation to speak in tongues, as after that, most of the congregation are more receptive to what the preacher is saying, believing that everything that happens in the church must now be from God, after everyone has spoken in tongues.

This is not dissimilar to asking everyone to pray for a church event beforehand, as psychologically, praying for an event will increase our motivation to attend. That is why to me, many prayer programmes for events are nothing more than yet another way to motivate people through creating a conviction that God must be involved with the event, simply because everybody is praying for it.

DEMONICALLY INSPIRED TONGUES

Yes, there are things such as demonically inspired tongues, but there has to be the genuine before there can be the fake.

But why would the enemy fake tongues? Because he is the great counterfeiter! He can only twist and destroy what God has created. The devil has never created anything else but sin and rebellion. Even sex is an invention of God. The devil can only twist it and corrupt it. Likewise, he can do the same with tongues.

When I was about twenty, we encountered a demon-possessed pagan priestess during our outreach. This woman could speak what others said was perfect Hebrew, and she mocked my feeble tongues with her fluent speaking in tongues.

I kept on repeating 'Poco loco'. She ridiculed that. I had no idea about what it meant, and it was only a few years later when I learnt that it is Spanish and means 'little crazy.'

That pretty much summed up the situation. We cast out demons from a woman who wanted to stop them tormenting her, but she wasn't ready to give her life to Jesus.

That is a little crazy, as Jesus says in Matthew 12:43-45,

> "When an unclean spirit goes out of a man, he goes through dry places, seeking rest, and finds none. Then he says, 'I will return to my house from which I came.' And when he comes, he finds it empty, swept, and put in order. Then he goes and takes with him seven other spirits more wicked than himself, and they enter and dwell there; and the last *state* of that man is worse than the first. So shall it also be with this wicked generation."

The next time someone from our team saw this young woman, she was many times worse than before. I felt sorry for her and could only hope that the fact that she had seen that the power of God was greater than the power of the enemy would one day bring her to Him.

I learnt an important lesson that day. I realised that the demonic powers are real, but that the demonic spirits must submit to the name of Jesus.

When I looked in the eyes of this woman, I could see into the filthy underworld of the demons. After that, I have never been scared of direct confrontation with the enemy.

There was absolutely *no* contest.

I am not contesting that demons are dangerous; of course they are, but the name of Jesus is enough to cast them out in a direct confrontation between the two kingdoms. It is because of this that the devil prefers to use deception, as it is through deceiving people that he can inflict more damage on us.

I also learned as Jesus said that unless the Holy Spirit moves in, there is absolutely no reason to cast out a demon; things will only get worse after that.

9

WORD OF KNOWLEDGE

Many leaders in the Charismatic movement seem willing to forgive William Branham almost anything because of his allegedly accurate words of knowledge. As Branham's ministry model still plagues the Pentecostal and Charismatic movements, it is important to have a look at it before establishing what the Bible says about the gift.

Branham didn't trigger the Healing Revival with his alleged word of knowledge; initially he relied on the vibrations of his hand to discern the sicknesses in people. It was supposed to be a heavenly sign that God was using him.

This sign of vibrations proved far from reliable, and the appearance of the 'word of knowledge' came in 1949.[1] And suddenly, after taking half a year away from ministry, Branham was able to know detailed and accurate information about people.

Branham constantly asserted that he had never met the people in the prayer line before, and yet he was able to tell them their names and addresses.[2]

Branham claimed that the sign of discernment was unique to him, and according to him, only one person would get that in any generation. According to Branham, "That'll never be until I die."[3]

Earlier on, we have looked at how it is nearly certain that Branham got his accurate 'words of knowledge' from the prayer cards that contained most, if not all, of that information. He wasn't lying when he told that he had not met these people—who all had numbered prayer cards, and Branham could call any number—but he had seen all, or at least some, of the prayer cards. And Branham didn't need to memorise the content of all of them, but only the content of a few. It was enough for the illusion to work if he memorised a few and ensured that the sick were standing in line in the right order, as that would have given an appearance that he could know accurate information about anyone, had he wanted to.

So, this model of Branham, nearly certainly generated by using memorising prayer cards, has become the unattainable gold standard that the word of knowledge ministers aim to gain. This model is so popular that I have heard ministers joking about knowing the exact sum of money that people have in their accounts and exhorting them to give more during an offering talk—and with no one lifting an eyebrow.

There is only one direct reference in the Bible to the gift of the word of knowledge, as listed by Paul in 1 Corinthians 8. Paul uses the words *logos gnosis*, but unhelpfully, he doesn't explain what he means by them. This alone wouldn't be enough to make any conclusive statement about what they stood for. That is why some scholars, mainly the ones who don't believe that the spiritual gifts still exist, say that *logos gnosis* is a teaching gift.

George Jeffreys, the founder of the Elim Pentecostal movement in Great Britain, defines the word of knowledge as,

> It is the bestowal of a word of knowledge on special occasions. It differs from the word of wisdom in that it miraculously supplies the mind with the knowledge of things. The former wisely decides after reviewing the matter under consideration, the latter reveals the matter itself.[4]

He warns,

> We have known persons who have sadly lacked the word of wisdom when dispensing the word of knowledge entrusted to them.[5]

Fortunately, there are many instances in the Bible that illustrate what the word of knowledge is.

We can see a high-level word of knowledge by Daniel in a situation where his life, and the lives of all wise men, the astrologers, the magicians and soothsayers in Babylon, were in danger. King Nebuchadnezzar had seen a dream and demanded not just for the interpretation but also for the revelation of what he had seen; otherwise he would kill all the wise men.

> The king answered and said to Daniel, whose name was Belteshazzar, "Are you able to make known to me the dream which I have seen, and its interpretation?"
>
> Daniel answered in the presence of the king, and said, "The secret which the king has demanded, the wise men, the astrologers, the magicians, and the soothsayers cannot declare to the king. But there is a God in heaven who reveals secrets, and He has made known to King Nebuchadnezzar what will be in the latter days. Your dream, and the visions of your head upon your bed, were these: As for you, O king, thoughts came to your mind while on your bed, about what would come to pass after this; and He who reveals secrets has made known to you what will be. But as for me, this secret has not been revealed to me because I have more wisdom than anyone living, but for our sakes who make known the interpretation to the king, and that you may know the thoughts of your heart." (Daniel 2:26-30)

I don't think Daniel actually re-saw the dream, but God told him what the dream was about.

In the Gospel of John, Jesus sees Nathanael under the fig tree.

> Jesus saw Nathanael coming toward Him, and said of him, "Behold, an Israelite indeed, in whom is no deceit!" Nathanael said to Him, "How do You know me?" Jesus answered and said to him, "Before Philip called you, when you were under the fig tree, I saw you." Nathanael answered and said to Him, "Rabbi, You are the Son of God! You are the King of Israel!" Jesus answered and said to him, "Because I said to you, 'I saw you under the fig tree,' do you believe? You will see greater things than these." (John 1:47-50)

That is a 'word' of knowledge, but in a visual form. In Mark 2:5-8, Jesus declares the sins of a paralysed man forgiven.

> When Jesus saw their faith, He said to the paralytic, "Son, your sins are forgiven you." And some of the scribes were sitting there and reasoning in their hearts, "Why does this Man speak blasphemies like this? Who can forgive sins but God alone?" But immediately, when Jesus perceived in His spirit that they reasoned thus within themselves, He said to them, "Why do you reason about these things in your hearts?"

Often, a word of knowledge is an insight into what is taking place in someone's heart, and Jesus sees straight into the heart of the scribes. Then He heals the paralytic to demonstrate that He has the authority to forgive sins.

Again, John 4 tells a story about Jesus meeting a woman at a well in Samaria. He asks her for water, which leads to a conversation between Jesus and the woman.

Jesus tells the woman,

> "Go, call your husband, and come here." The woman answered and said, "I have no husband." Jesus said to her, "You have well said, 'I have no husband,' for you have had five husbands, and the one whom you now have is not your husband; in that you spoke truly." The woman said to Him, "Sir, I perceive that You are a prophet." (John 4:16-19)

The woman now perceives Jesus as a prophet, but in fact, Jesus isn't really prophesying; He's telling her current state of affairs, and what has already taken place. This is a word of knowledge.

I often find myself talking to people with words of knowledge, as God directs me straight to the real issues in people's lives. That is an excellent way to use the gift in everyday life. What is astonishing to me is that often I don't even know that I am operating in the word of knowledge, until the people I am talking to react, and I find out, that all this time, the Holy Spirit has been directing the conversation. Often, there is a sense of God's presence over the conversation, but

I am not aware of giving out any particular word of knowledge. Perhaps the whole conversation is a word of knowledge in those situations!

It seems to me that Paul was making a great effort to entice the Christians in Corinth to desire other spiritual gifts, and not just the gift of speaking in tongues, and, in the process, he ended up giving us a glimpse of the diverse ways of how the Holy Spirit works in our lives.

Also, he used two words that the Corinthians Christians loved— knowledge and wisdom—and told them that they were something the Holy Spirit was willing to give everyone liberally, and not just to some elite Christians.

How would you define what Jesus said to the Samaritan woman? Is it a prophecy? Not really. It doesn't really concern the future. What is it? It is revelatory knowledge about her present-day situation—in other words, a word of knowledge. A word of knowledge reveals the present-day situation— the way things are.

It might not always be a specific word as such that I need to utter, but it provides a revelatory point for conversations.

In ministry situations, I often get a word of knowledge about someone, but rather than sharing the word, I turn it into a question.

"Does this ring a bell?" kind of approach rather than, "Thus says the Lord!" opens the person's heart for ministry. It doesn't make it any less impactful but respects the other person's freedom and privacy.

Also, this is a good way to grow in the gift, as the stakes are lower. Often, what happens is that when the person opens up, this is followed by a word of wisdom or prophecy. It builds confidence when you realise that the initial word of knowledge —information that you wouldn't have known—is correct. You can then prophesy or give a word of wisdom more boldly, and the recipient is also more receptive to the work of the Holy Spirit.

The word of knowledge is an excellent safety check if you are about to prophesy to someone you don't know very well. It assures that you are on right track.

Often, you realise that God has given you the gift of the word of knowledge when in conversations with people, unexpected things pop into your mind. If this is accompanied with a sense of God's presence, you should be able to share them with the person you are talking to through directing the conversation to the issue the word of knowledge is about, without even mentioning that it is a word of knowledge.

When Jesus spoke to the Samaritan woman, He didn't first tell her that she has had five husbands, and that the current man she is with isn't in fact her husband. Instead, He simply asked her to bring her husband, and the woman responded by saying that she is not married. It was only when the woman's heart had been opened with the conversation linked to marriage that Jesus shared what we would normally call a word of knowledge. Jesus' focus was to express love to her, rather than to show off with an amazing revelation. It was only because He discerned that the woman was receptive to truth—after all, she responded with telling the truth that she is not married—that Jesus took the further step of sharing the word of knowledge.

It is likely that, in many ways, Jesus' ministry to the woman was the factor that opened the hearts of Samaritans to the gospel, so that in Acts the disciples were able to spread the Good News to Samaria easily.

But the ministry in the stage performance model is entirely focused on showing off with the words of knowledge, and with no respect for the privacy of the person ministered to.

FALSE WORDS OF KNOWLEDGE

There is such a thing as false words of knowledge. This doesn't mean that their content is necessarily wrong, but their source is wrong. For example, illusionists and magicians are trained to read anyone's body language and involuntary signs and expressions that people give without even realising it.

The spiritualist movement that started in the mid-1850s in America produced many spiritualists that were able to give accurate but false words of knowledge.

One of the mediums, who worked in the late 19th century, recounted his experiences after he renounced his profession.

> The spirits of our deceased relatives and friends announced themselves, and generally gave a correct account of their earthly lives. I must confess, however, that, whenever we attempted to pry into the future, we usually received answers as ambiguous of those of Grecian oracles.[6]

It is fascinating how this spiritualist's experience resembles Branham's ministry. He was notorious for his accurate words of knowledge, but his prophetic ministry was a total failure.

I suspect that the reason for this is simple—the devil knows the past, but he doesn't know the future. The devil can see backwards quite clearly; only God can see forward fully and accurately. And that is why false words of knowledge are definitely in the devil's arsenal, even according to the testimony of this former spiritualist.

I am not in a position to make a final judgment on the source of Branham's ministry. That belongs to God. And He is the only one who can tell the future entirely accurately. But based on Branham's theology, I don't think God will judge me too harshly when I get to heaven, if I get this one wrong.

Let me give a rule of thumb: as the word of knowledge is a prophetic gift, the source behind it must be judged not only based on the word of knowledge, but also on the accuracy of the prophetic word or the word of wisdom that proceeds from it. That is because a word of knowledge on its own has very little value.

Many 'word of knowledge' ministries disturb me today. They seem to be able to give very accurate descriptions of what has already taken place, but the prophetic words uttered afterwards are highly unreliable.

A false but accurate-sounding word of knowledge doesn't always need to have a demonic source.

In Victorian times, when a medium visited a new town, he was advised to visit the local cemetery and make a note of names, dates and any other information obtained from the tombstones.[7]

Nowadays, you can find similar information from people's social media feeds. You go to the Facebook page of the church or conference you will be speaking in, discover who is planning to attend and find out everything about their family. These are the people most likely to attend a conference. That's your material. One man tested all the words of knowledge given by a prominent 'word of knowledge' prophet during a specific event and discovered that all the 'words of knowledge' he had shared were freely available on the Facebook profile pages of people who had tagged the event in social media to tell everyone that they would attend that conference. So theoretically, this preacher could have taken all these accurate words of knowledge from the internet. Whether he did or didn't, we don't know. That is between him and God. But what is the prophetic value of information that can be poached from the internet?

Also, rather intriguingly, this particular prophet traces the authority of his ministry back to William Branham.

We should always use words of knowledge humbly—their main point is not to make us look good, so that we can assert our prophetic authority over people and tell them what to do. Often, you don't even need to mention that you have received this information supernaturally. But they are a helpful tool in ministering effectively, especially to people we don't know very well.

10

WORD OF WISDOM

There has been some confusion in the Church regarding the word of wisdom, with many non-Charismatic commentators seeing it as some sort of teaching gift.

Branham seemed to have some strange ideas about wisdom, as in a sermon preached on Sunday 1ˢᵗ April 1962 in the Branham Tabernacle, he said,

> Now, God is the Author of faith; Satan is the author of wisdom.[1]

Yet, it should be clear for anyone reading the Bible that faith and wisdom are intimately linked, as the fear of the Lord is the beginning of wisdom.

The Pentecostal and the Word of Faith movements haven't placed much weight on the value of wisdom in the past, often perceiving reason rather suspiciously. Obviously, times have changed, and these movements have their established theological seminaries. And Branham is an extreme example of the idolatry of unlearnedness that you can encounter in Pentecostal and Charismatic movements.

Proverbs 4:7 says,

> Wisdom is the principal thing; therefore get wisdom. And in all your getting, get understanding.

But when it comes to the word of wisdom, we aren't talking about man's learnedness, which does have much value—in the hands of God. Paul says,

> These things we also speak, not in words which man's wisdom teaches but which the Holy Spirit teaches, comparing spiritual things with spiritual. (1 Corinthians 2:13)

The wisdom Paul talks about is God's perspective in our lives.

But it is not always clear even in the Charismatic church what this gift of word of wisdom stands for.

Lester Sumrall, for example, clearly confuses this gift with the gift of prophecy. He writes,

> The word of wisdom is the revealing of the prophetic future under the anointing of God. In the Old Testament every seer (the former term for prophet) and every prophet who foretold the future was endowed with this gift.[2]

Sumrall has been forced to do this, as earlier on, he has downgraded the gift of prophecy to be merely "words of edification, exhortation, and comfort"[3], and now he has to restore the actual gift of prophecy back into the New Testament. But this is based on rather sloppy Bible reading, and a direct consequence of applying unbiblical categories to gifts.

Much better definition comes from George Jeffreys.

> It is a supernatural giving of a word of wisdom to believers by revelation, to the intent that they might advise, instruct, and speak the words of wisdom to the Church thereby making known the deep things of God.[4]

Clearly, Jeffreys is referring to Paul's teaching about spiritual wisdom. The best definition I have come across is from Matthew Poole, an English non-Comformist theologian of the 17th century.

> But it is most probable, that he meaneth by it what we ordinarily understand by wisdom, viz. a faculty, from a good

judgment of the circumstances of actions, to do them at the best time, and in the best manner, wherein they may be serviceable to their ends.[5]

What this definition needs is more emphasis on the fact that the Holy Spirit is intimately involved in sharing this wisdom, although it can also utilise our life experiences. The word of wisdom is God-given wisdom about what to do. It is less directive than prophecy and more concerned with applying God-given principles.

A word of wisdom makes sense to our reasoning and not just to our faith.

One of the best examples comes from Acts 15, where the apostles discuss whether Gentile believers should be circumcised, after Paul and Barnabas have come to them in Jerusalem.

After deliberation, James says,

> "Therefore I judge that we should not trouble those from among the Gentiles who are turning to God, but that we write to them to abstain from things polluted by idols, from sexual immorality, from things strangled, and from blood. For Moses has had throughout many generations those who preach him in every city, being read in the synagogues every Sabbath." (Acts 15:19-21)

This is nothing but a word of wisdom on an apostolic level. The main purpose of this decree was to ensure that the Jewish and Gentile Christians would be able to worship together in the same community. How much do we need this kind of wisdom today in the Church!

But word of wisdom doesn't just work in the Church. It also works outside the Church.

In Genesis 41, the Pharaoh sees two disturbing dreams, and eventually, Joseph is requested to interpret the Pharaoh's dream. After explaining the Pharaoh's dream, Joseph says, rather boldly,

> "Now therefore, let Pharaoh select a discerning and wise man, and set him over the land of Egypt. Let Pharaoh do this, and let

him appoint officers over the land, to collect one-fifth of the produce of the land of Egypt in the seven plentiful years. And let them gather all the food of those good years that are coming, and store up grain under the authority of Pharaoh, and let them keep food in the cities. Then that food shall be as a reserve for the land for the seven years of famine which shall be in the land of Egypt, that the land may not perish during the famine." (Genesis 41:33-37)

This is a great example of a word of wisdom. For years, Joseph has been managing a prison, and it was quite likely that he had to deal with issues such as severe food shortage. It is a wise word, based on experience, not a prophetic word, but applying a prophetic dream that God has shown to the Pharaoh. The Pharaoh sees his wisdom, appointing Joseph to be the man ruling the land of Egypt, which fulfils the prophetic vision given to Joseph many years ago.

As we can see, a word of wisdom is lined up with God's vision and His plan, and it furthers them. It is not just any wise word.

God can give you a word of wisdom that saves you through nearly insurmountable dangers.

In Matthew 22:15-22, the Pharisees plot to trap Jesus.

Then the Pharisees went and plotted how they might entangle Him in His talk. And they sent to Him their disciples with the Herodians, saying, "Teacher, we know that You are true, and teach the way of God in truth; nor do You care about anyone, for You do not regard the person of men. Tell us, therefore, what do You think? Is it lawful to pay taxes to Caesar, or not?"

But Jesus perceived their wickedness, and said, "Why do you test Me, you hypocrites? Show Me the tax money." So they brought Him a denarius. And He said to them, "Whose image and inscription is this?" They said to Him, "Caesar's." And He said to them, "Render therefore to Caesar the things that are Caesar's, and to God the things that are God's." When they had heard these words, they marveled, and left Him and went their way. (Matthew 22:15-22)

There is a subtext in Jesus' words the Sadducees and Pharisees would probably have been aware of, but which we miss, as we aren't that aware of the Temple system. There was another coin with another portrait, also used in Israel.

The temple tax could be paid in one currency only, and when you came to the Temple, you had to exchange your money to acquire that currency. The payment could be made only in Tyrian currency, the *tetra drachma*. It had the highest percentage of silver, and therefore it was the most inflation-resistant currency available.

Jews used the Tyrian coins for sacred purposes, despite the images of the god Melqart and the eagle on the coins—and the inscription declaring Tyre a holy city of asylum. But this is the same Baal that Queen Jezebel served.

No wonder that Jesus turned the tables of moneylenders in Matthew 21 and said that the Temple had become a den of robbers. The Temple officials had brought idolatry to the centre of worship. It was the Tyrian coin with an image of Baal that the Temple officials used, and it seems that they used to rob the Jews through setting unfavourable exchange rates.

Like Ahab, who had been deceived by the riches of Tyre, the Jewish leaders of Jesus' time had been deceived by the mammon of Tyre. They had even come up with an understanding that *Yahweh*, who had commanded the Jews not to make any images of Himself, didn't object using an image of a false god on the Temple coin, as it wasn't an image of Him.

Deuterenomy 4:15-16 says,

> Take careful heed to yourselves, for you saw no form when the Lord spoke to you at Horeb out of the midst of the fire, lest you act corruptly and make for yourselves a carved image in the form of any figure

So, the Jewish leaders were saying that because they didn't actually worship Baal, it was fine to use the coin with his image on it. Not only did Jesus avoid their trap through a word of wisdom, He also showed to them indirectly that they were hypocrites.

Some time ago I met a pastor who was undergoing a change in his ministry. He was running a local church, and I had prophesied that God was bringing transformation into his ministry. Since that, some people had become Christians through the ministry of their church, and they had joined the church. Also, there was a newfound passion for prayer in his church, especially amongst men, and he found that extraordinary, as they had never shown much desire for spiritual growth.

But now he had a new dilemma. For fifteen years, he had prepared his sermons in advance. He would ask God for a word, and once he got that, he would meticulously prepare his sermon.

What was happening was that he had now been receiving the topics from the Holy Spirit only on Sunday morning, and he now had very little time to prepare.

The Holy Spirit gave me a supernatural insight into his situation.

"God is changing the dynamics of your preaching." That was a word of knowledge about his predicament.

"But what about my sermon preparation? I'm used to prepare my sermons well in advance."

"How many years have you been preparing sermons?" I asked.

"For fifteen years."

"Your next sermon has been fifteen years in the making", I said. That was a word of wisdom. It was clear to me that the God wanted him to rely on his sermon preparation less, and more on the inspiration of the Holy Spirit, and the way He was doing it was to remove the option to prepare well in advance.

I told him that it was likely that the Holy Spirit would give him the topic even later.

I saw him a few weeks later. Guess what. The Holy Spirit had given him the inspiration for his message only half an hour before the service. Now he had even less time to prepare. But even the congregation members who knew that he hadn't had any time to prepare gave excellent feedback, as there had been no sign for the lack of preparation. How could there have been—he had been preparing for that sermon for fifteen years!

"I don't need to be a prophet to tell you that the preparation time will become even shorter," I told him. That was yet another word of wisdom. "God is pressing you to increase your trust to follow a lot more intuitive dynamic in your preaching that responds to the needs of whoever is present in the congregation." I saw him a month later. "God gave me the word only when I stepped behind the pulpit to preach", he said. But his preaching had gone well, and there had been a different flow to it.

Through taking away the crutch of sermon preparation God was coaching him to become a better preacher. He had prepared long enough; now it was time trust in the flow of the Spirit.

Often, a word of wisdom works with the word of knowledge and prophecy. Its nature is revelatory, but it gives people a lot more space to act according to their understanding, rather than being straitjacketed by a directive prophecy.

Often, there is a clear sense of God's presence, and you sense how the Holy Spirit is directing you toward the right ideas in the library of your experiences, but elevating those ideas, so that you end up saying much wiser things than you could have imagined in the beginning of the conversation.

I try to avoid directive prophecy as much as I can. I know that is not what most would expect prophets to do, but I want every Christian to learn to hear from the Holy Spirit directly, rather than from a mediator, a prophet. At best, a prophet can assist you on a journey, but it is your journey to make, and the only way to finish well is to have a personal, intimate relationship with God.

I have had situations where people come to me and ask about accepting a new job or if someone is the right person to marry, and often God reveals the right answer to me, but rather than telling the people the right answer, I don't tell it to them. Instead, I take an opportunity to teach them how to seek God's will for themselves.

Any marriage will be a lot stronger if the man and the woman have sought God for themselves and got the answer from God rather than from some prophet. There have been occasions when it has been clear to me that the person they are dating is the wrong one, but rather than telling them that he or she is the wrong one, I have prepared them for the inevitable breakup by outlining biblical principles. Often people who ask if someone is the right one to marry are really fishing for a blessing for their own decision rather than genuine direction from God. So, in those situations, it is much better to ask these people to pray and study the Bible, so that they will find the answer themselves. Often, the answer is easy to find, but a hopeful heart can be rather self-deceiving.

In situations like these, the word of wisdom is a lot better than prophecy, in a sense that it teaches people to become more responsible for their own lives.

Once, a young woman came to me, and said, "I want to be closer to God."

"Do you pray every day?" I asked. That was a word of knowledge turned into a simple, practical question.

"No", she answered.

"How do you expect to be close to God unless you give Him your undivided attention?" I asked.

The New Testament prophets haven't been called to be mediators between men and God, but to equip men and women to hear from God directly.

A word of wisdom is the greatest aid against the temptation to 'prophesy' to others, when you have nothing prophetic to say that you have received from God. Nearly always, a word of wisdom is better than prophecy. The truth is that no one needs a mediator between themselves and Jesus. As I get older, I have become less interested in giving anyone prophetic words, and a lot more interested in helping Christians build an intimate relationship with the Holy Spirit and developing their spiritual gifts. And mentoring and coaching are some of the main areas where the word of wisdom operates. Each mentoring relationship is unique, and every time we meet with people we mentor, the Holy Spirit is able to give from His wisdom that He has accumulated in us through experiences, as we have sought to follow Him.

To many Christians, a word of wisdom might sound a lot less impressive than a word of knowledge or prophecy, but often it is far more useful.

11

DISCERNING SPIRITS

The Pentecostal movement began with an outpouring of the Holy Spirit, but it didn't take long before its leaders had to begin to fight against demonic influences.

In his sermons William Seymour referred to counterfeits and deceiving spirits. It is evident that he came across both of them in Azusa Street.

Seymour was aware that many people came to Azusa Street imitating the work of the Holy Spirit. His solution was studying the Bible more carefully.

He said,

> We must rightly divide the Scriptures and compare scripture
> with scripture so that there be no confusion and no deceptive
> teaching or wrong teaching may creep in.[1]

Unfortunately, serious Bible study is something that is missing from the Charismatic movement, where most Christians rely on their leaders to do the Bible study on their behalf and often elevate the word of their leaders above the authority of the Scripture.

One of the greatest threats against Azusa Street came from the spiritualists who were attracted to the mission. Seymour singled them out and labelled them as counterfeits. Because of their presence in Pentecostalism, the movement was quickly identified with "free loveism", which was a 'liberation movement' for women. Free loveism gave women the freedom to choose their sexual partners.

Not all spiritualists were free lovers, but nearly all free lovers were spiritualists. So, there was a presence of known spiritualists at the Azusa Street Mission.[2]

Studying the history of the Azusa Street Revival, we can see that a move of God doesn't automatically protect us from demonic influences. That is why it is vital for anyone exercising the gifts to study the whole Bible carefully.

Take Branham, for example. He taught that sicknesses were caused by demons and cast demons out of Christians. But if we read the Scriptures, we soon realise that this isn't biblical teaching. And yet many Christians followed him, as they elevated Branham's word above the Bible.

The Bible says quite a few things about demons. But in the New Testament, there isn't a single instance where a Christian's sickness has been caused by demons. That a demonic sickness can torment a Christian is something the devil wants us to believe.

Another thing altogether is that our sins can inflict sicknesses over us because of bad lifestyle choices, and the collective sins of humankind do inflict sicknesses on even the innocent.

But the devil can attack our mind and thought processes and through that affect our lives.

WHAT IS THE GIFT OF DISCERNING SPIRITS?

The gift of discerning spirits is the ability to discern spiritual influences or presences in our life and environment.

Hebrews 4:12 says,

> For the word of God is living and powerful, and sharper than any two-edged sword, piercing even to the division of soul and spirit, and of joints and marrow, and is a discerner of the thoughts and intents of the heart.

Studying the Word of God brings us discernment, and first it begins to bring discernment regarding our own motivations—what is of soul and what is of the Holy Spirit.

This isn't the gift of discerning spirits as such, but fundamental discernment every Christian must have in their lives. For you to know what is of God in your life, you must also know what is of your own soul. And it is the Word of God, in partnership with the Holy Spirit, which begins to bring that separation, so that you will be able to discern your motivations more clearly.

But although knowing the Word is necessary for the gift of discerning spirits to function, the actual gift is a side product of spending lengthy times in the presence of God.

The gift of discerning spirits is a gift birthed in *God's* presence. It is a prophetic gift, and only useful when accompanied with the gift of prophecy and an ability to hear from God. Without the ability to hear from God, you can't really put the gift of discerning spirits into any productive use, and it can even lead you astray, as you will easily misinterpret the reasons behind a spiritual disturbance.

When we become sensitive to God's presence, we *also* become more sensitive to the presence of demonic influences around us.

You can be aware of the demonic, but that is not necessarily the gift of discerning spirits. For example, some artistic people are spiritually sensitive. The mediums can sometimes sense the presence of demons. But it is only through the power and the presence of the Holy Spirit that we can begin to discern what these powers really are. Becoming aware of demonic beings without the Holy Spirit giving you that awareness is dangerous, because you don't have the spiritual power to resist and discern their deception without the Holy Spirit.

The air in Finland where I come from is very clean. Every time I land at Heathrow Airport, I become very aware of how polluted the air of London is. But soon I get used to it again and hardly even notice it.

It takes clean air for you to take notice of the polluted air. Likewise, it takes experiencing the presence of God for you to begin to discern the demonic influences around you.

It is only when we meet with God that we become aware of our sinfulness. Most people aren't aware of their sinfulness but think they are more righteous than the average person.

In Luke 5, disciples have been fishing all night and caught nothing. Jesus instructs them to go fishing again.

> When He had stopped speaking, He said to Simon, "Launch out into the deep and let down your nets for a catch." But Simon answered and said to Him, "Master, we have toiled all night and caught nothing; nevertheless at Your word I will let down the net." And when they had done this, they caught a great number of fish, and their net was breaking. So they signaled to their partners in the other boat to come and help them. And they came and filled both the boats, so that they began to sink. When Simon Peter saw it, he fell down at Jesus' knees, saying, "Depart from me, for I am a sinful man, O Lord!" (Luke 5:5-8)

This was a miraculous catch. Up to this point Peter had perhaps thought that he was a good man, but now he becomes acutely aware of his sinfulness, as he encounters the supernatural power of God. But it doesn't seem that Jesus even mentioned the word sin.

It was only when I became a disciple of Jesus that I even began to be aware of how sinful I really am! That was because the Holy Spirit took hold of His temple, and His light began to shine in the darkest corners of my life.

WHAT DOES THE BIBLE SAY ABOUT DEMONS?

I have had many experiences about the kingdom of Satan, as I am in war against it. But when it comes to teaching about the devil and his kingdom, we must always begin from the Scriptures and not from our experiences, to ensure that no scheme of Satan will be able to deceive us, because our experiences can be misleading.

In John 8:44, Jesus says to the Pharisees,

> "You are of your father the devil, and the desires of your father you want to do. He was a murderer from the beginning, and does not stand in the truth, because there is no truth in him. When he speaks a lie, he speaks from his own resources, for he is a liar and the father of it."

If Satan is the father of all lies, there is a fair chance that many experiences people have about Satan are just that—lies.

When Jesus was tempted by the devil in the desert, He refused to listen to him, even when the devil was quoting the Scripture. He knew that if the devil was reading the Bible, he would somehow be twisting it. He knew that the devil is a liar and a murderer, and that he has a huge army of his kind at his disposal.

Hebrews 12:22 says,

> But you have come to Mount Zion and to the city of the living God, the heavenly Jerusalem, to an innumerable company of angels

According to the Bible, there are so many angels that they are nearly impossible to count!

Revelation 12:7-9 tells about war that took place in heaven.

> And war broke out in heaven: Michael and his angels fought with the dragon; and the dragon and his angels fought, but they did not prevail, nor was a place found for them in heaven any longer. So the great dragon was cast out, that serpent of old, called the Devil and Satan, who deceives the whole world; he was cast to the earth, and his angels were cast out with him.

So, Satan was cast out with the angels that followed him in rebellion. And Revelation 12:3-4 gives us the proportion of angels that followed Satan.

> And another sign appeared in heaven: behold, a great, fiery red dragon having seven heads and ten horns, and seven diadems on his heads. His tail drew a third of the stars of heaven and threw them to the earth.

That is one third of an innumerable number of angels. That is a huge number, and according to the book of Revelation, these dark angels—demons—are now on earth.

The Bible refers to Satan as Beelzebub—the lord of the flies—who releases a horde of demons on anyone who wants to follow Jesus. So, why can't we see them if they are everywhere on earth? Hebrews 1:14 gives us the answer.

> Are they not all ministering spirits sent forth to minister for those who will inherit salvation?

Here the author writes about angels, but demons used to be angels—like the Holy Spirit, angels and demons are spirits, which means they don't have a physical body. They are invisible to us, but that doesn't mean they are not around us.

After Jesus was tempted by the devil in the desert, it says in Matthew 4:11,

> Then the devil left Him, and behold, angels came and ministered to Him.

There are times when God lifts the oppression of the enemy by sending His angels, like when an angel comes to strengthen Jesus in Gethsemane in Luke 22:43, just before He is betrayed by Judas.

> Then an angel appeared to Him from heaven, strengthening Him.

The angels are on our side of the battle and, often, God releases them to strengthen us. His army *always* fights on our behalf. This is an invisible battle that we can't see, but we can sense it through the gift of discerning spirits.

But we still face a fierce battle. In Ephesians 6:12 Paul says,

> For we do not wrestle against flesh and blood, but against principalities, against powers, against the rulers of the darkness of this age, against spiritual *hosts* of wickedness in the heavenly *places*.

There is a battle between you and the principalities; it is a close-contact wrestling match, close enough to smell the sweat and the blood of the opposition.

The Hebrew word *stn* vocalised as *satan* means something close to the English word opponent, in its root sense of "to place in the way", or to "obstruct". Neil Forsyth, Professor of English at the University of Lausanne, explains,

> Most uses of the root *stn* in the Old Testament already suggest this kind of darker meaning; the assumption is usually that the path is right and the opponent wrong. But the word does not necessarily refer to spiritual adversaries. In 1 Kings, for example, the word refers to an ordinary earthly enemy: "And *Yahweh* stirred up an adversary (*satan*) to Solomon, Hadad the Edomite." In the same chapter, Rezon, king of Damascus, is called "*satan* to Israel all the days of Solomon."[3]

God rarely obstructs us directly when He wants to increase our spiritual maturity; instead He lets the devil do it. When He tested Job, He didn't bring suffering into Job's life directly; instead, He lifted His protection.

But the devil often seeks to obstruct us through other people, and we must remember that we don't fight against flesh and blood.

The gift of discerning spirits helps us to shift our focus from Hadad the Edomite to Satan, who pulls the strings behind the scenes.

These stars of heaven that were thrown to earth seem to be one third of the angels that lost their heavenly glory but not all their spiritual power. The prophet Isaiah saw into the heart of their leader.

> How you are fallen from heaven, O Lucifer, son of the morning! How you are cut down to the ground, you who weakened the nations! For you have said in your heart: "I will ascend into heaven, I will exalt my throne above the stars of God; I will also sit on the mount of the congregation on the farthest sides of the north; I will ascend above the heights of the clouds, I will be like the Most High." Yet you shall be brought down to Sheol, to the lowest depths of the Pit. (Isaiah 14:12-15)

Ezekiel also refers to Satan working behind the scenes in the city of Tyre with words of God.

> "You were the anointed cherub who covers; I established you; you were on the holy mountain of God; you walked back and forth in the midst of fiery stones. You were perfect in your ways from the day you were created, till iniquity was found in you. By the abundance of your trading you became filled with violence within, and you sinned; therefore I cast you as a profane thing out of the mountain of God; and I destroyed you, O covering cherub, from the midst of the fiery stones. Your heart was lifted up because of your beauty; you corrupted your wisdom for the sake of your splendor; I cast you to the ground" (Ezekiel 28:14-17)

We can only imagine what level of spiritual opposition Paul had to come through to be inspired to write,

> Therefore take up the whole armor of God, that you may be able to withstand in the evil day, and having done all, to stand. Stand therefore, having girded your waist with truth, having put on the breastplate of righteousness, and having shod your feet with the preparation of the gospel of peace; above all, taking the shield of faith with which you will be able to quench all the fiery darts of the wicked one. And take the helmet of salvation, and the sword of the Spirit, which is the word of God; praying always with all prayer and supplication in the Spirit, being watchful to this end with all perseverance and supplication for all the saints. (Ephesians 6:13-18)

There are Christians who see the devil everywhere, and in one sense, they are right, because the devil's army works everywhere, but often, they see the devil in the wrong things, mostly in the area of culture. They still wrestle against flesh and blood, even when they often believe that they are wrestling against principalities.

A bigger problem today is that many in the Charismatic church worship the supernatural, and they are too scared of criticising anything at all in fear of criticising the Holy Spirit. To them, all supernatural must come from God. Yet, others conclude that all supernatural activity is demonic or manmade and shut it out. But shutting out supernatural altogether is also a mistake, as it doesn't stop the devil from working; it only robs us of the supernatural weapons given by the Holy Spirit and puts the Church in major disadvantage against the enemy.

IS THERE A JEZEBEL SPIRIT?

There is a belief in the Charismatic church about the existence of a 'Jezebel spirit', and according to the prevalent version of the belief, a Jezebel spirit seems to be nearly omnipresent. Usually, this teaching leaves unclear whether a Jezebel spirit is a singular spirit, or a *type* of a demonic spirit.

William Branham preached against the "Jezebel spirit" and the "Jezebel religion"[4] on many occasions, and he certainly propagated the idea about a Jezebel spirit more than most preachers, not least because he seemed to have a fairly low view of women. In Branham's thinking, the Jezebel spirit was a spirit of insubordination and seduction that affects women.

But most of the Jezebel teaching gives one demon that might exist far too much power, and it is based on misreading of two passages in the Bible. The Bible doesn't even mention a 'Jezebel spirit', so conjecturing its existence is speculation at best.

Queen Jezebel's story, that any teaching about a 'Jezebel spirit' is ultimately based on, is told in 1 and 2 Kings. She was a Phoenician princess, the daughter of Ethbaal, king of Tyre. Jezebel married King Ahab of the Northern Kingdom—Israel—during the time when the ancient Israel was divided into Israel in the north and Judah in the south.

Ahab was the son of King Omri, who had brought the northern Kingdom of Israel to great power, established Samaria as his capital, and whose historical existence is confirmed by ancient inscriptions on the Mesha Stele and the Black Obelisk of Shalmaneser III.

According to the biblical account, Ahab and Jezebel supported the worship of the deities Baal and Asherah, erecting shrines to them in Samaria, which was "evil in the sight of the Lord".

1 Kings 18 says that Jezebel had commanded that all the prophets of *Yahweh* in the kingdom of Israel be killed, while entertaining four hundred and fifty prophets of Baal and four hundred prophets of Asherah at her royal table. Elijah, prophet of *Yahweh*, had escaped Jezebel's persecution, however, and confronted King Ahab, demanding that all the prophets of Baal and Asherah meet him at Mount Carmel for a competition. The prophets of the pagan gods and Elijah met before "all the people", and Elijah had two altars set up, one dedicated to Baal, one to *Yahweh*, and a bull sacrificed upon each altar. The supporters of Baal called upon their god to send fire to consume the sacrifice, but nothing happened. When Elijah called on *Yahweh*, fire came down from heaven immediately and consumed the offering, whereupon the crowd fell to the ground, crying, "The Lord, he is the God." Elijah ordered the people to seize the prophets of Baal, and they were all slaughtered on his orders. Jezebel swore to kill Elijah in revenge.

It is from this story where the belief about the Jezebel spirit as some sort of spirit of intimidation and the archenemy of the prophets has been derived from. And it is not difficult to see the attraction of a theory about the raging Jezebel spirit to modern-day prophets who often face opposition when they rise in the church. It seems that many prophets can identify with Elijah!

The biblical account of Queen Jezebel is rather short, and many Charismatic writers have a lot more to say about the Jezebel spirit than that. It seems to me that many prophetic figures project their own bad experiences into 'a Jezebel spirit' that becomes some sort of Satan's associate minister No 1, doing Satan's bidding when he is otherwise obstructed.

There are many reasons why the current understanding in the Charismatic church about the Jezebel spirit is harmful to us.

First, the Jezebel spirit teaching has wrongly been used to oppress women in the Church.

Second, to understand what really went on between King Ahab, Queen Jezebel and Elijah, we need to ask an important question: *Why did Ahab marry Jezebel?*

1 Kings 16:29-33 says,

> In the thirty-eighth year of Asa king of Judah, Ahab the son of Omri became king over Israel; and Ahab the son of Omri reigned over Israel in Samaria twenty-two years. Now Ahab the son of Omri did evil in the sight of the Lord, more than all who were before him. And it came to pass, as though it had been a trivial thing for him to walk in the sins of Jeroboam the son of Nebat, that he took as wife Jezebel the daughter of Ethbaal, king of the Sidonians; and he went and served Baal and worshiped him. Then he set up an altar for Baal in the temple of Baal, which he had built in Samaria. And Ahab made a wooden image. Ahab did more to provoke the Lord God of Israel to anger than all the kings of Israel who were before him.

Ahab didn't become evil *after* he married Jezebel. It was because he *was* evil that he married her. In the ancient times, kings rarely married princesses because they fell in love with them. After all, they had concubines and mistresses for sex. It seems clear that, like most kings of his time, Ahab probably didn't marry for love. Instead, Ahab married Jezebel, as he wanted to make an alliance with Tyre.

Tyre was one of the wealthiest cities on earth. Isaiah prophesied about Tyre in Isaiah 23:7-9,

> Is this your joyous city, whose antiquity is from ancient days, whose feet carried her far off to dwell? Who has taken this counsel against Tyre, the crowning city, whose merchants are princes, whose traders are the honorable of the earth? The Lord of hosts has purposed it, to bring to dishonor the pride of all glory, to bring into contempt all the honorable of the earth.

It was the money of Tyre that attracted Ahab to make an alliance with Tyre rather than Jezebel's beauty. And it was the money of Tyre that caused Ahab to worship Baals. And it was the demonic beings behind these Baals, rather than a Jezebel spirit, that energised Jezebel's rage.

Revelation 2:18-29 makes a reference to Jezebel, as Jesus speaks to the church in Thyatira.

And to the angel of the church in Thyatira write, "These things says the Son of God, who has eyes like a flame of fire, and His feet like fine brass: 'I know your works, love, service, faith, and your patience; and as for your works, the last are more than the first. Nevertheless I have a few things against you, because you allow that woman Jezebel, who calls herself a prophetess, to teach and seduce My servants to commit sexual immorality and eat things sacrificed to idols. And I gave her time to repent of her sexual immorality, and she did not repent. Indeed I will cast her into a sickbed, and those who commit adultery with her into great tribulation, unless they repent of their deeds. I will kill her children with death, and all the churches shall know that I am He who searches the minds and hearts. And I will give to each one of you according to your works.

Now to you I say, and to the rest in Thyatira, as many as do not have this doctrine, who have not known the depths of Satan, as they say, I will put on you no other burden. But hold fast what you have till I come. And he who overcomes, and keeps My works until the end, to him I will give power over the nations—He shall rule them with a rod of iron; They shall be dashed to pieces like the potter's vessels—as I also have received from My Father; and I will give him the morning star. He who has an ear, let him hear what the Spirit says to the churches.'"

On surface level, this seems like a clear-cut case about seduction by sensuality and sexuality, but when you understand the historical context, you begin to see that the Christians in Thyatira weren't seduced by sex in the pagan temples at all. Instead, they were being seduced by the pagan *money*.

In most Greek cities, the pagan temple areas were the places where people did business, and Thyatira wasn't an exception. If you didn't participate in the pagan temple cult, you were effectively a second-class citizen, and unable to be part of the trade guilds.

And Thyatira was a city *defined* by the trade guilds.

The only group that didn't have to go to a pagan temple and could still do good business were the Jews. They had been granted certain exemptions by the Roman Empire. Originally, Christians had been seen as a Jewish sect and protected by these special exemptions, but by the time of writing the book of Revelation, the Jewish Christians had already been kicked out of the synagogue. So, now they were a group of their own with no special protection.

It seems evident that the historical figure John refers to as Jezebel had come up with a 'theology' that justified taking part in trading within the pagan temple areas.

Her theology, as spread by her counterparts in the Thyatira church, would have been especially attractive to members who were in the workers' guilds. To reject guild membership would cause one to suffer economic deprivation. However, to be part of a guild required participation in its pagan religious festivities.

The temptation to compromise one's Christian beliefs must have been strong for many church members.

So, the Christians in Thyatira were willing to compromise in the area of their sexuality and worship because of money. And if we miss that, we miss the whole point of what Jesus was saying to the Christians in Thyatira.

Today, parts of the Charismatic church are frightened of a single demon that might exist. But if something like a Jezebel spirit does exist, it would in fact be a *multitude* of demons, rather than a single demon. And if they do exist, based on the Bible, their main operation would be to provide a smokescreen for the spirits of mammon to operate.

Like the Christians in Thyatira, we have far too often compromised the gospel for the sake of money. We have even created a theology to justify it. Today's Charismatic church is entirely comfortable with a theology that accommodates serving God *and* money, even when Jesus clearly said that it is not possible. The right question regarding the operation of a Jezebel spirit would be to ask if there is anything in the teachings of Jesus we have compromised—like Ahab and some of the Christians in Thyatira did—because of money.

And many Christian leaders fail to see the connection between money and sexual sin, the connection that has been so vividly illustrated to us through Jezebel in the book of Revelation.

Paul writes in 1 Timothy 6:6-10,

> Now godliness with contentment is great gain. For we brought nothing into this world, and it is certain we can carry nothing out. And having food and clothing, with these we shall be content. But those who desire to be rich fall into temptation and a snare, and into many foolish and harmful lusts which drown men in destruction and perdition. For the love of money is a root of all kinds of evil, for which some have strayed from the faith in their greediness, and pierced themselves through with many sorrows.

The Charismatic church of today has pierced itself with many sorrows, because we love money. And because we love money, many lusts rule over us, and we remain vulnerable to many demonic influences. We are fire fighting against those lusts through battling a semi-imaginary Jezebel spirit, but until we leave the slavery to mammon behind, we will never be truly free.

GIFT OF DISCERNING SPIRITS IN THE BIBLE

We can see the gift of discerning spirits operating in many occasions in the Bible.

In Acts 5:1-11 Peter confronts Ananias and Sapphira who lied about giving everything they had got from selling a house. As a result, they both end up dead.

In verse 3, Peter says,

> "Ananias, why has Satan filled your heart to lie to the Holy Spirit?"

Undoubtedly, Peter was operating in the gift of discerning spirits, although he might not have called it as such.

In Acts 16:16-19, when Paul was at Philippi, a slave girl possessed with a spirit of divination followed Paul and cried out that Paul and his companions were the servants of the Most High God, and that they would proclaim to the Philippians the way of salvation.

Paul listened to her for three days, but finally, "greatly annoyed", he commanded the spirit to leave her. What followed was that her masters, who made a lot of money from her fortune telling, complained to the magistrates, who threw Paul to prison.

This is one of the most fascinating examples of the work of the Spirit in the Bible. Why didn't Paul cast the demon out straight away? Why did he wait for three days?

I believe that it was because through the gift of discerning spirits, Paul would have been suspicious of why the demonic spirit caused the slave girl to proclaim what on surface level seemed helpful to his cause.

Eventually, Paul must have had cast the demon out, as he didn't want to accept a testimony of a demon. But it seems that the demonic spirit was trying to trigger Paul to react, and it succeeded. As the result, Paul and his companions were thrown into prison.

Thankfully, God outplayed the enemy and used Paul to bring the Philippian jailer to faith. But here we can see a complex scheme by the enemy in operation, where nothing was what it seemed.

Can you see how important the gift of discerning spirits is? Eventually, Paul went for it, greatly annoyed, perhaps trusting God to pull him out of whatever trouble he would be thrown in.

CASTING OUT DEMONS

Exorcism is something most Christians only encounter in movies, but it seems to have been common in Jesus' times. In Luke 8:26-33, Jesus casts out a horde of demons from a man.

> Then they sailed to the country of the Gadarenes, which is opposite Galilee. And when He stepped out on the land, there met Him a certain man from the city who had demons for a long time. And he wore no clothes, nor did he live in a house but in the tombs. When he saw Jesus, he cried out, fell down before Him, and with a loud voice said, "What have I to do with You, Jesus, Son of the Most High God? I beg You, do not torment me!"
>
> For He had commanded the unclean spirit to come out of the man. For it had often seized him, and he was kept

under guard, bound with chains and shackles; and he broke the bonds and was driven by the demon into the wilderness. Jesus asked him, saying, "What is your name?" And he said, "Legion," because many demons had entered him. And they begged Him that He would not command them to go out into the abyss. Now a herd of many swine was feeding there on the mountain. So they begged Him that He would permit them to enter them. And He permitted them.

Then the demons went out of the man and entered the swine, and the herd ran violently down the steep place into the lake and drowned.

This is the only time recorded in the Gospels when Jesus asked for the name of a demon. Some people have made a principle out of this, claiming that we should always ask the name of a demon, if we are attempting to cast them out.

But when Jesus encountered Legion, He would have been perplexed, as He wasn't able to identify the demon. But that was because there were so *many* of them.

Jesus mostly didn't ask for the name of the demons, as He discerned immediately what type of spirits he was dealing with.

In Matthew 17:14-23, Jesus casts out a deaf and mute spirit from a boy, whose father claims him to be insane. In Mark 9:14-29 version of the same story, the father says that the boy has been possessed by a mute spirit.

What is the reason behind the two versions of the story? It is likely that the father, who was desperate for the boy's wellbeing, might have known that he was possessed, but there would have been many social reasons for which it would have been a lot better to say that he was insane. But I don't think we can read into this an idea that sicknesses are caused by demon possession, as both versions of the story make it very clear that even the disciples were aware that this was a case of demon possession and its side effects.

But the Gospels in fact include exorcism as part of the gift of working miracles, so we will return to the issue later on.

But there are three main points of advice that we can take from the Bible. Luke 10:17 says,

Then the seventy returned with joy, saying, "Lord, even the demons are subject to us in Your name."

The name of Jesus has the power and authority over demons, and we cast them out in His authority. Sometimes, this process takes longer than we would like. In Matthew 17:20-21 Jesus explains why the disciples couldn't cast out the demon.

> So Jesus said to them, "Because of your unbelief; for assuredly, I say to you, if you have faith as a mustard seed, you will say to this mountain, 'Move from here to there,' and it will move; and nothing will be impossible for you. However, this kind does not go out except by prayer and fasting."

A friend of mine, who worked as a Lutheran minister and then became a revivalist and launched his own denomination, once told me that he has never encountered many genuinely demon possessed people in the West. This is undoubtedly due to the long influence of the *name* of Jesus in our society. But they will become more frequent the more Christianity loses the influence in the West.

Demon possession is mostly linked to occult practices, but the occult manifests itself within the followers of many religions, including nominal Christianity. Perhaps the occult connection that was punishable with death in Judaism was the reason why the father of the boy who was possessed by the mute spirit was unwilling to volunteer that information to everybody.

In Luke 11:24-26 Jesus says,

> "When an unclean spirit goes out of a man, he goes through dry places, seeking rest; and finding none, he says, 'I will return to my house from which I came.' And when he comes, he finds it swept and put in order. Then he goes and takes with *him* seven other spirits more wicked than himself, and they enter and dwell there; and the last *state* of that man is worse than the first."

According to Jesus, there is not much point in casting out a demon from someone who isn't willing to submit to Jesus.

I don't think we should be looking out to find demon-possessed people in order to manifest God's power. But if these beings manifest in your church or environment, it is good to know that you can fully trust in the power of the name of Jesus. So, rather than looking for demon possessed people, I want to focus on the three main weapons the devil has against you. You can find them easily in the Bible, but it has taken me years to understand how they operate.

DEVIL'S THREE MAIN WEAPONS

The devil's three main weapons are fear, sin and deception. In John 8:44, Jesus says that the devil is a murderer and a liar. As a murderer, he releases violence against us, and this brings fear. As a liar, he releases deception against us. And since the temptation in the Garden of Eden, he has always tempted us to sin.

All these three weapons get their energy from a demonic presence that accompanies them. God has an unlimited Presence; the angels and demons have a limited spiritual presence, and their presence is qualitatively different from God's.

The presence of God bears fruit, and so does the presence of the enemy, but of a rotten kind, if we allow it to operate in our lives.

Galatians 5:22-23 says that the fruit of God's presence in our lives is love, joy, peace, forbearance, kindness, goodness, faithfulness, gentleness and self-control.

The fruit of demonic presence in our lives, if we allow it to affect us, are the works of fear, sin and deception.

I believe that each demon possesses all these three weapons of demonic presence—fear, sin and deception—but we experience that demonic presence through whatever their predominant activity is at the time.

In Ephesians 2:2, Paul writes about the pervasive presence of the demonic forces around us, and how it brings sin into our lives.

> And you He made alive, who were dead in trespasses and sins, in which you once walked according to the course of this world, according to the prince of the power of the air, the spirit who now works in the sons of disobedience, among whom also we all once conducted ourselves in the lusts of

our flesh, fulfilling the desires of the flesh and of the mind, and were by nature children of wrath, just as the others.

This doesn't mean that we can blame the devil for all our sins, but we must understand that the devil works through seducing our flesh—everything in us that is not submitted to God. This often includes our reason and emotions, as they are not automatically in submission to Him.

But the other thing Paul is saying is that the presence of the enemy around us is as pervasive as the air that we breathe. We are continually surrounded by it. Thank God He has given us His Holy Spirit to reside permanently within us!

This demonic atmosphere around us makes it harder to believe in the Word of God, makes us forget His promises, and seeks to disconnect us from the flow of the Holy Spirit within us through making it difficult for us to experience God's presence.

The Church desperately needs the gift of discerning spirits today, but carrying this gift has its own challenges. It makes you aware of the operations of the enemy around yourself, but also around others. This can be emotionally taxing, and operating in the gift of discerning Spirits can often feel like walking through the sewage system of your city, partially submerged in the sewage.

Paul writes in 2 Corinthians 2:10-11,

> Now whom you forgive anything, I also forgive. For if indeed I have forgiven anything, I have forgiven that one for your sakes in the presence of Christ, lest Satan should take advantage of us; for we are not ignorant of his devices.

How did Paul become aware of Satan's devices? It must have been through experience, as he defended himself and fought against them in the power of the Holy Spirit.

One big problem we have in the Charismatic movement is that we don't keep on renewing our minds with the Bible, but embrace all things supernatural without even considering discernment. But the devil and his demons are also supernatural. And so are their works.

If you desire the supernatural, the devil will give you the supernatural, but that supernatural will only deceive you.

What I find shocking is that many Charismatics seem to be willing to accept even the testimony of demons, as long as it's exciting enough! But accepting the supernatural from the enemy will open the doors of deception into our lives, and in the long run, bring destruction.

Weapon 1–Fear

Enemy is the master of attacking us through manipulating our emotions. This is because our emotions are more intertwined with our beliefs than we realise. Through affecting our emotions, the devil can affect what we believe and influence our behaviour. Robert C. Solomon, Professor of Philosophy, writes on the philosophy of emotions.

> Beliefs and emotions are related in many important ways: belief as precondition or presupposition of emotion, and belief as brought about by emotion (say, by way of wishful thinking or rationalisation).[5]

This is quite an illuminating point of view. I don't know if it happens to you, but when I feel low, facts look different from when I feel optimistic. When I feel low, nothing seems possible; when I feel hopeful, even impossible seems possible.

I reason in an entirely different way when I feel hopeful than when I feel depressed. That is because our emotions affect our beliefs. They affect our thought processes deeply, and they manifest in our thoughts.

Paul writes in Romans 12:2,

> And do not be conformed to this world, but be transformed by the renewing of your mind, that you may prove what is that good and acceptable and perfect will of God.

In Ephesians 4:20-24, Paul says that "the spirit of your mind" needs continual renewing.

> But you have not so learned Christ, if indeed you have heard Him and have been taught by Him, as the truth is in Jesus: that you put off, concerning your former conduct, the old man which grows corrupt according to the deceitful lusts, and be renewed in the spirit of your mind, and that you put on the new man which was created according to God, in true righteousness and holiness.

The Spirit-filled state of your mind is continually bombarded with deceitful lusts, fear and arguments. These attacks come from the inside—what Paul calls flesh—but also from demonic beings.

Paul writes in 2 Corinthians 10:3-5,

> For though we walk in the flesh, we do not war according to the flesh. For the weapons of our warfare are not carnal but mighty in God for pulling down strongholds, casting down arguments and every high thing that exalts itself against the knowledge of God, bringing every thought into captivity to the obedience of Christ

One of the main weapons the devil uses against you is releasing fear-filled arguments. These are some of the fiery arrows Paul asks us to use the shield of faith against in Ephesians 6:13-18. Their goal is to disconnect your mind from the continual indwelling of the Holy Spirit. If they achieve to do that, the devil knows he will be able to defeat you.

These fiery arrows are not just facts; they are burning with demonic poison. We accept them because they sound factual, but they are at best only partial facts and immersed in fear, and in other emotions such as anger and a sense of guilt.

The main goal of releasing fear and guilt is not necessarily to make you submit to them, but to make you vulnerable to sin and deception. Here, the enemy is using our psychological defence mechanisms against us.

The only way to combat demonic fear and guilt are the presence and promises of God; all attempts of self-defence without the Holy Spirit can lead to destructive or addictive behaviour.

Psychology reveals to us some of our inner workings, even when it is unable to grasp the spiritual world. Robert C. Solomon writes,

> But belief is too dispositional to capture the essence of emotion, thoughts are too episodic for emotions, which often turn out to be enduring processes rather than mere episodes. Thus a thought may punctuate and manifest an emotion, but it is in itself not a process.[6]

If you breathe in the demonic fear produced by the prince of the air and his vassals, the fearful emotion itself will become a factory for fear-filled thoughts, and your fear-filled mind will end up doing the devil's job for him.

I have the gift of discerning spirits, and I can often discern how a demonic disturbance seeks to encapsulate my mind like a bubble or a sphere that begins to interfere with my thought processes and produces a diversity of fears or other negative emotions.

When under this demonic disturbance, for example, on the way to work, I can fear a multitude of things from a relationship breakdown to financial ruin, and whatever else, depending on what news headlines I read in the paper. It is as if the atmosphere of fear was able to seep deep in my thought processes and dig up even my deepest subconscious fear, and articulate it clearly.

The enemy might not necessarily feed me these individual fear-filled thoughts, but instead, he surrounds me with a spiritual environment that begins to feed my imagination and reasoning processes. He doesn't need to read my mind, but simply surround it with his presence, and my imagination will do the rest.

This same process can happen at night, when a demonic atmosphere begins to interfere with your dreams.

Robert C. Solomon writes,

> Thus emotions are like judgment. And emotions necessarily involve judgments.[7]

Our reasoning and emotions aren't that separate from each other. Contrary to common understanding, emotions and thoughts don't displace each other. Instead, our judgments and emotions are strictly interwoven.[8] According to Robert C. Solomon,

> Emotions are interestingly similar to beliefs. We can now explain this similarity by claiming that emotions are judgments—normative and often moral judgments.[9]

So, the enemy often attacks our faith through manipulating our emotions that begin to warp our beliefs, which will in turn begin to affect our behaviour. But because emotions and beliefs are so interwoven, the enemy can also attack our emotions through arguments—the process also works in reverse.

The apostle Paul saw many arguments as spiritually loaded. He writes,

> For the weapons of our warfare *are* not carnal but mighty in God for pulling down strongholds, casting down arguments and every high thing that exalts itself against the knowledge of God, bringing every thought into captivity to the obedience of Christ, and being ready to punish all disobedience when your obedience is fulfilled. (2 Corinthians 10:4-6)

Emotions also appear to behave like arguments. Robert C. Solomon writes,

> Emotions are in fact assessments that are perceived as particularly important for the agent . . . For this reason, emotions play a crucial role in the process of decision-making.[10]

If the enemy can affect your emotions, he can influence your decision-making. Robert C. Solomon concludes,

> An emotion is a system of concepts, beliefs and attitudes, and desires, virtually all of which are context-bound, historically developed and culture specific.[11]

Our six basic emotions are: fear, disgust, surprise, sadness, happiness and anger. The devil can manipulate each one of these emotions to weaken our faith. I focus on fear here, because it is one of the main weapons of the enemy. But the devil can use all these emotions to disconnect us from the presence of God.

Manuel Castells, a Spanish sociologist, writes,

> Feelings process emotions in the mind in the context of a memory.[12]

I often find that the enemy seeks to use my memories against me. By bringing certain types of memories to my awareness, the enemy will also bring the mood associated with the memory.

My son used to go to a Church of England primary school in Chelsea, before he went on to a boarding school outside London. It was a great primary school, and I have many beautiful memories of taking him there and back in the bus 49.

For a while, after he had moved on to the secondary school, I felt haunted by a depressing sense of his absence every time I travelled to anywhere near his old school. There was a sense of irredeemable loss over those times we had spent together.

But then the Holy Spirit began to speak to me about this, and I began to see how the enemy was using my memories against me, trying to bring depression for something I should really be joyful about. I realised that the enemy was attempting to distort my memories in order to rob me of my joy.

Manuel Castells writes,

> The human mind is characterised by its capacity for future-thinking, which is its ability to relate foreseeable events with brain maps.[13]

Our emotions affect the way we see the future. Fear makes the future seem hopeless.

Jean Paul Sartre, an atheist existential philosopher, writes,

The meaning of realism, of naturalism, and of materialism lies in the past: these three philosophies are descriptions of the past as if it were present.[14]

Often, when the enemy fights against God's promises in your life, he leads you to focus on the material and financial limitations of your life. If he can make you think about your life mainly on materialistic terms, he can easily kill any God-given dream in your life through bringing a sense of determinism, so that you become a prisoner of the past. He will whisper to your ear: "Look at your life. Things might change, but they will change so slowly that you will never make it to the future God has promised to you." But God is the Master of multiplication. He doesn't multiply seeds from 1 to 2, but from 1 to 30 or 100. Matthew 13:8 says,

> But others fell on good ground and yielded a crop: some a hundredfold, some sixty, some thirty.

But the devil will tell you that you will only add from 1 to 2, and even that, only with the greatest of your effort.

Nehemiah said to the Jews that wept when the priests read the Law aloud to the people for the first time in Jerusalem:

> Do not sorrow, for the joy of the Lord is your strength.
> (Nehemiah 8:10)

Joy is a fruit of the Spirit, and it is indispensable in our battle against the enemy. The apostle Paul writes in 1 Corinthians 13:13,

> And now abide faith, hope, love, these three; but the greatest of these is love.

Hope, faith and love are all attributes of God Himself, and that is why, when we are full of His Spirit, we are also full of hope. And hope is the greatest weapon against depression and despair. But the fear of future is the opposite of hope for future.

Can you see why the devil loves prophecies spreading fear? Can you see why our media can't get enough of doom and gloom? The devil likes to feed our thought factories of fear, so that we would live our lives in an atmosphere of fear.

Manuel Castells writes,

> Metaphors are critical to connect language (thus human communication) and brain circuitry. It is through metaphors that narratives are constructed.[15]

The enemy attacks the emotions to colour the narratives and the metaphors through which we perceive our lives, and through connecting your emotions to false memories that are only partially based on reality.

The reality is that no matter what happened in the past, God is still with us, and God was in control even in the past. And He will also be in control in future.

Satan is an expert in fear, because he has lived in fear for thousands of years. He and his demonic army know every nuance of fear. They have been in the presence of God, they know who God really is, and they know that, one day, they will be judged.

The apostle James writes,

> You believe that there is one God. You do well. Even the demons believe—and tremble! (James 2:19)

The demons fear God, and this fear goes to their very core. Hence they can't help but to radiate fear. And a demonic spirit that spreads fear will also spread rebellion, unbelief and deception.

Because anxiety and fear feel unpleasant, people try to deal with them in a variety of ways. We don't just passively experience negative emotions; we also try to regulate those negative emotions by increasing pleasant ones.[16]

All Christian leaders are under heavy spiritual attack, at all times, but many of them are not even theologically open to an idea about a negative, supernatural force influencing them. Hence they respond to a supernatural attack in the natural, self-medicating against the symptoms but never really dealing with the real cause. This can lead to all sorts of addictive and destructive behaviour, including alcoholism, addiction to sex and pornography, and drug use.

Many Christian leaders give you an impression of having an active prayer life, but in practice they pray far too little to ever be able to develop the gift of discerning spirits.

Paul didn't demand absolutism, as he encouraged Timothy to drink a little bit of wine for his stomach, but he does remind us of the dangers of alcohol in Ephesians 5:18.

> And do not be drunk with wine, in which is dissipation; but
> be filled with the Spirit

Many affairs have begun with a drink in a wrong company. Personally, I am happy to have a glass of wine in a safe company, but for every glass I pay a price—I have come to realise that my gift of discerning spirits becomes insensitive for around two hours, and after that, I often have to pray to reclaim spiritual authority over my environment.

Many Christian leaders take a drink to combat the anxiety caused by demonic oppression, which doesn't really help but makes things only worse. Instead, they should rise up in prayer and spiritual warfare.

In Daniel 10, Daniel prays for twenty-one days, and finally, the archangel Gabriel appears to him, revealing that although Daniel's prayer had been answered straight away, he had been delayed, as he had to fight his way through the army of the prince of Persia.

Daniel 10:2-3 says,

> In those days I, Daniel, was mourning three full weeks. I ate
> no pleasant food, no meat or wine came into my mouth,
> nor did I anoint myself at all, till three whole weeks were
> fulfilled.

It fits my experience that you can't fight spiritual warfare effectively if you are drinking even a bit, and when I am under a heavy spiritual attack, I cut all alcohol from my life, as I don't have any time to waste in lack of spiritual discernment. But you shouldn't be legalistic about this, as legalism is even more lethal to our walk in the Spirit than alcohol.

Daniel didn't do full fasting here, but it is noteworthy that the most enlightening glimpse into the heavenly battle that we have in the Old Testament came when he abstained from alcohol.

Similarly, many prescription drugs seem to be able to dull the gift of discerning spirits.

Anxiety leads to all sorts of negative side effects. For example, it may reduce openness to new ideas through cognitive freezing and resistance to change.[17]

So, we can see how fear is also an attack against the gift of creativity God has given to us.

Research in cognitive psychology demonstrates that high stress and anxiety are associated with biased information processing and a tendency to pay closer attention to threatening information.[18]

With Charismatic Christians, fear often leads to believing false prophecies, and there is a whole industry of false prophecy banking on fear.

Many Christians are addicted to scaremongering prophecies, even when they know that earlier prophecies by the same 'prophets' have been proven false. This is because their mind-set is saturated with fear.

1 John 4:18 says,

> There is no fear in love; but perfect love casts out fear, because fear involves torment. But he who fears has not been made perfect in love.

This isn't a word of judgment for those who feel fear, but a word of encouragement. But isn't it interesting that the apostle John positions fear as the enemy of God that must be overcome by the power of God?

I used to be of the opinion that a little bit of fear in my life didn't really matter. But I have come to realise that fear can easily bring disobedience into our lives. Abraham sinned because of fear. King Saul sinned and lost his anointing because of fear.

Also, fear opens up all kinds of other emotions and wrestles our mind out of submission to the Holy Spirit. It weakens our resistance against the demonic powers and the power of sin. Sometimes, the devil just hates to see you blessed and wants to rob you of joy, so he attacks you with fear.

There are many negative emotions, but fear is perhaps the most destructive one, as it is very deceitful, and we don't always realise that it opens the door to demonic influences in our lives.

Weapon 2—Sin

The devil's second main weapon is sin. Eventually, succumbing to fear leads to sin, although sin doesn't need fear to be active because of flesh—our sinful nature.

Some years ago, I was coming out of a lengthy season of battling demonic fear and intimidation. The spiritual atmosphere felt a little bit lighter, and, one day, I found myself wondering what the enemy might put on my way next. I didn't have to reflect long, as I received an instant answer from the Holy Spirit.

"First he will give you what you don't want; then he will give you what you want."

It took me years to figure out what this means exactly. Initially, I thought that this means that after a season of testing the devil would tempt me with success. This is also true, but I don't think that is what the Holy Spirit meant.

What I have just described is one of the *main* traps of the enemy, and he will use it against you many times a day.

Even when we are full of the Spirit, we still have our soul and natural human emotions, and the enemy is an expert in tricking the natural processes of our mind.

I have had to resist the enemy through many seasons of spiritual disturbance, up to the point where I have come to experience demonic attacks as a sort of negative, demonic force field. I have learned to resist these demonic force fields in the Spirit, but, nevertheless, they have an impact on my soul.

The Holy Spirit in me can defend me against these demonic attacks, but my soul and my emotions are still affected. I still feel the negative oppression of these demonic force fields, even when my active using of the shield of faith protects me. It is like walking across an enemy territory, always alert of the potential attack of the enemy, and sometimes encountering the enemy at a close distance. Emotionally, this takes its toll.

I have discovered that I am at my most vulnerable when it comes to sin nearly immediately after a demonic attack has lifted and my emotions begin to regain their positivity. It is as if the lifting of the oppression caused my soul to temporarily take over, and for a time, I can become a *soulish* Christian. I sigh of relief, but then I realise that the oppressive attack of fear is often followed by the seductive attack on my positive emotions that I am regaining. You can easily miss that if you begin to associate the demonic attacks with fear, but forget that he also attacks with seduction.

First he will give you what you don't want; then he will give you what you want. My soul doesn't want fear and oppression, but there are many other things it does.

Paul writes,

> I say then: Walk in the Spirit, and you shall not fulfill the lust of the flesh. For the flesh lusts against the Spirit, and the Spirit against the flesh; and these are contrary to one another, so that you do not do the things that you wish. (Galatians 5:16-17)

After a negative spiritual attack, our positive emotional levels are low, and our soul desires an uplifting. That is when we are especially vulnerable to the desires of our flesh.

But anxiety and fear don't only cause us to look for physical or emotional pleasures; they also cause us to react in a negative way.

For years, I felt agitated every time we were about to travel on air. I am normally quite a laid-back person, but I found taking my family to the airport on time to be a particularly stressful situation, and I often reacted impatiently and angrily to any delays in my schedule. For years, I put it down to added stress of travel and the fact that missing a flight for being late can be quite expensive.

But as I began to develop the gift of discerning spirits, I realised that, most times, when we were getting ready to fly, a tangible demonic atmosphere descended upon us. This negative atmosphere caused me to react angrily. I made a decision not to engage with that negative atmosphere at all. I simply focused on just being still and connecting with the presence of the Holy Spirit within me, and this evil presence would lift usually within twenty minutes. When it operated around us, any minor disagreement would blow up. With it gone, there were no disagreements at all.

We tend to think that the enemy will only attack our ministry. But he will always attack our family and relationships, as shipwreck in those areas will sabotage your whole life.

James 3:6 says,

> And the tongue is a fire, a world of iniquity. The tongue is so set among our members that it defiles the whole body, and sets on fire the course of nature; and it is set on fire by hell.

The enemy is always looking for a fault line in our defence, the hidden weaknesses and wounds in our soul. If he can connect his demonic fire to these weaknesses, he can make the power of hell blow up in us.

This doesn't mean that the Holy Spirit would leave us, or that we would suffer from demonic possession; only we are not living in the power of the Holy Spirit, but let the enemy influence our actions, much like Peter did, when he rebuked Jesus who had just told the disciples that He would soon die on the cross.

> But He turned and said to Peter, "Get behind Me, Satan! You are an offense to Me, for you are not mindful of the things of God, but the things of men." (Matthew 16:23)

Another scheme of Satan is to bombard us with thoughts of guilt. These thoughts of guilt have a heavily oppressive nature, and accepting them can be extremely harmful to us. Thankfully, there is a lot more teaching about grace in the Church than there used to be. But the effect of these guilt-filled thoughts can be that we become insensitive to natural thoughts of guilt, as we become so used to these attacks. In many parts of the Church, this has led to accepting all kinds of behaviour that is clearly sinful. I have seen many teachers that have taught holiness in the past become completely unbothered about sin in their lives and in the life of the church. Once you push all emotions of guilt away and brand it all as an attack from the enemy, you actually remove one of the major defence mechanisms that God has given to us—our conscience. That is why we must resist these attacks in the power of the Holy Spirit, rather than in the power of our mind, as the way our natural mind works is that these attacks will lead either to depression or lack of sensitivity when it comes to habitual sins.

Weapon 3—Deception

The third part of the devil's main strategy against us is deception. In one of the most shocking passages in the Bible, Jesus says,

> "Beware of false prophets, who come to you in sheep's clothing, but inwardly they are ravenous wolves. You will know them by their fruits. Do men gather grapes from thorn bushes or figs from thistles? Even so, every good tree bears good fruit, but a bad tree bears bad fruit. A good tree cannot bear bad fruit, nor can a bad tree bear good fruit. Every tree that does not bear good fruit is cut down and thrown into the fire. Therefore by their fruits you will know them. Not everyone who says to Me, 'Lord, Lord,' shall enter the kingdom of heaven, but he who does the will of My Father in heaven. Many will say to Me in that day, 'Lord, Lord, have we not prophesied in Your name, cast out demons in Your name, and done many wonders in Your name?' And then I will declare to them, 'I never knew you; depart from Me, you who practice lawlessness!'" (Matthew 7:15-23)

Jesus doesn't deny that these people achieved all these great things in His name. But He says He never *knew* them.

Can there be a more terrible fate than believing that you are serving God—even with signs and wonders—and to discover on the last day that it has all been in vain? This is the enemy's master work of deception.

The devil has no issue with you if he can deceive you. He will let you find out on the last day that you have been led astray.

Have you ever met ministers who appear to function in the spiritual gifts, but they seem to be completely devoid of love in their personal life? These ministers only pray on stage, but their personal prayer life is dead.

1 John 4:1-6 says,

> Beloved, do not believe every spirit, but test the spirits, whether they are of God; because many false prophets have gone out into the world. By this you know the Spirit of God: Every spirit that confesses that Jesus Christ has come in the flesh is of God, and every spirit that does not confess that Jesus Christ has come in the flesh is not of God. And this is the *spirit* of the Antichrist, which you have heard was coming, and is now already in the world. You are of God, little children, and have overcome them, because He who is in you is greater than he who is in the world. They are of the world. Therefore they speak *as* of the world, and the world hears them. We are of God. He who knows God hears us; he who is not of God does not hear us. By this we know the spirit of truth and the spirit of error.

According to John, the prophets of God are the ones that confess that Jesus came in the flesh. Like Paul, he seems to have been fighting against a rising Gnostic heresy. Paul writes in 1 Corinthians 12:1-3,

> Now concerning spiritual *gifts*, brethren, I do not want you to be ignorant: You know that you were Gentiles, carried away to these dumb idols, however you were led. Therefore I make known to you that no one speaking by the Spirit of God calls Jesus accursed, and no one can say that Jesus is Lord except by the Holy Spirit. (1 Corinthians 12:1-3)

A false prophet can easily say that Jesus is Lord, but here Paul is probably referring to someone who exhibits the ecstatic behaviour of spirit possession. If that person can't declare the Lordship of Jesus, he or she isn't possessed by the Holy Spirit but by a demonic being.

It seems that even demon-possessed people might have made their entry into the church of Corinth.

Translators have had difficulties in translating the Greek words *anathema Iesous*, and they tend to translate it as "Jesus is/be cursed", assuming that Jesus is the subject and the other term the predicate, but, in reality, the meaning of the phrase is ambiguous. But comparing it with Greek inscriptions of curses, it seems it should really be translated "May Jesus curse".[19]

This would make perfect sense in the light of the many references to magic and clear pre-Gnostic tendencies in Corinth. In essence, Paul is saying that, unlike the pagans who used magical formulas to curse their enemies, you can't curse people if you are speaking in the Holy Spirit.

WHERE GOD BUILDS A CHURCH, THE DEVIL BUILDS A CHAPEL

The Protestant reformer Martin Luther said that where God builds a church, the devil builds a chapel. Apart from the Azusa Street Revival, Southern California has been the birthing place of many religious movements. Katherine Tingley had a theosophical temple in Point Loma, and this movement has made a large impact on the New Age movement. Also, there was the Christian Science Temple of Mary Baker Eddy.

The Jesus People Movement began in San Francisco in the late 1960s, and it strengthened the emerging signs and wonders emphasis in the Charismatic movement. But it started in the same area of the city than the New Age and occult loving hippie movement.

The Royal Borough of Kensington & Chelsea in London, where I have lived for over twenty years, has seen the release of the Alpha Course into the world by the Holy Trinity, Brompton, and the church planting explosion of Kensington Temple in the late 1980s and 1990s. But just a few hundred yards from Kensington Temple, there is the birthing place of one of the main streams of the modern Wicca movement.

We can see that where God is moving supernaturally, the enemy is always manufacturing a counterfeit movement next door, trying to bring it in to the Church. And more often than not, we look for the devil in the world, but we are completely blind and oblivious to his works in the Church.

The gift of discerning spirits must be the most misunderstood gift out of the nine gifts. Today, it is also one of the most needed, as it is our guardian and protector in the supernatural world. William J. Seymour, the pastor of the Azusa Street church, where the Pentecostal revival started, said,

> The Corinthian church was one of Paul's most gifted churches, and just as it is today, where a church is very gifted, the only safeguard from deceptive spirits is by rightly dividing the Word of God, to keep out fanaticism.[20]

The enemy can deceive us in a multitude of ways. Much of that deception can be dealt with through Bible study and regular prayer. But if you are operating in the gifts of the Spirit, the enemy will attack your gift of receiving from God with his weapon of deception. For example, he will try to lure you to accept his deception as prophetic revelation, so that you will begin to be fed from the wrong source. He will achieve that by feeding thoughts into your mind that sound like a revelation to you.

I went through a season when nearly every day thoughts that emanated a vague sense of spiritual power would come to my awareness. Normally, their content would be that something specific would happen. They sounded much like prophetic thoughts, but instantly, I could hear another inner voice, proclaiming much louder: "That was not me!" That was the voice of the Holy Spirit. This happened frequently, and I began to realise that the enemy was attacking my prophetic gift with false revelation.

Receiving false revelation and accepting it will eventually either wreck your ability to hear from God or make you into a false prophet.

God's words carry His presence. Always disregard any thoughts that seem revelatory but don't come enveloped in His presence. This will save you from a lot of trouble, as the enemy will attempt to abduct your increasing spiritual awareness. Thoughts from God, soul and the enemy all carry energy but they all have distinguishably different presence. As you learn to discern the nature of the energy source behind the thought, you will learn to discern its origin.

The Holy Spirit never speaks a word that doesn't come enveloped in His presence. The devil can camouflage as an angel of light, but he can't fake God's presence.

Words spoken by the enemy are either full of poison, or when he masquerades as the angel of light, like empty shells, devoid of life. They have a presence of restlessness about them.

The enemy might recite the Bible, as he did to Jesus when He was tempted, but he can never manufacture the unique sense of peace and energy that accompanies the presence of God.

DISTURBING DREAMS

Often, Christians begin to open to the gift of discerning spirits through dreams. They begin to see disturbing dreams that appear to have a demonic origin. But more often than not, it is not that demonic beings are producing the actual dream; rather it is the dreamer that is subconsciously reacting to a demonic influence in their lives and visualising that influence through dreams.

If you see dreams that appear to be a product of demonic interference, you should see it as an opportunity to begin to develop your dormant gift of discerning spirits.

Think about the places you have visited and people you have met recently. Could any of them have any occult influences?

Nearly without a fail, if I meet anyone who has had any occult influences in their lives, or if I visit a place with strong demonic links, this will be manifested in my dreams.

Once, I was on my way to work when I got a phone call. It was a friend I had seen at a Christian conference a week earlier. I met him later on that day.

We talked, and he opened up about his past, about the time before he had become a Christian. It turned out that his parents had exposed him to the occult in young age. I gave him a prophecy and then left.

After around half an hour, a deep sense of restlessness and depression came over me. A few hours later it was becoming clear that I was under an intensifying demonic attack. When I got home, I went to pray, as I was puzzled about what was going on. It was after around ten minutes of prayer that I remembered my meeting with him and realised that the demonic presence I felt must be somehow connected to him.

I called him, and he told me that he had been under intense demonic oppression and had found it very difficult to pray. I prayed for him and cast out every demonic influence out of his life.

Around ten minutes later, the demonic oppression lifted, and the freedom of the Holy Spirit arrived. I thought that this episode was over.

A day later I was in bed, ready to sleep. I began to sense a strong demonic disturbance in the room. I closed my eyes and I could see three dark figures appearing. They stood around the bed, silent. I opened my eyes. They were still there.

I was tired, so I fell asleep. That night I saw the most terrible dreams about child killings and horrible things I don't really want to remember. I had never seen anything that disgusting in my dream world before.

Through the gift of discerning spirits, I have come to understand that many a restless dream, full of anxieties, is nothing more than a side product of a demonic presence in my environment.

DISCERNING PEOPLE'S SPIRITUAL STATES

The gift of discerning spirits helps you to discern people's spiritual states. Sometimes you get a sense that something is not right with a person. It doesn't mean that you tell them or anyone else that, but it helps you to apply caution at the right time.

Once, I was negotiating with someone over quite a sizable business deal, but I felt that this person should not be trusted. I ended up not going ahead, but someone I know did. This person ended up breaking every promise he had made to my friend, and this caused a lot of trouble.

This doesn't mean that you should ever accuse anyone of anything, just because of how you feel. It just means that you proceed more cautiously than normally and inspect everything carefully.

When it comes to discerning negative spirituality, this can just be a deep sense of unease. But this gift doesn't only work with evil spiritual influences, but you can often also discern the friends of God and feel immediately that they are trustworthy, as they are part of your family in Christ.

There are times when I have seen people's sins in visual form. I used to meet one pastor regularly, and nearly every time I met him, I could see filthy symbols and images around his mouth. As I prayed over this, the Holy Spirit spoke to me and said that his marriage was dead. Some years later, he left his wife, and it was revealed that he had a multitude of adulterous relationships at the time.

I met with one pastor regularly, and one time when I met with him, I felt like I wanted to vomit. This was a physical reaction to the demonic sin in his life. It felt as if the demon influencing his life kicked me in the stomach. I didn't call his sin, although God showed it to me, but I believe that God showed it to me to protect me. No one knew about that sinful entanglement in his life at the time; it only became visible later.

DEVELOPING THE GIFT OF DISCERNING SPIRITS

I have identified nine steps in the development of a fully mature gift of discerning spirits.

1. Studying the Bible on a daily basis

If you want to develop the gift of discerning spirits, you must study the Bible regularly. God has given us His revelation in the Scripture. Reading the Bible prayerfully begins to develop the discernment within us. In Joshua 1:8, God speaks to Joshua who is getting ready to enter the Promised Land and encounter his enemies.

> This Book of the Law shall not depart from your mouth, but you shall meditate in it day and night, that you may observe to do according to all that is written in it. For then you will make your way prosperous, and then you will have good success.

Only when we study the Scripture diligently, we will be able to have a good success in defeating our enemies.

2. Cultivating a lifestyle of experiencing God's presence

Reading the Scripture is necessary, but it is not enough. We must also spend time in the tangible presence of God, and learn to open the streams of the living water—the presence and the power of the Holy Spirit—within us.

The gift of discerning spirits needs a continual flow of the Holy Spirit's presence within us to operate. It is perhaps the most energy-consuming of the gifts. Sometimes, it feels like walking around the city with an active, spiritual nuclear reactor within you!

3. Discerning your emotions

With the help of what the Scripture says about your emotions and the protection of God's grace and the power of the Holy Spirit, you will be able to discern and analyse your emotions.

Many Christians seek to ignore their emotions and motivations, trying to combat the negative ones with faith. But you must also understand your emotional life and its key dynamics. If you feel depressed, rather than ignoring it, acknowledge it, and seek to understand why. What has caused you to feel depressed? Is there any specific reason? Or if you feel angry, why do you feel angry? Try to go a little bit deeper than the superficial motivations. The real reasons for your anger are nearly always deeper than what you are reacting to. At the root of our soulish and fleshy reactions are often nearly forgotten experiences—memories that influence and direct our behavioural patterns without us discerning it.

4. Resisting negative emotions and sensations with faith and the presence of God

But the analysis of your own emotions and motivations isn't enough. We must learn to use the shield of faith and hide ourselves in the presence of God. Psalm 27:5 says,

> For in the time of trouble He shall hide me in His pavilion; in the secret place of His tabernacle.

God's presence is our shield and our protection against the schemes of Satan.

5. *Separating emotions from the spiritual force energising them*
As you seek to remain protected by the shield of God's presence, over time, you will begin to sense how the emotions and loaded half-facts the enemy uses to attack you will become separated from the spiritual force behind them. As they become disconnected from their power source, they will begin to lose their power on you.

6. *Experiencing the spiritual forces as negative force fields or spheres*
After you experience that sense of disconnection, you often begin to experience the demonic spiritual beings as something like negative force fields. You will sense how their pressure on your mind increases and decreases. They come at you like waves that hit the shore when a storm begins to rage, but slowly, as you resist, they begin to recede.

Some of the emotions will still keep on getting through your defence, especially during intensive attacks.

But at this stage, you don't need to, or shouldn't, even engage with these emotions and demonically charged thoughts at all. Instead, you should wait under the shield of faith and God's presence, until the most intensive phase of the attack is over, and then you can pray and counterattack.

In the meantime, you should focus on reconnecting and maintaining the flow of the Holy Spirit's power and presence into your life. You are no more fighting against these forces actively; instead you are focused on the Lord, and His presence fights for you.

Psalm 46:10 says,

Be still, and know that I am God.

It is at this stage when you begin to realise that the devil's main goal is to disconnect you from the flow of the presence of God in your life. But you are a temple of the Holy Spirit, and you don't need to leave His temple. Instead, you are hiding in His pavilion.

This is a place where the storms of life no more affect your mind as strong as they used to. They might still be coming at you, but your security is the Lord and His presence.

7. Learning to operate with the gift
The gift of discerning spirits is both for everyday life and ministry. In my prayer life, I wait for the disturbance of the demonic spirits to lift before I practise any active prophetic listening. In my everyday life, I resist whatever reaction the demonic disturbance seeks to impose on me. In ministry, I am mindful of the spiritual environment, and factor it in.

There are situations in everyday life that will have completely different consequences depending on the spiritual atmosphere.

You can often discern the presence and operation of a demonic influence in the room where you minister, as you are confronted with impure or negative thoughts, or fear and discouragement. Often, I feel the presence of the demonic forces as a tangible, heavy wall that tries to shout at me and tell me that it's unbreakable.

One of the main dangers when you are seeking to minister in the supernatural is that the enemy is also operating in that dimension. This gives particular challenges when it comes to operating in the prophetic gift.

Often when I minister in a church, I encounter strong spiritual resistance. In that situation, I dare not to receive or share any new revelation, but operate from the revelation of the Word and specific prophetic revelation that God has given to me *before* that event. I sense the atmosphere through the gift of discerning spirits. It is only when I feel that the spiritual resistance is lifting that I step into the prophetic flow.

Prophetic ministry is ministry in His presence, and if I don't sense His presence, I can't really accept any prophetic revelation.

There are two main reasons: first, you can be deceived. Second, even if you aren't deceived, your listeners can be deceived.

Matthew 13:19 says,

> When anyone hears the word of the kingdom, and does not understand it, then the wicked one comes and snatches away what was sown in his heart.

I have realised that, often, people aren't receptive to a word, and the evil one snatches it, before it has any time to make any impact.

But I can 'hammer' the atmosphere with the revelation God has already given to me beforehand and create a new atmosphere where listeners become receptive. That is why it is so important to prepare for any ministry time in prayer, so that you will have the confidence to stick with the word that God has given you in advance, no matter how much the enemy attempts to intimidate you. In this kind of ministry, I can spend hours in the Holy Spirit speaking to me about an event, but this only gives me the ability to deliver His word faithfully.

8. Learning to tolerate continual spiritual disturbance

One of the hardest things about this gift is that you will often feel and experience these spiritual disturbances, which can be emotionally and even physically taxing. Often, you have been called to live and minister in an environment where sin has created strongholds in people's lives, so this is mostly not something you can easily escape from. You will simply need to learn to tolerate emotional discomfort at times.

9. Learning to rest again in God's presence

You need regular times of rest in God's presence. You must be able to remember that your ministry is not just warfare, but at the heart of it is rest in God's presence and fellowship with Him.

Psalm 23:5 says,

> You prepare a table before me in the presence of my enemies.

There is a lot of spiritual disturbance in the world and around you. Sometimes, you have been called to confront those forces around you, at other times to ignore them.

When special force soldiers are dropped behind the enemy line, they have a clear mission. They don't engage with the enemy on the way, unless it is obstructing the accomplishment of their mission.

You have been called to move every spiritual mountain that stands on the way, but you should ignore the ones that are on the wayside.

In Joshua 1:7, when God instructs Joshua regarding taking over the Promised Land, He says,

> "Only be strong and very courageous, that you may observe to do according to all the law which Moses My servant commanded you; do not turn from it to the right hand or to the left, that you may prosper wherever you go."

The enemy is always distracting you, trying to get you involved in battles that only deviate from your mission. Unless you are careful with the gift of discerning spirits, the enemy will turn it against you. Mark 1:35-38 says,

> Now in the morning, having risen a long while before daylight, He went out and departed to a solitary place; and there He prayed. And Simon and those who were with Him searched for Him. When they found Him, they said to Him, "Everyone is looking for You." But He said to them, "Let us go into the next towns, that I may preach there also, because for this purpose I have come forth."

Above all, the enemy will attack your ability to worship, your relationships and the purpose you were born for. But Jesus didn't let even the apparent needs of people deviate Him from His worship and His purpose.

What the disciples were really saying was that Jesus was popular and they quite liked to be famous by association, but Jesus didn't care for that.

The devil is a master in manufacturing apparent needs and storms around you. We must keep on loving people. But we must also ensure that we are continually being filled with the Holy Spirit, as otherwise, we will start giving from our own well, which will soon dry out, rather than letting the streams of the living water of God's presence flow through us.

One of the things that can happen during times of spiritual warfare is that you begin to associate a strong presence of God with warfare. It has happened to me and caused me to feel anxious and weary when I begin to experience God's presence, not looking forward to the attack I know His presence will be protecting me from. That is why you must always be rediscovering the joy in the presence of God.

MINISTERING TO PEOPLE WITH THE GIFT OF DISCERNING SPIRITS

The gift of discerning spirits is vital for effective prophetic ministry, especially in situations where you don't have time to seek God's guidance in His presence.

For example, if you are ministering prophetically, there will always be a large number of people who come forward to be prayed for. You will not have met any of these people before. I use the gift to discern their spiritual state. There are times when I receive a prophecy for them, but I can discern that they aren't ready to receive it, because their commitment to Jesus is not steadfast enough. There is a call over their life, but they are not ready to receive it yet.

At other times, people come to ask you to confirm a prophecy they say someone else has given to them, but you discern that all they are doing is to camouflage their heart's desire with religious language. It is amazing how many people seem to think that a prophet's blessing could somehow make a difference if God has already disagreed with you.

Sometimes, I can discern that people are lying to me; at other times I can discern a sin in their lives.

I rarely tell them what I am seeing. Instead, I use what I discern as a material for diagnostic, direct, but non-condemning questions, no matter what the issue. After all, these people are seeking God at some level, even if they aren't ready to spill the secrets of their heart to me. 1 Peter 4:8 says,

And above all things have fervent love for one another, for "love will cover a multitude of sins."

The gift of discerning spirits is not a gift of exposing people, but a gift for helping them to be set free.

If you sense that there is a demonic influence in someone's life, you should take the following steps.

1. Proceed cautiously until certain

It is fine and advisable to take your time. Ministering in the gift of discerning spirits can sometimes feel like stepping from a room full of light into a dark room. It takes a bit of time for your eyes to adjust, but soon you will begin to see the contents of the room.

2. Ask questions – don't prophesy

One of the most destructive things you can do to people is to 'prophesy' what you see through the gift of discerning spirits, or proclaim it as a word of knowledge. This will only bring people under condemnation. So, you should almost never proclaim to the person you are ministering to exactly what you see. Instead, you can use what you see as material for questions.

3. Don't let the darkness dictate your ministry

The devil is a liar, and often the enemy will seek to dictate the way you will minister by releasing deception, fear or uncomfortable emotions. Don't let him deceive you, so that you will react to whatever he will project unto you, or the person you are praying for.

Instead, observe the person, the disturbance, and the flow of the Holy Spirit within you. You need to be aware of all three. It is not your job to react to whatever the enemy is doing, but to submit to the work of the Holy Spirit in you.

4. Connect with the flow of the Spirit within you

The presence of God is there within you to protect you and to guide you to all truth. Jesus says in John 14:26,

"But the Helper, the Holy Spirit, whom the Father will send in My name, He will teach you all things, and bring to your remembrance all things that I said to you."

You must wait for the Helper within you to come. Wait for God's presence to begin to flow within you before attempting to minister in any deeper way.

5. Minister in the flow of the Spirit

Every encounter with a demonic presence or influence is a spiritual battle. Hence you should only minister in the flow of the Holy Spirit.

6. Pray afterwards

Every encounter with the enemy takes its toll on you. If you worked in the London sewage system and went home, you would probably want to have a thorough wash before attempting to kiss your wife or husband! In a similar way, ministering with the gift of discerning spirits demands a time of prayer afterwards. Otherwise, these encounters with demonic influences in other people's lives can have a negative influence in your life.

Unless you are careful, you will end up carrying the depression, anxieties, fears, negative thoughts and so on of the people you have ministered to.

Often, we minister to people who are walking through the valley of the shadow of death. But after ministering to them, we must not stay in the valley, but climb back on the mountain of God's presence.

12

FAITH

If you study the history of ideas, you will soon realise that the theological ideas and frameworks haven't been impacted just by the Bible, but they reflect the prevalent secular and religious ideologies of their time, either through resisting or embracing them. But either way, through assimilation or through rejection, the prevailing modes of thought in society tend to influence theology and Christian ideas.

So, for example, Paul's letters argue against bringing Jewish legalism *and* Greek philosophy and paganism into Christianity. Unless we understand that he's fighting on two or even three fronts, and not just one, we can easily misinterpret his writings.

There are eras that have deeply affected theology, but the questions the theologians were answering then might no more be relevant. For example, the focus of medieval theologians on logic is still deeply affecting us without us even realising it.

Often, it is only the passing of time that will give us the perspective to see more clearly what is from God and what was a product of a particular intellectual era.

One of the major streams that has affected Charismatic Christianity is the Word of Faith movement, and the Healing Revival was very much influenced by it.

This seems clear to most, but what has been lost to the mists of the 19th and the early 20st century is that the Word of Faith movement itself was profoundly affected by New Thought.

Kate Bowler, Assistant Professor of the History of Christianity in North America at Duke Divinity School writes about New Thought.

New thought represents a cluster of thinkers and metaphysical ideas that emerged in the 1880s as the era's most powerful vehicle of mind-power. Three aspects of New Thought became foundational to the twentieth century's view of mind-power.[1]

First, New Thought assumed unity between God and humanity, perceiving that separation between them was only relative and not absolute.[2]

Bowler writes,

> As many New Thought authors worked inside a Christian framework, they explored "salvation" not as a act imposed from above by God, but rather an act of drawing out humanity's potential.[3]

New Thought saw the material world as subject to the mind and began to perceive faith as something that could bend reality.

> Second, New Thought taught that the world should be reimagined as thought rather than substance. The spiritual world formed absolute reality, while the material world was the mind's projection.[4]

Third, they thought that human beings shared God's creative power of thought and words.

> Third, New Thought argued that people shared in God's power to created by means of thought. People shaped their own worlds by their thinking, just as God had created the world using thought. Positive thoughts yielded positive circumstances, and negative thoughts yielded negative circumstances.[5]

Phineas P. Quimby (1802–66) is usually cited as the founder or the earliest proponent of New Thought. A native of Portland, Maine, Quimby was a clockmaker with little traditional education. After observing the power of the mind to heal through hypnosis, suggestion and the placebo effect, Quimby began to practise hypnotism and developed the view that illness was simply a matter of the mind. He opened an office for mentally aided healing in Portland, Maine in 1859. One of Quimby's students was Mary Baker Eddy, who went on to found the Christian Science movement.[6]

E.W. Kenyon, who is considered to be the father of the Word of Faith movement, brought the New Thought way of thinking into teaching about healing. F.F. Bosworth, who would later on work with Branham, then carried the New Thought framework to healing revivals.

Later on, there was a shift from an emphasis on healing to focus on prosperity in New Thought.[7] This shift was followed by a similar shift in the Christian camp, which led to prosperity gospel.

It is vital to understand that behind the Word of Faith understanding of faith is a belief that man's mind has the ability to bend physical reality. The word of faith was seen as the *law* of faith, or as "faith force".

But this is distinctly different understanding of faith than what the Bible gives to us. In the Bible, faith is a gift from God, and the gift of faith is a gift given by the Holy Spirit. In the Word of Faith teaching you hear a lot about the "spirit man". This goes back to Kenyon's teaching about the "spiritual man" that is born again, but rather than the apostle Paul, who teaches that we are a temple of God's Spirit, in Kenyon's teaching our reborn spirit remains very much in charge. This leads to a very different understanding about faith than in the Bible. But faith is such an ambiguous word; we use it for saving faith and for the gift of faith, so when anyone speaks about faith, we often accept the teaching without any questions.

WHAT IS THE GIFT OF FAITH?

The gift of faith is separate from saving faith, although even the saving faith is a gift.

In 1 Samuel 14, Jonathan, King Saul's son, and his servant approach the garrison of the Philistines. The whole of Israel is oppressed by the Philistines, and they have only one sword. It is in Jonathan's hand.

Then Jonathan said to the young man who bore his armor, "Come, let us go over to the garrison of these uncircumcised; it may be that the Lord will work for us. For nothing restrains the Lord from saving by many or by few." So his armorbearer said to him, "Do all that is in your heart. Go then; here I am with you, according to your heart."

Then Jonathan said, "Very well, let us cross over to these men, and we will show ourselves to them. If they say thus to us, 'Wait until we come to you,' then we will stand still in our place and not go up to them. But if they say thus, 'Come up to us,' then we will go up. For the Lord has delivered them into our hand, and this will be a sign to us." (1 Samuel 14:6-10)

They get the sign, attack the garrison, and bring a victory to the Israelites. We don't see Jonathan act in a similar way in all circumstances, but for some reason, he believes that God would give them that garrison. And he asks God for a sign, which is an insane sign, as attacking the garrison would have looked like madness, but it is given.

Most of us would have asked for the sign to be that all the Philistines would flee!

David behaves in a very similar way when he attacks Goliath. In 1 Samuel 17:26, David says,

"For who is this uncircumcised Philistine, that he should defy the armies of the living God?"

But this reckless faith has been birthed out of deep revelation. Ultimately, the gift of faith draws on a deep understanding of who God is and what He is capable of doing, but this faith is usually released to a specific situation.

This faith is energised by the power of the Holy Spirit. Its object isn't random but revealed.

In Mark 11:23, Jesus says to His disciples:

"For assuredly, I say to you, whoever says to this mountain, 'Be removed and be cast into the sea,' and does not doubt in

his heart, but believes that those things he says will be done,
he will have whatever he says."

It is likely that Jesus spoke about the Temple Mountain and the cult
of sacrifices linked to it, and then He went to remove that mountain
by dying on the cross.

But there is a second meaning to the text—if God gives you faith
for removing a particular mountain, you will be able to remove that
mountain—but not just any mountain. The gift of faith has a *specific*
object.

The gift of faith is a special faith for particular things. Hebrews
11:1 says,

> Now faith is the substance of things hoped for, the evidence
> of things not seen.

Faith has a specific object; it is not something we can use for just
anything. That is why a genuine prophetic word will usually release
the gift of faith for that particular thing and not for any other thing.

George Jeffreys, the founder of Elim Pentecostal Movement in
Britain, writes,

> We have known faith given in this manner to have lifted the
> servants of God entirely out of themselves, until they could
> believe for the impossible to happen. We have also known
> the same men, without this special endowment, to appear as
> helpless as children.
>
> At one time the preacher is ministering to the sick in the
> ordinary realms of faith with very little apparent results; at
> another he is moving against them, clothed with this special
> faith, and helpless cripples are healed to the astonishment of
> even the minister himself. Without this special faith he might
> feel weak and tired before the smallest of congregations, but
> with it he feels that monster congregations are in the palms
> of his hands. This special quality of faith seems to come upon
> certain of God's servants at times of great need.[8]

Hebrews 11 gives us perhaps the best glimpse into the workings of the gift of faith in the Bible.

It shows that is only God's word that has creative power, and we understand this by faith.

> By faith we understand that the worlds were framed by the word of God, so that the things which are seen were not made of things which are visible. (Hebrews 11:3)

Hebrews 11 shows that the gift of faith leads to specific action. Each hero of faith mentioned in the chapter believed in a specific promise of God.

> By faith Abraham, when he was tested, offered up Isaac, and he who had received the promises offered up his only begotten son, of whom it was said, "In Isaac your seed shall be called," concluding that God was able to raise him up, even from the dead, from which he also received him in a figurative sense. (Hebrews 11:17-19)

Abraham's faith would have been madness without the specific promise of God. We can see how the gift of faith is always energised by revelation from God.

Hebrews 11:30 says,

> By faith the walls of Jericho fell down after they were encircled for seven days.

We can see everywhere how the gift of faith can only be applied based on specific revelation. You can't apply it to all things randomly.

Let's go back to Matthew's version about moving the mountain. Mark puts Jesus' teaching about moving the mountain by faith in the context of a fig tree. Matthew, on the other hand, puts it in the context of casting out a demon from a young boy.

> And when they had come to the multitude, a man came to Him, kneeling down to Him and saying, "Lord, have mercy on my son, for he is an epileptic and suffers severely; for he

often falls into the fire and often into the water. So I brought him to Your disciples, but they could not cure him." Then Jesus answered and said, "O faithless and perverse generation, how long shall I be with you? How long shall I bear with you? Bring him here to Me." And Jesus rebuked the demon, and it came out of him; and the child was cured from that very hour. Then the disciples came to Jesus privately and said, "Why could we not cast it out?"

So Jesus said to them, "Because of your unbelief; for assuredly, I say to you, if you have faith as a mustard seed, you will say to this mountain, 'Move from here to there,' and it will move; and nothing will be impossible for you. However, this kind does not go out except by prayer and fasting." (Matthew 17:14-21)

This is partially an enigmatic story, and we have often been misled by its possible interpretations. It gives an impression that our faith has the capacity to do anything we like if we only have right kind of faith. But this must be seen in the context of Matthew 10, where Jesus sends the twelve disciples out and gives them authority to cast out demons.

This was a *specific* commission; Jesus had given them an authority over demons. So, it seems clear that Jesus rebuked them because they lacked faith in the authority of *Jesus*. The disciples still didn't understand who Jesus was, and what His authority was based on.

In my view, every Christian should have a gift of faith, and in fact every Christian needs it, and has it, at least for some things. In my experience, the gift of faith can be released by four factors:

1. Knowing who God is
As my main gift is prophecy, I often rely on the prophetic gift to release faith. But a while ago, I went through a season when every time I asked for revelation regarding my life, I got a simple answer. The Holy Spirit simply said, "Trust in Me." Initially that was annoying. How was I supposed to trust in God when He had not yet told me what would happen?

But then I realised that a subtle shift had taken place in my mind. I had learned to rely on prophetic revelation, whereas God simply wanted me to trust in Him and His faithfulness. What He was telling me was that I should know Him better by now and know that He's faithful, and that I shouldn't ask Him to explain every detail of His plan. It should have been enough for me to trust Him.

Psalm 23:1 says,

> The Lord is my shepherd; I shall not want.

It was enough for David to know who God is to know that He would look after his every need.

2. Knowing God's Word

Often, the gift of faith is triggered when we read the Bible, and the Holy Spirit begins to remind us of His promises.

That is why reading the Bible is so important. How can you believe in God's promises if you don't know what they are?

3. Prophetic promises

Prophetic words, visions and dreams release the gift of faith for their fulfilment. My own gift of faith has been largely energised by prophetic words. I have a firm faith in certain, specific things, but I find it difficult to have faith on anything God has not spoken to me about.

4. Being in God's presence

This is slightly different from knowing God. You can know God but not spend time in His presence. But each time you time spend in God's presence, the gift of faith is released into your life.

FAITH AND HEALING

One problem we have in the Charismatic church is that many attempt to operate all the gifts through faith, when in fact, the gift of faith is just one of the nine gifts.

Often, we talk about faith healers, which implies that it is faith that brings healing. But it is a lot better to operate through the gifts of healings when it comes to healing.

Yet, it seems undeniable that in many instances, it is faith that brought healing, at least in the Gospels. And obviously, we need faith for the gifts of healings to operate.

But there is a remarkable shift from the Gospels to Acts.

In times of the Gospels, Jesus sent the apostles in His *delegated* authority. The disciples had not yet been baptised in the Holy Spirit. That is why the healing stories of the Gospels might not be as useful model for healing ministry as many tend to believe.

Jesus said to His disciples in John 16:7, the night before His crucifixion,

> "Nevertheless I tell you the truth. It is to your advantage that
> I go away; for if I do not go away, the Helper will not come
> to you; but if I depart, I will send Him to you."

Can you see what a difference the Holy Spirit brings? No more are the disciples depending on the delegated authority of Jesus; now they are carrying the Holy Spirit, who has all the authority.

There is a difference in the dynamics between the Spirit-filled Church and the band of disciples that only had the delegated authority of the *name* of Jesus.

The disciples who trusted in the name of Jesus could cast out demons only through fasting and prayer; the disciples filled with the Spirit could cast out demons straight away in the power of the Spirit.

If you watch any horror films about exorcisms, you will soon realise that all the priests have in those films is the name of Jesus. It still has authority, but not at the level of a Spirit-filled believer.

We can see the difference clearly in Acts.

When Peter prays for the lame man in Acts 3:6, he says,

> "In the name of Jesus Christ of Nazareth, rise up and walk."

Many years later, when Paul prays for the cripple who had never walked in Acts 14:9, he says, "Stand up straight on your feet!" And he does. Paul doesn't even refer to the name of Jesus. He is walking in the power of the Holy Spirit and exercising the authority that the Holy Spirit has given to him in that situation.

In the Gospels, exorcists other than disciples cast out demons in the name of Jesus. These people hadn't been filled with the Holy Spirit, and yet the name of Jesus was powerful enough to cast demons out.

There is an enormous power in the name of Jesus alone, but our faith goes further when we are filled with the Holy Spirit.

Unfortunately, much of the faith in the Body of Christ today is only knowledge-based, without the anointing of the Holy Spirit, and without the gift of faith. But when we begin to move in the gift of faith, it is no more our faith, but the faith of God, that is moving through us. And God has unlimited resources of faith.

Faith hits at the heart of the enemy's kingdom, destroying fear and unbelief. Energised by the power of God, it believes the impossible. But this faith is not random; it is *focused*. It only believes in the promises of God.

In the Kingdom of God, there is no faith that is independent of God's Word or His Spirit.

At the heart of the gift of faith is an unshakable trust in God's goodness and trustworthiness that flows from the very presence of God. Deep faith rises only from knowing God.

Your faith increases through testing, and it is through testing that God can stretch the capacity of your faith.

New wine needs new wineskins, and nowhere is it more applicable than when it comes to faith. The Holy Spirit gives the gift of faith, but for that faith to stay and increase in us, our capacity to believe—against all evidence—must be increased.

Paul expresses that faith in 2 Corinthians 4:7-14,

> But we have this treasure in jars of clay to show that this all-surpassing power is from God and not from us. We are hard pressed on every side, but not crushed; perplexed, but not in despair; persecuted, but not abandoned; struck down, but not destroyed. We always carry around in our body the death of Jesus, so that the life of Jesus may also be revealed in our

body. For we who are alive are always being given over to death for Jesus' sake, so that his life may also be revealed in our mortal body. So then, death is at work in us, but life is at work in you.

It is written: "I believed; therefore I have spoken." Since we have that same spirit of faith, we also believe and therefore speak, because we know that the one who raised the Lord Jesus from the dead will also raise us with Jesus and present us with you to himself.

Paul writes here about the spirit of faith. Can you see how the gift of faith is very different from the gift of working miracles and healing?

Faith often operates regardless of a lack of visible evidence; the gifts of healings and the working of miracles produce immediate results. Often, the gift of faith helps us through times of suffering and trials. It is the greatest gift for times of great difficulties.

1 Peter 1:6-9 says,

> In all this you greatly rejoice, though now for a little while you may have had to suffer grief in all kinds of trials. These have come so that the proven genuineness of your faith—of greater worth than gold, which perishes even though refined by fire—may result in praise, glory and honor when Jesus Christ is revealed. Though you have not seen him, you love him; and even though you do not see him now, you believe in him and are filled with an inexpressible and glorious joy, for you are receiving the end result of your faith, the salvation of your souls.

The gift of faith can work in so many different ways in our life, but it always gets its power from God. It is a great protector against fear and attacks from the enemy.

In Acts 23, Paul has been arrested in Jerusalem.

> But the following night the Lord stood by him and said, "Be of good cheer, Paul; for as you have testified for Me in Jerusalem, so you must also bear witness at Rome." (Acts 23:11)

This revelation releases faith in Paul's life to appeal to Caesar. It gives him faith to get through a shipwreck without losing anyone aboard. Paul knows that no matter what happens, he will make it alive to Rome—somehow—simply, because God has promised it.

If you never put your life on the line, you will never reap the reward of faith, and your faith will never grow. The testing of our faith can be tough, and many lose hope in the process.

The gift of faith is there to sustain you, until you receive what God has promised to you—both in this age and in heaven.

We need to put the gift of faith back into its place as one of the nine spiritual gifts. It is a vital gift, but rather than releasing instant miracles, its main purpose is to get us through difficult times and times of testing, so that God's purposes will be released through our lives.

13

WORKING MIRACLES

If you follow any media produced by the Charismatic church at all, you will soon hear stories of gold dust descending on people from heaven, miraculous gold teeth and diamonds appearing out of thin air, and of angel feathers and miracle oil landing on people. Some people will even tell you that they have been teleported around the world! One well-known Charismatic 'miracle worker' sells handkerchiefs that are supposedly anointed with oil that his body has generated.

Or if you are a Catholic, you will have heard stories about stigmata and weeping statues of Mary, and many miracles taking place around relics.

What should we make of these stories? Are these what the Bible calls signs? Are these the signs of the gift of working miracles? Or are they just made-up stories? In fact, what is a miracle?

One of the problems we face is that not everything that looks like a miracle actually is one. Our world is full of illusionists and magicians, and sometimes, I wonder how much of that kind of activity has seeped into our churches. With most of the miracle stories circulating around, there is no evidence independent from the storyteller that these events actually took place. Now, this is perfectly fine with visionary experiences, but here we are talking about events that should somehow alter the material world and leave at least some traces.

So, we hear about supernaturally created diamonds and gold dust, but no one is actually able to reproduce any of these diamonds for inspection. But I tell you, if a God-given diamond would land on my feet from heaven, I wouldn't sell it but keep it for the rest of my life! Yet no one seems to be in possession of these diamonds afterwards, so that we could inspect them.

When it comes to many Charismatic 'miracle workers', there is a remarkable similarity with the proponents of Gnosticism, when it comes to the type of Christ they claim to serve.

The *Gnostic Gospels* are a collection of over fifty ancient texts based upon the teachings of several spiritual leaders, which were written from the 2nd to the 4th century. These gospels are not part of the standard Biblical canon, but they are part of what is called the New Testament Apocrypha. There is a diversity of reasons for the Church Fathers rejecting them as non-authentic or false gospels.

The *Infancy Gospel of Thomas* is a falsely attributed gospel about the childhood of Jesus that is believed to be from the 2nd century. It was part of a popular genre of work, written to satisfy a hunger among early Christians for more miraculous and anecdotal stories of the childhood of Jesus than the Gospel of Luke provided.

In the *Infancy Gospel of Thomas* Jesus appears like a magician.

> This little child Jesus when he was five years old was playing at the ford of a brook: and he gathered together the waters that flowed there into pools, and made them straightway clean, and commanded them by his word alone. And having made soft clay, he fashioned thereof twelve sparrows. And it was the Sabbath when he did these things (or made them). And there were also many other little children playing with him.
>
> And a certain Jew when he saw what Jesus did, playing upon the Sabbath day, departed straightway and told his father Joseph: "Lo, thy child is at the brook, and he hath taken clay and fashioned twelve little birds, and hath polluted the Sabbath day." And Joseph came to the place and saw: and cried out to him, saying: "Wherefore doest thou these things on the Sabbath, which it is not lawful to do?"
>
> But Jesus clapped his hands together and cried out to the sparrows and said to them: "Go!"

And the sparrows took their flight and went away chirping. And when the Jews saw it they were amazed, and departed and told their chief men that which they had seen Jesus do.

In the Gnostic Gospels Jesus performs miracles just because He can, often to show off. Similarly, much of the Charismatic world wants to perform miracles simply to show off and to create excitement.

Paul writes in 1 Corinthians 4:18-20,

Now some are puffed up, as though I were not coming to you. But I will come to you shortly, if the Lord wills, and I will know, not the word of those who are puffed up, but the power. For the kingdom of God is not in word but in power.

The 'miracle workers' talk a lot about power—on stage—and some have taken their talk about power to the streets, recording their miraculous works on video—thereby following the illusionists, who took their illusions from stage to the streets before them.

But how are these people in real life? I mean not on stage and not performing. I know many Christian ministers who are 'miracle workers' on stage but have zero power off stage. I also know many Christians who are nobodies in the eyes of the Church, but if anyone asks them to pray in the real life, they rise up to the challenge, and their prayer brings a real transformation.

One of the first things I do when I hear about a new miracle worker entering the Charismatic market is to have a look at their theology. What do they actually teach? If their teaching is based on, for example, the ability of man's mind to bend reality, it is not much for them to believe in man's ability to bend the truth and facts.

WHAT ARE MIRACLES?

Years ago, in Finland, I drove an old car along the motorway and lost control of it. The car began to spin, and it hit the road railing on the other side of the road. This was fortunate, as the railing that was only used in that curve obstructed me from rolling down the hill and hitting the many large trees of the forest below. The car bounced from the railing and collided with the side of a car approaching from the opposite direction. Again, that was fortunate, as had the car collided with the front of the other car, both its driver and myself would have been dead. The impact of the collision made my car do a somersault, after which it spun on the road. When the car stopped, I was hanging from the seatbelt upside down.

I saw some blood on the steering wheel and what was left of the windscreen in front of me. I made my way out of the car and saw how the fuel had started to leak from the tank. I had blocked all the traffic, and by now, there were other drivers coming out of their cars. They came to help me. I lay there, on the road, relieved to be alive, and waited for an ambulance.

The firemen came first. The first one came to me, and leaned over me. He said,

> It is a miracle that you are alive.

On that road, there was only one route my car could take for me to stay alive after I lost control. But that route was not straightforward at all, as the car had to bounce off the railing at exactly the right time to hit the side of the other car—but not the front. And without colliding with the other car, my car might have somersaulted over the railing on the other side and hit one of the large rocks or trees.

This was one of the turning points in my life. I realised that the fact I had survived the crash might mean that my life had a higher purpose.

But was my fortunate escape really a miracle? And even if God was involved, could I legitimately call this a miracle? Couldn't this be simply attributed to luck?

Before moving on, there are two things to consider. First of all, the fireman must have seen hundreds of car wrecks in his life. He was a specialist. If you went to a doctor and he said that your survival was a miracle, would you believe it?

Secondly, there is an interesting detail about the crash. I was nearly completely uninjured—apart from a deep wound on my left elbow that was stitched at the hospital. It healed, but it left a visible, ugly scar. In my book *Five Movements: Winning the Battle for Your Prophetic Gift*

I tell about forty ways God used to teach me about the prophetic to lead me together with my wife. My wife has a similar scar on her left elbow, in a nearly identical location—a result of a rather different accident. I have always thought that we were marked to be together.

The Gospel of John refers to miracles as signs, and to me, this was a sign that my life had a purpose. And to me, the scar is a sign of two things—the miracle of survival and the miracle of God bringing me together with my wife—for a purpose.

But here the miracle is dependent on the vantage point. My vantage point is God's foreknowledge and His ability to deliver exactly what He has promised. Yet, someone else could look at it and not see a miracle at all. And the consensus of the secular world is that the area for miracles keeps on shrinking, as we know scientifically more and more about the universe. The prevailing, secular view is that there are no miracles, but only natural events that haven't been explained yet.

But in this chapter we are talking about the gift of working miracles. I didn't perform a miracle at all; I was the object of it. But did my father work a miracle, as God had shown him two weeks earlier that I would be in an accident, and he had been praying for my safety ever since?

RATIONALISM AND MIRACLES

Apart from the Pentecostals and Charismatics, the rest of the Protestant church is often rather sceptical when it comes to the gift of working miracles, although it is less sceptical when it comes to God's ability to perform miracles.

Without realising it, most Christians in the West are victims of the rationalistic philosophy. According to the rationalistic worldview, man can understand the universe by beginning from himself, without any recourse to outside knowledge, specifically outside knowledge or revelation from God.[1]

This development of the scientific worldview was mirrored in the development of liberal theology. Francis A Schaeffer, an American theologian and philosopher, writes,

Where did liberal theology stand in that same period? As I mentioned, liberal theology simply echoed the surrounding rationalistic consensus. In this period the liberal theologians were also optimistic. They believed on the basis of rationalistic scholarship that they could find the historical Jesus while eliminating the supernatural from the biblical account.

They believed that they could take reason, apply it to the Bible, and come up with the historical Jesus while getting rid of the supernatural element they found in the biblical account. By presupposition they were naturalists, and the supernatural made them uncomfortable. But notice that basically they were simply following exactly that which the secular thinkers had already said.[2]

In the last few hundred years miracles have been largely pushed out from any academic theological work. What is tragic is that the scientific rationalists have long since confessed that their project of attempting to explain the world completely through rational laws has failed, but theology has largely failed to respond to that.

In most universities, theology is taught as one of the many ways of seeking partial truths. This is still part of the rationalist project. Theology might be acceptable, but not if it ventures into the area of hard sciences like physics or biology.

But in recent years, our scientific understanding has been changing.

Rev Adrian Low, Emeritus Professor of Computer Education at Staffordshire University and Assistant Curate of Abbots Bromley, Blithfield, Colton, Cowlick, and Great Haywood, writes in 'When God plays biased dice', a fascinating article in *Church Times* of 31st July 2015 about the quantum physics and the inbuilt randomness in every fundamental particle of the universe.

Low writes,

> Suppose, however, that what Einstein saw as an annoying randomness is actually where God is constantly at work in the world: God influencing the smallest of everything . . .
>
> What if the immensity of God is that every fundamental particle, everywhere, is in God's hands, and that the laws

that self-constrain God are not merely Newton's or Einstein's equations, but primarily are the statistics of particle movement—statistics that provide God with a means, designed into nature, to interact with the world?[3]

Paul saw something similar but through revelation knowledge. He writes in Colossians 1:17 (NLV):

> Christ was before all things. All things are held together by Him.

Quantum physics gives us the scientific model of the universe where "the ground of our being" can at least in principle be sustained by God, and where He has not been shut out from the universe He has created. Low adds,

> The probability that a big lump of matter will relocate a significant distance is almost zero, but not zero; it is very rare indeed—the bigger the lump, and the further the distance, the rarer it is. It is like an army of soldiers on the parade ground each being told to move in a random direction, and all of them choosing to move in the same direction, so that the whole army moves.[4]

Low continues,

> So, feeding five thousand, healing broken cells, stilling a storm, and turning water into wine are not impossible in term of physics: they are just extraordinarily rare."[5]

He concludes,

> But, if you are God, with a handle on the universe of particles, you have the opportunity to play that rare-moment card when you choose.[6]

According to Low, frequent huge miracles would undermine the predictability too much, and it's better to run with many small miracles. But whether God produces miracles through particle design or not is irrelevant to us. What is important is to understand, that according to physics, material miracles aren't actually scientifically impossible, simply because our universe might not be as closed a system as we think it is.

But this conversation about miracles is by no means new. Saint Augustine writes in the early 5th century in *The City of God*:

> Why, they say, are those miracles, which you affirm were worked formerly, worked no longer? I might, indeed, reply that miracles were necessary before the world believed, in order that it might believe . . . But they make these objections for the sole purpose of insinuating that even these former miracles were never worked.[7]

Then he proceeds to list a series of healings and exorcisms that appear well documented, some of which he has personally witnessed to.

WORKING OF MIRACLES IN THE GOSPELS

In the Gospel of John, the miracles are referred to as "signs", with an idea that they are witnessing to the divinity of Jesus.

The theology of the Signs and Wonders movement has been built on that with an idea that the signs and wonders are a necessary witness for the authenticity of the gospel. And that is how the miracle workers justify the weirdest of signs.

"It is all there to show that there is a supernatural God", they say.

We need to be careful about this. As we have seen throughout the book, not everything that is supernatural is automatically from God.

Jesus says in Matthew 24:24,

> "For false christs and false prophets will rise and show great signs and wonders to deceive, if possible, even the elect."

So, we can see that signs and wonders aren't automatically a sign that God is working.

When we assess miracle workers, we need to look at three things: the teaching and doctrine of the miracle worker, their lifestyle, and the presence of God in their ministry, or the lack of it. For example, John Alexander Dowie, whom the whole teaching about sicknesses being demons originates from, had no problem with teaching at Masonic Halls, and eventually, he declared that he was the returning biblical Elijah.[8]

John Alexander Dowie meets all the signs of a false prophet, yet many Christians respect him as an authentic prophet of God.

It seems that we are capable of ignoring all the warnings given in Scripture when someone is offering us what we want.

The Gospels describe three kinds of miracles performed by Jesus: exorcisms, healings, and wonders that affect the natural world.

The Gospel of John describes miracles as signs that are meant to help us believe. But these signs are not something that by themselves should be adequate for believing.

There is a huge misunderstanding in the Charismatic church regarding the purpose of miracles. Many preach that we should believe in miracles—often against all evidence—because we believe in Jesus.

But in the New Testament it was the other way around—people believed in Jesus because they saw the miracles.

John 1:43-50 tells the story about Jesus meeting Nathanael for the fist time.

> The following day Jesus wanted to go to Galilee, and He found Philip and said to him, "Follow Me." Now Philip was from Bethsaida, the city of Andrew and Peter. Philip found Nathanael and said to him, "We have found Him of whom Moses in the law, and also the prophets, wrote—Jesus of Nazareth, the son of Joseph." And Nathanael said to him, "Can anything good come out of Nazareth?" Philip said to him, "Come and see."
>
> Jesus saw Nathanael coming toward Him, and said of him, "Behold, an Israelite indeed, in whom is no deceit!" Nathanael said to Him, "How do You know me?"
>
> Jesus answered and said to him, "Before Philip called you, when you were under the fig tree, I saw you."
>
> Nathanael answered and said to Him, "Rabbi, You are the Son of God! You are the King of Israel!"

> Jesus answered and said to him, "Because I said to you, 'I saw you under the fig tree,' do you believe? You will see greater things than these." And He said to him, "Most assuredly, I say to you, hereafter you shall see heaven open, and the angels of God ascending and descending upon the Son of Man."

Jesus seems to be saying that Nathanael has believed in Him because of a small miracle, but that he would be seeing much larger ones.

After Jesus turns water into wine, it says,

> This beginning of signs Jesus did in Cana of Galilee, and manifested His glory; and His disciples believed in Him. (John 2:11)

So, perhaps the miracles that matter in your life are the ones where the Lordship of Jesus is manifested to you personally.

Only a small number of wedding guests would have actually witnessed this miracle—it was only the closest to Jesus who believed in Him, because they saw Him perform the miracle.

Professor Christopher D. Marshall sees miracles similar to parables.

> How can Mark use the miracles to convey a challenge to faith, yet remain so equivocal with respect to the effect of miracles on those who witness them? The key to this lies in the observation that in Mark the miracles display a markedly similar character to the parables. The miracles are to Jesus' actions what the parables are to his teaching: messages or puzzles that require interpretation.[9]

Matthew 13:10-15 says about the purpose of parables.

> And the disciples came and said to Him, "Why do You speak to them in parables?" He answered and said to them, "Because it has been given to you to know the mysteries of the kingdom of heaven, but to them it has not been given. For whoever has, to him more will be given, and he will have abundance; but whoever does not have, even what he has

will be taken away from him. Therefore I speak to them in parables, because seeing they do not see, and hearing they do not hear, nor do they understand. And in them the prophecy of Isaiah is fulfilled, which says:

'Hearing you will hear and shall not understand, and seeing you will see and not perceive; for the hearts of this people have grown dull. Their ears are hard of hearing, and their eyes they have closed, lest they should see with their eyes and hear with their ears, lest they should understand with their hearts and turn, so that I should heal them.'"

So, according to Jesus, parables are like judgments. They separate those who are open to God from those who are not. It seems there is something similar about miracles. They are also judgments.

Paradoxically, it seems that the seasons of revival we often celebrate in the Charismatic church are also judgments. I have experienced three major revivals in my lifetime, and what strikes me is that there is always a great falling away after a revival, even if that falling away might seem impossible during the revival. It is as if through a miracle or a revival God was calling Christians closer to Him, to follow Him more unconditionally than ever before, and He was using miracles and revivals to force us to make a decision. I have seen that when God manifests Himself supernaturally in our lives, it will always take us either closer to Him or further away from Him.

Matthew 11:2—24 is very clear about this.

Then He began to rebuke the cities in which most of His mighty works had been done, because they did not repent: "Woe to you, Chorazin! Woe to you, Bethsaida! For if the mighty works which were done in you had been done in Tyre and Sidon, they would have repented long ago in sackcloth and ashes. But I say to you, it will be more tolerable for Tyre and Sidon in the day of judgment than for you. And you, Capernaum, who are exalted to heaven, will be brought down to Hades; for if the mighty works which were done in you had been done in Sodom, it would have remained until this day. But I say to you that it shall be more tolerable for the land of Sodom in the day of judgment than for you."

We can see that if miracles don't bring repentance, they will bring a harsher judgment. Sometimes, I wonder if God is *withholding* revivals and miracles from us in His grace, as He knows we are not ready for repentance, and He wants to save us from judgment.

MIRACLES OF PROVISION AND NATURE

If you look at the miracles affecting the natural world in the Gospels, one thing stands out—miracles of provision.

Mark 8:13-21 says,

> And He left them, and getting into the boat again, departed to the other side. Now the disciples had forgotten to take bread, and they did not have more than one loaf with them in the boat.
>
> Then He charged them, saying, "Take heed, beware of the leaven of the Pharisees and the leaven of Herod." And they reasoned among themselves, saying, "It is because we have no bread."
>
> But Jesus, being aware of it, said to them, "Why do you reason because you have no bread? Do you not yet perceive nor understand? Is your heart still hardened? Having eyes, do you not see? And having ears, do you not hear? And do you not remember? When I broke the five loaves for the five thousand, how many baskets full of fragments did you take up?"
>
> They said to Him, "Twelve."
>
> "Also, when I broke the seven for the four thousand, how many large baskets full of fragments did you take up?"
>
> And they said, "Seven."
>
> So He said to them, "How *is it* you do not understand?"

The disciples still didn't understand the main purpose of the miracle of Jesus feeding the five thousand: that the disciples would believe in God's ability to provide in all circumstances.

The feeding of the five thousand and the turning of water into wine were all about demonstrating Jesus' Lordship over the earth and His ability to provide for us.

This is what Jesus meant when He said that if we seek the Kingdom of God, all things would be added to us. Sometimes, following Jesus calls for abandoning normal ways of provision, and that is exactly what the disciples would have to do after the Pentecost, when they started spreading the Gospel to all nations.

There would come a time when they all would be in need of miracles, and those miracles would take a different shape and form depending on their circumstances.

When Peter escapes from prison in Acts 12 with the help on an angel, it is an escape provided miraculously.

There is another type of miracle, which is also linked to nature. These types of miracles are often ambiguous, and they rarely convince a sceptic.

Some years ago, there was a Passion play at Trafalgar Square in London on Easter Friday. Thousands of people were gathered there. But it was a really rainy day, and it rained really hard most of the afternoon. Thousands of us must have been praying, and five minutes before the play started, the rain stopped, and it began to rain only minutes after the play had finished over an hour later. What was fascinating was that there was a circular spot of clear, blue sky just above Trafalgar Square, but the rest of the London skyline was covered in dark rain clouds, and there was a heavy downpour in most parts of London. My friends were running an event just a few miles away at the same time, and heavens had opened and completely flooded their event.

Was that a miracle? I'd definitely like to think so. But if a sceptic would disagree, I don't have a problem with that. But the absence of rain for the duration of the play certainly helped many people to see a wonderful presentation of the gospel.

Another time, we were at the Verona Arena in Italy to watch an open-air opera. My wife had been dreaming about being there for a long time, and we had finally made it to Verona, but unfortunately, we had booked our non-refundable tickets for an evening when it started to rain in the beginning of the opera. As it is an outdoor arena and the instruments the orchestra uses are invaluable, the show can get cancelled even if it rains a few drops.

The first part stopped and restarted a few times, as it began to rain heavily, and the orchestra kept on leaving and returning with their instruments when the rain started and stopped. We began to pray, as they were considering cancelling the show altogether. But then the rain stopped altogether. The second and third part played uninterrupted. But all around the arena, there were hundreds of lightning strikes, as the thunderstorm ravaged the surrounding area, but stayed away from directly above the arena. It was a bit like what we saw in Trafalgar Square but late at night, with the storm avoiding the arena. But the nearest lighting strikes kept on hitting the ground less than a mile away.

Was that a miracle? I'd like to think so. But hundreds of people in that place would have considered themselves simply fortunate—or who knows, maybe they were also praying with us for the show to be able to go on!

EXORCISM

The working of the miracles in the Bible included exorcism. What complicates our understanding is that, at the time of writing of the Gospels and the epistles, the Greek word *dunamis* (powers) referred to three things: healings, miracles and exorcism.[10]

So, we can't be completely certain whether the grouping of healing, miracles and exorcism is simply a result of the way the ancient Greek language worked rather than anything else.

Paul hardly refers to exorcism, perhaps because he writes to the churches, and to him, demonic beings operate mainly as external forces of principalities and powers, as God has redeemed His people from internal oppression—possession by demons—through the work of the cross.

So, most of exorcism in the New Testament takes place either in the Gospels or in Acts, as the apostles begin to spread the gospel.

Luke 11:14-22 says,

> And He was casting out a demon, and it was mute. So it was, when the demon had gone out, that the mute spoke; and the multitudes marveled. But some of them said, "He

casts out demons by Beelzebub, the ruler of the demons." Others, testing Him, sought from Him a sign from heaven. But He, knowing their thoughts, said to them:

"Every kingdom divided against itself is brought to desolation, and a house divided against a house falls. If Satan also is divided against himself, how will his kingdom stand? Because you say I cast out demons by Beelzebub. And if I cast out demons by Beelzebub, by whom do your sons cast them out? Therefore they will be your judges. But if I cast out demons with the finger of God, surely the kingdom of God has come upon you. When a strong man, fully armed, guards his own palace, his goods are in peace. But when a stronger than he comes upon him and overcomes him, he takes from him all his armor in which he trusted, and divides his spoils."

Exorcism demonstrates that the Kingdom of God is more powerful than Satan's kingdom. We need to know that; otherwise we won't have the courage to follow Jesus unconditionally.

Some years ago, I had a colleague at work. Her son had become a heroin addict, and she was really worried about her. We started meeting up with our work group and prayed for him regularly. I remember one time when the Holy Spirit led us to cast out demonic powers from his life.

Not soon after, drug dealers came after him and threatened to smash his knees, as he owed them money. He was forced to leave the city and go to rehab, where his life was turned around. He rediscovered his faith, graduated from university and got married.

Our little group of prayer warriors, led by a mother who felt love for her son, raided the palace of the enemy and took the spoils!

But we can see here how all working of the miracles happens through prayer or proclamation in the power of the Holy Spirit.

What is interesting about exorcism and spiritual warfare that is closely linked to it is that we can command the enemy to leave. There is not a single verse in the Bible where we can command God or the angels, but in the power of the Holy Spirit, we can command the enemy to leave.

Psalm 91:11-12 says,

> For He shall give His angels charge over you, to keep you in all your ways. In their hands they shall bear you up, lest you dash your foot against a stone.

Some Charismatic ministers claim that we can command the angels, but that is not the case. Instead, it is God who commands the angels, as they are His servants, but thankfully, He often commands them to serve us!

MIRACULOUS HEALINGS

There is an overlap between the gifts of healing and the gift of working miracles. As we have seen, the Gospels use the same Greek word for healings and miracles.

It is hard to say much more about this, although some would probably reserve the more spectacular healings to the area of the gift of working miracles. At least, it would be fair to say that resurrecting the dead in the New Testament belongs to the area of the gift of working miracles.

Acts 20:7-12 says,

> Now on the first day of the week, when the disciples came together to break bread, Paul, ready to depart the next day, spoke to them and continued his message until midnight. There were many lamps in the upper room where they were gathered together. And in a window sat a certain young man named Eutychus, who was sinking into a deep sleep. He was overcome by sleep; and as Paul continued speaking, he fell down from the third story and was taken up dead.
>
> But Paul went down, fell on him, and embracing him said, "Do not trouble yourselves, for his life is in him." Now when he had come up, had broken bread and eaten, and talked a long while, even till daybreak, he departed. And they brought the young man in alive, and they were not a little comforted.

It is comforting to know that even Paul found it impossible to keep everyone in the congregation awake! But even at that moment, a sceptic could have said that it was a natural recovery.

Some years ago we started to pray for a couple that had been trying to get a baby for seven years. We prayed for them for quite a while, until they got their first baby. And not soon after, they got their second baby! It would have been their prayers that would have touched God's heart, but because of us joining them in prayer, they named the second baby boy after me. As far as they were concerned, their babies were miracle babies.

One of the miracles that is repeated in the Bible is the barren woman having children, as God hears the prayers of the parents.

Because of the sceptics, many Charismatics have begun to prophesy about creative miracles—of incontestable proofs of God's miraculous healing power.

In their view of the Kingdom, as the Kingdom keeps on coming, we should get to the point where no one would be able to contest God's power and existence. So, they prophesy about a time when people will grow organs, limbs, and so on, and some even say that these things are already happening.

But if you follow these stories closely, it seems that these things always happen in another country and, definitely, no one ever has any visual proof. I find it impossible to believe that with hundreds of stories, there is never any visual proof of the existence of these creative miracles.

Now, I am not saying that they couldn't theoretically happen. I am not even saying that they have never happened. I am not saying that they are not happening right now. What I am saying is that most of these stories aren't true.

But miraculous healings don't automatically lead to people coming to faith. As we have seen, they can also lead to a harsher judgment.

Mark 6:1-6 says,

> Then He went out from there and came to His own country, and His disciples followed Him. And when the Sabbath

had come, He began to teach in the synagogue. And many hearing Him were astonished, saying,

"Where did this Man get these things? And what wisdom is this which is given to Him, that such mighty works are performed by His hands! Is this not the carpenter, the Son of Mary, and brother of James, Joses, Judas, and Simon? And are not His sisters here with us?"

So they were offended at Him. But Jesus said to them, "A prophet is not without honor except in his own country, among his own relatives, and in his own house." Now He could do no mighty work there, except that He laid His hands on a few sick people and healed them. And He marveled because of their unbelief. Then He went about the villages in a circuit, teaching.

The neighbours of Jesus witnessed to some of the miracles, the Pharisees witnessed to many of them, but neither group believed in Jesus. And if they found it difficult to believe that He was a prophet of God, they would have found it impossible to believe that He is the Son of God.

So, if even with Jesus there were no incontestable miracles that caused all people to believe in God, will we fare any better?

In Luke 16:19-31, Jesus tells a parable about a rich man and a poor man, who used to beg at the rich man's gate, entering the afterlife with the rich man in hell and the poor man in paradise. In the parable, the rich man begs Abraham to send the poor man to warn his brothers, but Abraham says,

> "If they do not hear Moses and the prophets, neither will they be persuaded though one rise from the dead." (Luke 16:31)

COMING OF THE KINGDOM

Isaiah 35:4-6 prophesies,

> Say to those who are fearful-hearted, "Be strong, do not fear! Behold, your God will come with vengeance, with the recompense of God; He will come and save you." Then the

eyes of the blind shall be opened, and the ears of the deaf shall be unstopped. Then the lame shall leap like a deer, and the tongue of the dumb sing. For waters shall burst forth in the wilderness, and streams in the desert.

This is a Messianic prophecy, and we can see how miracles signal the coming of the Kingdom.

But this coming of the Kingdom today must be interpreted in the context of the early church, as it is the book of Acts that demonstrates what the coming of the Kingdom means. And regardless of the coming of the Kingdom and the miracles, most of the apostles were still martyred.

The book of Acts doesn't offer us a dominionist coming of the Kingdom that many preach today, seeking to deliver to us miracles that can't be questioned.

There is a warning to the dominionist church, whose archetype is the church in Rome, in Revelation 17.

Revelation 17:1-2 says,

> Then one of the seven angels who had the seven bowls came and talked with me, saying to me, "Come, I will show you the judgment of the great harlot who sits on many waters, with whom the kings of the earth committed fornication, and the inhabitants of the earth were made drunk with the wine of her fornication."

The verse 18 gives us the location of the harlot.

> And the woman whom you saw is that great city which reigns over the kings of the earth.

At the time, it was the city of Rome that ruled over the kings of the earth. The prostitute in the Old Testament prophetic language is Israel. The prostitute in the New Testament language is the Church.

John is greatly astonished, as he is shown a church in Rome that, rather than being persecuted, is now in power and prostituting all that Jesus stood for with the kings. And that harlot church would be the mother of all prostitutes, so there would be similar churches all across the world.

The book of Revelation gives a clear prophecy about the Church prostituting with the kings for power that has already come to pass, and we shouldn't take it lightly.

Many Charismatics today expect the miraculous to lead to the takeover of the world by the Church in this age. But as the book of Revelation shows to us, the 'takeover of the world' by the Church often leads to prostituting the Church.

MIRACLES IN REVIVAL ATMOSPHERE

Many Christians feel apprehensive about the stage managing miracle workers and hence they talk about revival atmosphere, where God will move spontaneously, as long as we create that atmosphere.

Hence if God is being worshipped, the Holy Spirit might just begin to move. In a sense, this goes back to the experience of the First Pentecost and Azusa Street.

What is good is that this usually takes some of the focus away from the Charismatic leader, even if these sessions are usually managed by the Charismatic leaders, so they don't have the same sense of idolatry than events focusing on the gifts of the leaders.

But we can't say that this is the gift of working miracles, because the gift of working miracles seems to have been given to individuals.

Also, there is a problem with these kinds of events that we need to tackle. Allow me to be frank here. I came to Kensington Temple in London for the first time in August 1994, when the leaders of the church had just imported the Father's Blessing from Toronto.

It was a month full of meetings with church seeking God nearly every weeknight. I had no idea about this going on there, and I didn't even know anything about Kensington Temple, but a friend of mine had recommended me to visit there.

It was certainly a miraculous visit. Senior Minister of Kensington Temple, Colin Dye, had a word of knowledge about a young Finnish man, and I came forward. He blessed me to the ministry of their church over five years before I actually joined their team, and I would work over sixteen years in his team. To me, what happened there was definitely a move of God. But that doesn't mean that all the phenomena linked to that move would definitely be from God.

In 1 Samuel 19, King Saul is seeking David to kill him. The Holy Spirit has already departed from him, and he had been disturbed by an evil spirit. 1 Samuel 19:22-24 tells how Saul comes to Naioth in Ramah.

> And *someone* said, "Indeed *they are* at Naioth in Ramah." So he went there to Naioth in Ramah. Then the Spirit of God was upon him also, and he went on and prophesied until he came to Naioth in Ramah. And he also stripped off his clothes and prophesied before Samuel in like manner, and lay down naked all that day and all that night. Therefore they say, "Is Saul also among the prophets?"

Saul's heart was not right with God, and his reaction to the Spirit of God being upon him—think about this as a revival atmosphere—was impure. This is the precise problem with the revival atmosphere. Not everything that takes place in a revival atmosphere is from God. Much of that is the reaction of soul, and we can see how both Paul and John write about demonic spirits manifesting in their public meetings, and tell us how to discern them.

The problem of the Charismatic church is that we assume that everything that seems supernatural or miraculous that happens in our meetings is from God. But that is not the case. We still need discernment and the gift of discerning spirits to know what is really going on.

IS IT AN APOSTOLIC GIFT?

In Acts 19 the apostle Paul was at Ephesus.

> Now God worked unusual miracles by the hands of Paul, so that even handkerchiefs or aprons were brought from his body to the sick, and the diseases left them and the evil spirits went out of them. (Acts 19:11-12)

We can see the two elements of healing and exorcism strongly linked to miracles here. We can also see how many try to copy these unique events as methods today.

Paul writes in 2 Corinthians 12:12,

> Truly the signs of an apostle were accomplished among you with all perseverance, in signs and wonders and mighty deeds.

So, we can see how the working of miracles is an apostolic gift, although it is not limited to the apostles.

But what is striking about the miracles in the Bible is that they are not multipliable. From Genesis to the book of Revelation, each miracle is a unique gift from God. Yet, there are some similarities and we can see certain patterns, as the Gospel writers have testified.

But this uniqueness defies any classification. In one sense, what the Bible is saying is that what miracles include is everything that you can think of—if you need it to fulfil God's purposes.

We can see Daniel not eaten by the lions in the lions' den. That is a miracle. But I wouldn't want to try to repeat that! We can see his friends thrown in the furnace and protected by an angel. That is a miracle. But I wouldn't want to repeat that either.

And generations of Christians have tried to walk on water, without succeeding, not unless they are in a northern nation such as Finland, and the water has frozen.

In the Bible, miracles are something God releases when nothing else works, and they are needed to fulfil His plan.

There is not a singular show-off miracle in the Bible. They all have a purpose, and in most cases, they take place in times of extreme need.

Jesus is tempted by the devil in Matthew 4:1-11.

> Then Jesus was led up by the Spirit into the wilderness to be tempted by the devil. And when He had fasted forty days and forty nights, afterward He was hungry. Now when the tempter came to Him, he said, "If You are the Son of God,

command that these stones become bread." But He answered and said, "It is written, 'Man shall not live by bread alone, but by every word that proceeds from the mouth of God.'"

Then the devil took Him up into the holy city, set Him on the pinnacle of the temple, and said to Him, "If You are the Son of God, throw Yourself down. For it is written: 'He shall give His angels charge over you,' and, 'In their hands they shall bear you up, Lest you dash your foot against a stone.'"

Jesus said to him, "It is written again, 'You shall not tempt the Lord your God.'" Again, the devil took Him up on an exceedingly high mountain, and showed Him all the kingdoms of the world and their glory. And he said to Him, "All these things I will give You if You will fall down and worship me."

Then Jesus said to him, "Away with you, Satan! For it is written, 'You shall worship the Lord your God, and Him only you shall serve.'"

Then the devil left Him, and behold, angels came and ministered to Him.

The first two temptations were all about Jesus abusing His position as the Son. Throughout the Bible, we can see how God never released miracles unless there was a need, and the stories about exorcism, healings and miraculous provision are all about God meeting a need.

They take place in situations where nothing else will work. In the Old Testament, God reveals Himself to Moses as Yahweh—"I am", or "I will be who I will be".

Ultimately, God's will and purpose is the birthplace of all miracles.

God is saying through His name that He will be what we need Him to be at any given situation, so we don't need to worry, as long as we are with Him.

God is saying that He will meet any need that we will encounter on the way, as we follow Jesus, through being what He needs to be in order to fulfil His plan.

That is why every miracle is unique.

The gift of working miracles is where compassion and faith come together. We can all experience miracles in our lives, but those who are operating in the gift of working miracles are the ones who have so identified with the cause of the Kingdom that they are regularly in a need of a miracle hence God releases many miracles through their lives.

Many make the mistake in believing that if we can have one miracle, we should be able to manufacture them at will.

That is because we erroneously link miracles with faith. If we only had more faith, we would have more miracles. But according to Jesus, that is not the case. Jesus says in Luke 4:25-27,

> But I tell you truly, many widows were in Israel in the days of Elijah, when the heaven was shut up three years and six months, and there was a great famine throughout all the land; but to none of them was Elijah sent except to Zarephath, in the region of Sidon, to a woman who was a widow. And many lepers were in Israel in the time of Elisha the prophet, and none of them was cleansed except Naaman the Syrian."

It says that all in the synagogue, where Jesus spoke, were filled with wrath and wanted to kill Him, but He went His way.

Here Jesus refers to two types of miracles. The first one was a creative miracle, where the oil and the flour didn't run out in the widow's house, because she was hosting Elijah during drought. Elijah was hiding in the enemy's land in broad daylight, because Sidon was the mother city of Tyre, and Queen Jezebel was a princess of Sidon.

This was offensive to the Jews, as Jesus pointed out that God had performed a miracle to a foreigner. But she was integral to God's purposes, as Elijah was central to God's plan.

Naaman was a commander of the Syrian army, and he was healed of leprosy. He was yet another enemy of Israel. As a result, he found faith in the God of Israel.

Ultimately, miracles have less to do with faith and more to do with God's purposes. Miracles happen when we pray "Your Kingdom come, Your will be done", and line up our lives with that prayer.

The paradox is that faith school presents that this is the very prayer that prevents miracles from happening and seeks to build a factory for miracles by faith. But it is lining up with the Kingdom of God that will produce miracles. Each miracle will be individual and different, according to the needs of the Kingdom. Hence we have the apostle Paul who survives a shipwreck and is resurrected after stoning, but ends up being martyred in Rome. Late in Paul's life, he writes in 2 Timothy 4:6-8,

> For I am already being poured out as a drink offering, and the time of my departure is at hand. I have fought the good fight, I have finished the race, I have kept the faith. Finally, there is laid up for me the crown of righteousness, which the Lord, the righteous Judge, will give to me on that Day, and not to me only but also to all who have loved His appearing.

Many miracles had kept Paul in the fight and in the race, but now he was finishing it. God was about to lift His protection over Paul's physical life, so that he would be able to experience the greatest miracle of them all, the resurrection. But the way to the resurrection would go through an execution.

Today, our faith has become hopelessly this-worldly, and many are attempting to build a paradise on earth.

But Hebrews 13:14 says,

> For here we have no continuing city, but we seek the one to come.

The miracles God gives to us are part of His plan for eternity, and He is ready to release them as long as we line up with His plan.

Ultimately, what will release miracles is *love* that derives its energy from the Holy Spirit. That is why the working of miracles is releasing *supernatural* love.

14

FINISHING WELL

I have worked in a large Pentecostal church for over sixteen years and been involved in Pentecostal and Charismatic churches most of my life. During that time, a huge number of leaders have been lost to alcohol, drugs, money and adultery of all kinds.

In the late 1960s, God used Lonnie Frisbee to spark the Signs and Wonders movement that followed from the Jesus People Movement—the last cultural revival that the Western Church has experienced.

Like many hippies that converted to Christ, Lonnie Frisbee read the Gospels and simply believed them. So, he believed in signs and wonders because they were in the Bible. His was the simple gospel about the Kingdom, and it was effective.

The signs and wonders thinking was further developed by John Wimber and Vineyard, and it has impacted the Charismatic movement worldwide.

Lonnie Frisbee, on the other hand, died of HIV after numerous homosexual encounters, never overcoming his homosexual addiction.

A. A. Allen, the famous healing revivalist, was found dead in his hotel room, surrounded by alcohol and pills.

Today, I know many ministers who have once operated in the power of the Holy Spirit but are now struggling with alcohol, sex or drugs. And nearly on a weekly basis we hear about some ministry failure.

The list seems endless, and it is still getting longer.

You might think that all this is due to our fallen nature, and to a certain extent, it can all be explained with that.

Paul writes in Romans 7:22-25,

> For I delight in the law of God according to the inward man. But I see another law in my members, warring against the law of my mind, and bringing me into captivity to the law of sin which is in my members. O wretched man that I am! Who will deliver me from this body of death? I thank God—through Jesus Christ our Lord!

But thank God, that is not the whole picture! Romans 8:1 says,

> There is therefore now no condemnation to those who are in Christ Jesus, who do not walk according to the flesh, but according to the Spirit.

The only way to combat our flesh is to walk in the Spirit.

But what happens if God's presence departs? And why does God's presence depart? And by this I mean that the streams of the living water become blocked in our life. It doesn't seem to me that the presence of God would depart simply because of our flesh, as we are carrying our flesh, until we die.

The presence of God departed from King Saul's life because of fear that led to disobedience. When God's presence departed from King Saul's life, he first looked for someone who was carrying it and hired David to play harp for him. Many leaders who have lost their anointing initially surround themselves with anointed wingmen—until those wingmen also lose their anointing because they follow their leader to sin.

But you can't live off the presence of God someone else is carrying, and eventually, King Saul departed from God's presence altogether. But the anointing that King Saul carried had opened him to the supernatural dimension, and he ended up consulting occult sources for counsel.

Often, when the presence of God departs, people seek to substitute the emotional high, relaxation, or peace they have experienced with something else, and end up becoming addicted to things that can also provide an emotional high or release—alcohol, sex or drugs. Others become greedy, as they seek for a variety of emotional experiences, and producing those experiences takes a lot of money.

It is dangerous to ask for anointing from the Holy Spirit, but it is even more dangerous to lose it. Hebrews 6:4-6 says,

> For it is impossible for those who were once enlightened, and have tasted the heavenly gift, and have become partakers of the Holy Spirit, and have tasted the good word of God and the powers of the age to come, if they fall away, to renew them again to repentance, since they crucify again for themselves the Son of God, and put Him to an open shame.

The flowing of the Holy Spirit in our lives is blocked when we refuse to take heed of God's clear call to love our neighbour. Charles Finney, leader in the Second Great Awakening in the United States, writes in his *Lectures on Revivals of Religion*:

> Revivals are hindered when ministers and churches take wrong growing in regard to any question involving human rights. If the church fails to speak out against such an issue as slavery, she is perjured, and the Spirit of God departs from her. One of the reasons for the low state of religion at the present time is that many churches have taken the wrong side on the subject of slavery, have suffered prejudice to prevail over principle, and have feared to call this abomination by its true name.[1]

Finney had a rather different view on how revivals die than many revivalists of today. In his view, unless a revival begins to work through acts of love, it will soon die.

The flowing of the Holy Spirit in our lives can also be blocked by deception.

Matthew 16:1-12 says,

> Then the Pharisees and Sadducees came, and testing Him asked that He would show them a sign from heaven. He

answered and said to them, "When it is evening you say, 'It will be fair weather, for the sky is red'; and in the morning, 'It will be foul weather today, for the sky is red and threatening.' Hypocrites! You know how to discern the face of the sky, but you cannot discern the signs of the times. A wicked and adulterous generation seeks after a sign, and no sign shall be given to it except the sign of the prophet Jonah." And He left them and departed. Now when His disciples had come to the other side, they had forgotten to take bread.

Then Jesus said to them, "Take heed and beware of the leaven of the Pharisees and the Sadducees." And they reasoned among themselves, saying, "It is because we have taken no bread." But Jesus, being aware of it, said to them, "O you of little faith, why do you reason among yourselves because you have brought no bread? Do you not yet understand, or remember the five loaves of the five thousand and how many baskets you took up? Nor the seven loaves of the four thousand and how many large baskets you took up? How is it you do not understand that I did not speak to you concerning bread?—but to beware of the leaven of the Pharisees and Sadducees."

Then they understood that He did not tell them to beware of the leaven of bread, but of the doctrine of the Pharisees and Sadducees.

The flow of the Holy Spirit in our lives will also be blocked when we are chasing for signs and wonders without any regard for the Word of God.

Today, I am afraid that the leaven that was put there by New Thought, spiritualism, freemasonry and many other false doctrines has worked its way through the bread, and now the bread we offer has become inedible.

And yet we keep on eating it.

The Charismatic church is ripe for reformation when it comes to spiritual gifts. May this be the generation that refuses to accept what is available at the Charismatic stage managed market of 'gifts' and return back to the Source!

But thankfully, this Source is never far from us.

Now when He was asked by the Pharisees when the kingdom of God would come, He answered them and said, "The kingdom of God does not come with observation; nor will they say, 'See here!' or 'See there!' For indeed, the kingdom of God is within you." (Luke 17:20-21)

Your Kingdom Come. Your will be done. Amen.

ENDNOTES

INTRODUCTION

1. Candy Gunther Brown, *Testing Prayer*, 1 edition (Cambridge, Mass.: Harvard University Press, 2012), 1.
2. James Robinson, *Divine Healing: The Years of Expansion, 1906-1930: Theological Variation in the Transatlantic World* (Pickwick Publications, 2014), 146.

CHAPTER 1: FROM COMMUNITY TO STAGE PERFORMANCE

1. Candy Gunther Brown, ed., *Global Pentecostal and Charismatic Healing* (Oxford; New York: Oxford University Press, USA, 2011), 3.
2. Cary McMullen, 'The Ledger of Lakeland', "Inside Todd Bentley's Florida Outpouring," ChristianityToday.com, accessed February 23, 2016, http://www.christianitytoday.com/ct/2008/september/4.18.html.
3. Douglas J. Nelson, *For Such a Time as This: The Story of Bishop William J. Seymour and the Azusa Street Revival, a Search for Pentecostal/Charismatic Roots* (University of Birmingham, 1981), 194.
4. Dr Shani Orgad, *Media Representation and the Global Imagination* (Cambridge ; Malden, MA: Polity, 2012), 190.
5. Chas H. Barfoot, *Aimee Semple McPherson and the Making of Modern Pentecostalism, 1890-1926*, 1st edition (London: Routledge, 2011), 209.
6. Ibid., 232.
7. Ibid., 327.
8. Ibid., 236.

9. Ibid., 395.

10. Ibid., 407.

11. Ibid., 439.

12. "Exposed: Magicians, Psychics and Frauds - Exposed: Magicians, Psychics and Frauds - Exposed: Magicians, Psychics and Frauds, 2014-2015, Storyville - BBC Four," BBC, accessed February 5, 2016, http://www.bbc.co.uk/programmes/p029bgws/p029bgkj.

13. Simone Natale, *Supernatural Entertainments:Victorian Spiritualism and the Rise of Modern Media Culture* (Penn State University Press, 2016), 1–2.

14. Ibid., 3.

15. Ibid., 138.

CHAPTER 2: THE FALSE MINISTRY MODEL

1. "Paul Keith Davis: A New Season - The Church Is Entering an Age of Militancy and Spiritual Confrontation," accessed February 6, 2016, http://www.elijahlist.com/words/display_word.html?ID=13291.

2. ChasingRiver, *The Real Jesus - Part 4 - by Bill Johnson*, accessed February 6, 2016, https://www.youtube.com/watch?v=vHcRI60j0HI.

3. C. Douglas Weaver, *The Healer-Prophet* (Macon, Ga.: Mercer University Press, 2004), 141.

4. Ibid.

5. Bill Johnson and Eric Johnson, *Momentum: What God Starts, Never Ends*, Original edition (Shippensburg, Pa.: Destiny Image Publishers, 2013), 67.

6. Derek Prince, *Protection from Deception* (New Kensington, PA: Whitaker House,U.S., 2008), 42–43.

7. William Branham, "William Branham, The Spoken Word, 2:24-28" (Spoken Word Publications, Jeffersonville IN, 1972).

8. Weaver, *The Healer-Prophet*, 111.

9. William Branham, "Revelation Chapter Four, Part III, Vol. 13 of The Revelation of Jesus Christ" (Spoken Word Publications, Jeffersonville IN, n.d.), 676.

10. Weaver, *The Healer-Prophet*, 62.

11. Ibid., 65.

12. William Branham, *Obey the Voice of the Angel,"* Sermon Delivered in Minneapolis MN, 1949.

13. Gordon Lindsay, *William Branham: A Man Sent from God* (W. Branham, 1950), 173.

14. William Branham, *Expectations,* n.d.

15. William Branham, "How the Gift Came to Me," *The Voice of Healing,* April 1948.

16. "1933 7 Visions of William Branham | William Branham," accessed February 6, 2016, http://www.williambranham. com/1933-7-visions-of-william-branham/.

17. Lindsay, *William Branham.*

18. Johnson and Johnson, *Momentum,* 70.

19. David Edwin Harrell Jr, *Oral Roberts: An American Life* (San Francisco, CA: Harpercollins, 1987), 166.

20. Ibid.

21. Ibid., 456.

22. Matt Bai, *All the Truth Is Out: The Week Politics Went Tabloid* (New York: Knopf Publishing Group, 2014), xv.

23. Ibid., 228.

CHAPTER 3: WHAT IS SUPERNATURAL LOVE?

1. Orgad, *Media Representation and the Global Imagination,* 194.

CHAPTER 4: 1 CORINTHIANS AND THE GIFTS

1. Robert Larmer, ed., *Questions of Miracle* (Montreal Que.: McGill-Queen's University Press, 1997), xiii.

2. Brown, *Testing Prayer,* 66.

3. John Wesley, *Works: Miscellaneous* (B. Waugh and T. Mason, 1831), 444.

4. James D. G. Dunn, *Unity and Diversity in the New Testament: An Inquiry Into the Character of Earliest Christianity,* New edition edition (London: SCM Press, 2012), 299.

5. Brown, *Testing Prayer,* 72.

CHAPTER 5: WAR BETWEEN TWO KINGDOMS

1. Bill Johnson, *The Essential Guide to Healing* (Grand Rapids, Mich.: Chosen Books, 2011), 65.
2. Ibid.
3. Ibid., 66.
4. Ibid., 113.
5. Johnson and Johnson, *Momentum*, 120.
6. Ibid., 132.
7. General Stanley McChrystal et al., *Team of Teams: New Rules of Engagement for a Complex World* (Portfolio Penguin, 2015), 12–13.

CHAPTER 6: THE GIFTS OF HEALINGS

1. Brown, *Testing Prayer*, 1.
2. Ibid., 30.
3. Barfoot, *Aimee Semple McPherson and the Making of Modern Pentecostalism, 1890-1926*, 107–108.
4. William K. Kay and James Robinson, *Divine Healing: The Formative Years: 1830-1890:Theological Roots in the Transatlantic World* (Eugene, Or.: Pickwick Publications, 2011), 15.
5. Ibid., 29.
6. Rolvix Harlan, *John Alexander Dowie and the Christian Catholic Apostolic Church in Zion.* (R.M. Antes, 1906), 157.
7. Barfoot, *Aimee Semple McPherson and the Making of Modern Pentecostalism, 1890-1926*, 227.
8. James R Goff JR, *Fields White Unto Harvest* (University of Arkansas Press, 1988), 44.
9. Robinson, *Divine Healing*, 27.
10. Barfoot, *Aimee Semple McPherson and the Making of Modern Pentecostalism, 1890-1926*, 92.
11. Harrell, *Oral Roberts*, 7.
12. Ibid., 106.
13. Robert Pierce Shuler, *"McPhersonism": A Study of Healing Cults and Modern Day "Tongues" Movements Containing Summary of Facts as to Disappearance and Re-Appearance of Aimee Semple McPherson* (The author, 1924), 122–123.
14. Ibid., 123.

15. Barfoot, *Aimee Semple McPherson and the Making of Modern Pentecostalism, 1890-1926*, 227.

16. Ibid., 34.

17. Ibid., 31.

18. Ibid., 147.

19. Harrell, *Oral Roberts*, 164.

20. Ibid.

21. Ibid., 166.

22. Ibid., 456.

23. Ibid., 451.

24. Barfoot, *Aimee Semple McPherson and the Making of Modern Pentecostalism, 1890-1926*, 285.

25. Weaver, THE *Healer-Prophet*, 62.

26. Ibid.

27. Ibid., 63.

28. Ibid., 75.

29. Ibid., 63.

30. F. F. Bosworth, *Christ the Healer*, Revised edition (Grand Rapids, MI: Chosen Books, 2008), 16–17.

31. Ibid., 17.

32. Ibid., 18.

33. Ibid., 29.

34. Harrell, *Oral Roberts*, 403.

35. Katia Moskvitch, "Why Does Food Taste Different on Planes?," accessed February 8, 2016, http://www.bbc.com/future/story/20150112-why-in-flight-food-tastes-weird.

36. Brown, *Testing Prayer*, 4.

37. Herbert Benson et al., "Study of the Therapeutic Effects of Intercessory Prayer (STEP) in Cardiac Bypass Patients: A Multicenter Randomized Trial of Uncertainty and Certainty of Receiving Intercessory Prayer," *American Heart Journal* 151, no. 4 (April 2006): 934–42, doi:10.1016/j.ahj.2005.05.028.

38. Brown, *Testing Prayer*, 96.

39. Ibid., 12.

40. Ibid., 278–279.

41. Ibid., 281–282.

42. Brown, *Testing Prayer*.

43. Ibid., 188.

44. "CHM: Personal Ministry - Christian Healing Ministries," accessed February 8, 2016, http://www.christianhealingmin.org/index.php?option=com_content&view=article&id=424&Item-id=482.

45. George Jeffreys, *Healing Rays* (Kessinger Publishing Co, 2003), 155.

46. Ibid., 2–3.

47. Ibid., 37–38.

48. Ibid., 170–171.

49. Ibid., 56–57.

50. Ibid., 57–58.

51. "Modern Pentecostalism - A. J. Pollock," accessed February 8, 2016, http://biblecentre.org/content.php?mode=7&item=439.

52. John Wimber and Kevin N. Springer, *Power Healing*, Reprint edition (San Francisco: HarperOne, 2009), 16.

53. Ibid., 154.

54. Ibid., 238–239.

CHAPTER 7: THE GIFT OF PROPHECY

1. "Apostolic-Prophetic Movement," *Wikipedia, the Free Encyclopedia*, August 24, 2015, https://en.wikipedia.org/w/index.php?title=Apostolic-Prophetic_Movement&oldid=677553740.

2. David Pytches, *Some Said It Thundered* (Hodder & Stoughton Religious, 1990), 1.

3. Ibid., 89.

4. Ibid., 90.

5. "Historical Weather For 1983 in Kansas City, Missouri, USA - WeatherSpark," accessed February 8, 2016, https://weatherspark.com/history/30837/1983/Kansas-City-Missouri-United-States.

6. Ibid.

7. Ibid.

8. "Visions and Revelations. Mike Bickle with Bob Jones, Kansas City, Missouri. Transcribed from Five (1) Hour Tapes," Fall

1988, 86.

9. Ibid., 44.
10. Ibid., 45.
11. Ibid., 50.
12. Ibid., 58.
13. Ibid.
14. Ibid., 74.

CHAPTER 8: TONGUES AND THEIR INTERPRETATION

1. StPaulsLondon, 'The Kingdom of God with the Rt Revd Dr Tom Wright', sec. 1:26:28, accessed February 29, 2016, https://www.youtube.com/watch?time_continue=1584&v=rLiy-WlS9mA.
2. Dunn, Unity and Diversity in the New Testament, 302.
3. Ibid., 299.
4. Ibid., 301.
5. "Mithras Liturgy," Wikipedia, the Free Encyclopedia, December 25, 2015, https://en.wikipedia.org/w/index.php?title=Mithras_Liturgy&oldid=696701414.
6. H. F. J. Horstmanshoff et al., eds., Kykeon: Studies in Honour of H.S. Versnel (Leiden; Boston: Brill, 2002), 79.
7. Ibid., 78–79.
8. Ibid., 80.
9. Andrew B. Newberg et al., "The Measurement of Regional Cerebral Blood Flow during Glossolalia: A Preliminary SPECT Study," Psychiatry Research: Neuroimaging 148, no. 1 (November 2006): 67–71.

CHAPTER 9: WORD OF KNOWLEDGE

1. Weaver, The Healer-Prophet, 76.
2. Ibid., 77.
3. Ibid., 78.
4. George Jeffreys, Pentecostal Rays: The Baptism and Gifts of the Holy Spirit (Elim Publishing, 1933), 121–122.
5. Ibid., 122.
6. Ruth Brandon, The Spiritualists: The Passion for the Occult in the Nine-

teenth and Twentieth Centuries (New York: Alfred a Knopf, 1983), 46.

7. Ibid.

CHAPTER 10: WORD OF WISDOM

1. "Wisdom Versus Faith -- 62-0401 -- Sermon Preached by William Branham," accessed July 15, 2016, http://branham.ru/message/message64e1.html?sermonum=820.
2. Lester Sumrall, Gifts & Ministries of the Holy Spirit (New Kensingon, PA: Whitaker House,U.S., 2005).
3. Ibid., 58.
4. Jeffreys, Pentecostal Rays, 120.
5. "1 Corinthians 12 Matthew Poole's Commentary," accessed February 11, 2016, http://biblehub.com/commentaries/poole/1_corinthians/12.htm.

CHAPTER 11: THE GIFT OF DISCERNING SPIRITS

1. William Seymour and Roberts Liardon, The Great Azusa Street Revival: The Life and Sermons of William Seymour (Embassy Publishing, 2014), 157.
2. Barfoot, Aimee Semple McPherson and the Making of Modern Pentecostalism, 1890-1926, 152–153.
3. Neil Forsyth, The Old Enemy: Satan and the Combat Myth, Reprinted Ed edition (Princeton, N.J.: Princeton University Press, 1989), 113.
4. "Jezebel Religion -- 61-0319 -- Sermon Preached by William Branham," accessed July 18, 2016, http://branham.ru/message/message9c9c.html?sermonum=748.
5. Robert Solomon, Not Passion's Slave: Emotions and Choice (New York: OUP USA, 2003), 181.
6. Ibid., 182.
7. Ibid., 188.
8. Fabrizio Macagno, Emotive Language in Argumentation (Cambridge University Press, 2014), 63.
9. Ibid., 64.
10. Ibid., 65.
11. Ibid., 66.
12. Manuel Castells, Communication Power, 2 edition (Oxford University

Press, Usa, 2013), 140.

13. Ibid., 141.

14. Jean-Paul Sartre, *Being and Nothingness: An Essay on Phenomenological Ontology*, 2 edition (London: Routledge, 2003), 225.

15. Castells, *Communication Power*, 142.

16. Bethany Albertson, *Anxious Politics* (Cambridge University Press, 2015), 9.

17. Ibid., 46.

18. Ibid.

19. R. W. L. Moberly, *Prophecy and Discernment*, 1 edition (Cambridge, UK; New York: Cambridge University Press, 2008), 172–173.

20. Seymour and Liardon, *The Great Azusa Street Revival*.

CHAPTER 12: THE GIFT OF FAITH

1. Kate Bowler, *Blessed: A History of the American Prosperity Gospel* (New York: OUP USA, 2013), 13–14.

2. Ibid., 14.

3. Ibid.

4. Ibid.

5. Ibid.

6. "New Thought - ReligionFacts," accessed February 26, 2016, / new-thought.

7. Bowler, *Blessed*, 33–34.

8. Jeffreys, *Pentecostal Rays*, 124.

CHAPTER 13: THE GIFT OF WORKING MIRACLES

1. *The Church Before the Watching World*, p. 17

2. *The Church Before the Watching World*, p. 18

3. "When God Plays Biased Dice," accessed July 22, 2016, https://www.churchtimes.co.uk/articles/2015/31-july/comment/opinion/when-god-plays-biased-dice.

4. Ibid.

5. Ibid.

6. Ibid.

7. St Augustine of Hippo, *The City of God* (Peabody, Mass:

Hendrickson, 2009), 739.

8. "John Alexander Dowie," *Wikipedia, the Free Encyclopedia*, May 13, 2016, https://en.wikipedia.org/w/index.php?title=John_Alexander_Dowie&oldid=720024842.

9. Christopher D. Marshall, *Faith as Theme in Mark's Narrative*, New Ed edition (Cambridge; New York: Cambridge University Press, 2008), 60.

10. Edited by William K. Kay and Robin A. Parry, *Exorcism and Deliverance: Multi-Disciplinary Studies* (Milton Keynes: Paternoster, 2009), 56.

CHAPTER 14: FINISHING WELL

1. Barfoot, *Aimee Semple McPherson and the Making of Modern Pentecostalism, 1890-1926*, 303.

REFERENCES

"1 Corinthians 12 Matthew Poole's Commentary." Accessed February 11, 2016. http://biblehub.com/commentaries/poole/1_corinthians/12.htm.

"1933 7 Visions of William Branham | William Branham." Accessed February 6, 2016. http://www.williambranham.com/1933-7-visions-of-william-branham/.

Albertson, Bethany. *Anxious Politics.* Cambridge University Press, 2015.

"Apostolic-Prophetic Movement." *Wikipedia, the Free Encyclopedia,* August 24, 2015. https://en.wikipedia.org/w/index.php?title=Apostolic-Prophetic_Movement&oldid=677553740.

Bai, Matt. *All the Truth Is Out: The Week Politics Went Tabloid.* New York: Knopf Publishing Group, 2014.

Barfoot, Chas H. *Aimee Semple McPherson and the Making of Modern Pentecostalism, 1890-1926.* 1st edition. London: Routledge, 2011.

Benson, Herbert, Jeffery A. Dusek, Jane B. Sherwood, Peter Lam, Charles F. Bethea, William Carpenter, Sidney Levitsky, et al. "Study of the Therapeutic Effects of Intercessory Prayer (STEP) in Cardiac Bypass Patients: A Multicenter Randomized Trial of Uncertainty and Certainty of Receiving Intercessory Prayer." *American Heart Journal* 151, no. 4 (April 2006): 934–42.

Bosworth, F. F. *Christ the Healer.* Revised edition. Grand Rapids, MI: Chosen Books, 2008.

Bowler, Kate. *Blessed: A History of the American Prosperity Gospel.* New York: OUP USA, 2013.

Brandon, Ruth. *The Spiritualists: The Passion for the Occult in the Nineteenth and*

Twentieth Centuries. New York: Alfred a Knopf, 1983.

Branham, William. *Expectations*, n.d.

Branham, William. "How the Gift Came to Me." *The Voice of Healing*, April 1948.

Branham, William. *Obey the Voice of the Angel*," Sermon Delivered in Minneapolis MN, 1949.

Branham, William. "Revelation Chapter Four, Part III, Vol. 13 of The Revelation of Jesus Christ." Spoken Word Publications, Jeffersonville IN, n.d.

Branham, William. "William Branham, The Spoken Word, 2:24-28." Spoken Word Publications, Jeffersonville IN, 1972.

Brown, Candy Gunther, ed. *Global Pentecostal and Charismatic Healing*. Oxford; New York: Oxford University Press, USA, 2011.

Brown, Candy Gunther. *Testing Prayer*. 1 edition. Cambridge, Mass.: Harvard University Press, 2012.

Castells, Manuel. *Communication Power*. 2 edition. Oxford University Press, Usa, 2013.

ChasingRiver. *The Real Jesus - Part 4 - by Bill Johnson*. Accessed February 6, 2016. https://www.youtube.com/watch?v=vHcRI60j0HI.

"CHM: Personal Ministry - Christian Healing Ministries." Accessed February 8, 2016. http://www.christianhealingmin.org/index.php?option=com_content&view=article&id=424&Itemid=482.

Dunn, James D. G. *Unity and Diversity in the New Testament: An Inquiry Into the Character of Earliest Christianity*. New edition. London: SCM Press, 2012.

"Exposed: Magicians, Psychics and Frauds - Exposed: Magicians, Psychics and Frauds - Exposed: Magicians, Psychics and Frauds, 2014-2015, Storyville - BBC Four." BBC. Accessed February 5, 2016. http://www.bbc.co.uk/programmes/p029bgws/p029bgkj.

Forsyth, Neil. *The Old Enemy: Satan and the Combat Myth*. Reprinted Ed edition. Princeton, N.J.: Princeton University Press, 1989.

Goff, James R, JR. *Fields White Unto Harvest*. University of Arkansas Press, 1988.

Harlan, Rolvix. *John Alexander Dowie and the Christian Catholic Apostolic Church in Zion*. R.M. Antes, 1906.

Harrell, David Edwin, Jr. *Oral Roberts: An American Life*. San Francisco, CA: Harpercollins, 1987.

Hippo, St Augustine of. *The City of God*. Peabody, Mass: Hendrickson, 2009.

"Historical Weather For 1983 in Kansas City, Missouri, USA - WeatherSpark." Accessed February 8, 2016. https://weatherspark. com/history/30837/1983/Kansas-City-Missouri-United-States.

Horstmanshoff, H. F. J., H. W. Singor, F. T. van Straten, and Johan Strubbe, eds. *Kykeon: Studies in Honour of H.S. Versnel*. Leiden; Boston: Brill, 2002.

Jeffreys, George. *Healing Rays*. Kessinger Publishing Co, 2003.

Jeffreys, George. *Pentecostal Rays: The Baptism and Gifts of the Holy Spirit*. Elim Publishing, 1933.

"Jezebel Religion -- 61-0319 -- Sermon Preached by William Branham." Accessed July 18, 2016. http://branham.ru/message/ message9c9c.html?sermonum=748.

"John Alexander Dowie." *Wikipedia, the Free Encyclopedia*, May 13, 2016. https://en.wikipedia.org/w/index.php?title=John_Alexander_ Dowie&oldid=720024842.

Johnson, Bill. *The Essential Guide to Healing*. Grand Rapids, Mich.: Chosen Books, 2011.

Johnson, Bill, and Eric Johnson. *Momentum: What God Starts, Never Ends*. Original edition. Shippensburg, Pa.: Destiny Image Publishers, 2013.

Kay, William K., and James Robinson. *Divine Healing: The Formative Years: 1830-1890: Theological Roots in the Transatlantic World*. Eugene, Or.: Pickwick Publications, 2011.

Lakeland', Cary McMullen, 'The Ledger of. "Inside Todd Bentley's Florida Outpouring." ChristianityToday.com. Accessed February 23, 2016. http://www.christianitytoday.com/ct/2008/ september/4.18.html.

Larmer, Robert, ed. *Questions of Miracle*. Montreal Que.: McGill-Queen's University Press, 1997.

Lindsay, Gordon. *William Branham: A Man Sent from God*. W. Branham, 1950.

Macagno, Fabrizio. *Emotive Language in Argumentation*. Cambridge

University Press, 2014.

Marshall, Christopher D. *Faith as Theme in Mark's Narrative*. New Ed edition. Cambridge; New York: Cambridge University Press, 2008.

McChrystal, General Stanley, David Silverman, Tantum Collins, and Chris Fussell. *Team of Teams: New Rules of Engagement for a Complex World*. Portfolio Penguin, 2015.

"Mithras Liturgy." *Wikipedia, the Free Encyclopedia*, December 25, 2015. https://en.wikipedia.org/w/index.php?title=Mithras_Liturgy&oldid=696701414.

Moberly, R. W. L. *Prophecy and Discernment*. 1 edition. Cambridge, UK; New York: Cambridge University Press, 2008.

"Modern Pentecostalism - A. J. Pollock." Accessed February 8, 2016. http://biblecentre.org/content.php?mode=7&item=439.

Moskvitch, Katia. "Why Does Food Taste Different on Planes?" Accessed February 8, 2016. http://www.bbc.com/future/story/20150112-why-in-flight-food-tastes-weird.

Natale, Simone. *Supernatural Entertainments:Victorian Spiritualism and the Rise of Modern Media Culture*. Penn State University Press, 2016.

Nelson, Douglas J. *For Such a Time as This: The Story of Bishop William J. Seymour and the Azusa Street Revival, a Search for Pentecostal/Charismatic Roots*. University of Birmingham, 1981.

Newberg, Andrew B., Nancy A. Wintering, Donna Morgan, and Mark R. Waldman. "The Measurement of Regional Cerebral Blood Flow during Glossolalia: A Preliminary SPECT Study." *Psychiatry Research: Neuroimaging* 148, no. 1 (November 2006): 67–71.

"New Thought - ReligionFacts." Accessed February 26, 2016. /new-thought.

Orgad, Dr Shani. *Media Representation and the Global Imagination*. Cambridge ; Malden, MA: Polity, 2012.

Parry, Edited by William K. Kay and Robin A. *Exorcism and Deliverance: Multi-Disciplinary Studies*. Milton Keynes: Paternoster, 2009.

"Paul Keith Davis: A New Season - The Church Is Entering an Age of Militancy and Spiritual Confrontation." Accessed February 6, 2016. http://www.elijahlist.com/words/display_word.html?ID=13291.

Prince, Derek. *Protection from Deception*. New Kensington, PA: Whitaker House, U.S., 2008.

Pytches, David. *Some Said It Thundered*. Hodder & Stoughton Religious, 1990.

Robinson, James. *Divine Healing: The Holiness-Pentecostal Transition Years, 1890-1906: Theological Transpositions in the Transatlantic World*. Eugene, Or.: Pickwick Publications, 2013.

Robinson, James. *Divine Healing: The Years of Expansion, 1906-1930: Theological Variation in the Transatlantic World*. Pickwick Publications, 2014.

Sartre, Jean-Paul. *Being and Nothingness: An Essay on Phenomenological Ontology*. 2 edition. London: Routledge, 2003.

Schaeffer, Francis A. *Church Before the Watching World*. 1st UK Paperback Edition. London: Inter-Varsity Press, 1972.

Seymour, William, and Roberts Liardon. *The Great Azusa Street Revival: The Life and Sermons of William Seymour*. Embassy Publishing, 2014.

Shuler, Robert Pierce. *"McPhersonism": A Study of Healing Cults and Modern Day "Tongues" Movements Containing Summary of Facts as to Disappearance and Re-Appearance of Aimee Semple McPherson*. The author, 1924.

Solomon, Robert. *Not Passion's Slave: Emotions and Choice*. New York: OUP USA, 2003.

StPaulsLondon. *The Kingdom of God with the Rt Revd Dr Tom Wright*. Accessed February 29, 2016. https://www.youtube.com/watch?time_continue=1584&v=rLiy-WlS9mA.

Sumrall, Lester. *Gifts & Ministries of the Holy Spirit*. New Kensingon, PA: Whitaker House, U.S., 2005.

"The Infancy Gospel of Thomas." Accessed July 25, 2016. http://gnosis.org/library/inftoma.htm.

"Visions and Revelations. Mike Bickle with Bob Jones, Kansas City, Missouri. Transcribed from Five (1) Hour Tapes," Fall 1988.

Weaver, C. Douglas. *The Healer-Prophet*. Macon, Ga.: Mercer University Press, 2004.

Wesley, John. *Works: Miscellaneous*. B. Waugh and T. Mason, 1831.

"When God Plays Biased Dice." Accessed July 22, 2016. https://www.churchtimes.co.uk/articles/2015/31-july/comment/opinion/when-god-plays-biased-dice.

Wimber, John, and Kevin N. Springer. *Power Healing*. Reprint edition. San Francisco: HarperOne, 2009.

"Wisdom Versus Faith -- 62-0401 -- Sermon Preached by William Branham." Accessed July 15, 2016. http://branham.ru/message/message64e1.html?sermonum=820.

OTHER BOOKS BY IHERINGIUS

Marko Joensuu
Five Movements: Winning the Battle for Your Prophetic Gift
The Red Scorpion: A True Russian Mafia Story
Cloud 913

Claudio Ferro
Angels and Demons: Modern and Ancient Spiritual Warfare

David Muyiwa Adeola
The Gatekeeper: Bringing a Revolution and a Mind-shift to Your
Personal Prayer Life and Prayer Movements in the Nations

IHERINGIUS

iheringius.com

Lightning Source UK Ltd.
Milton Keynes UK
UKOW02f2029030916

282110UK00002B/33/P